IMAGES
of America
ELMORE AND GENOA

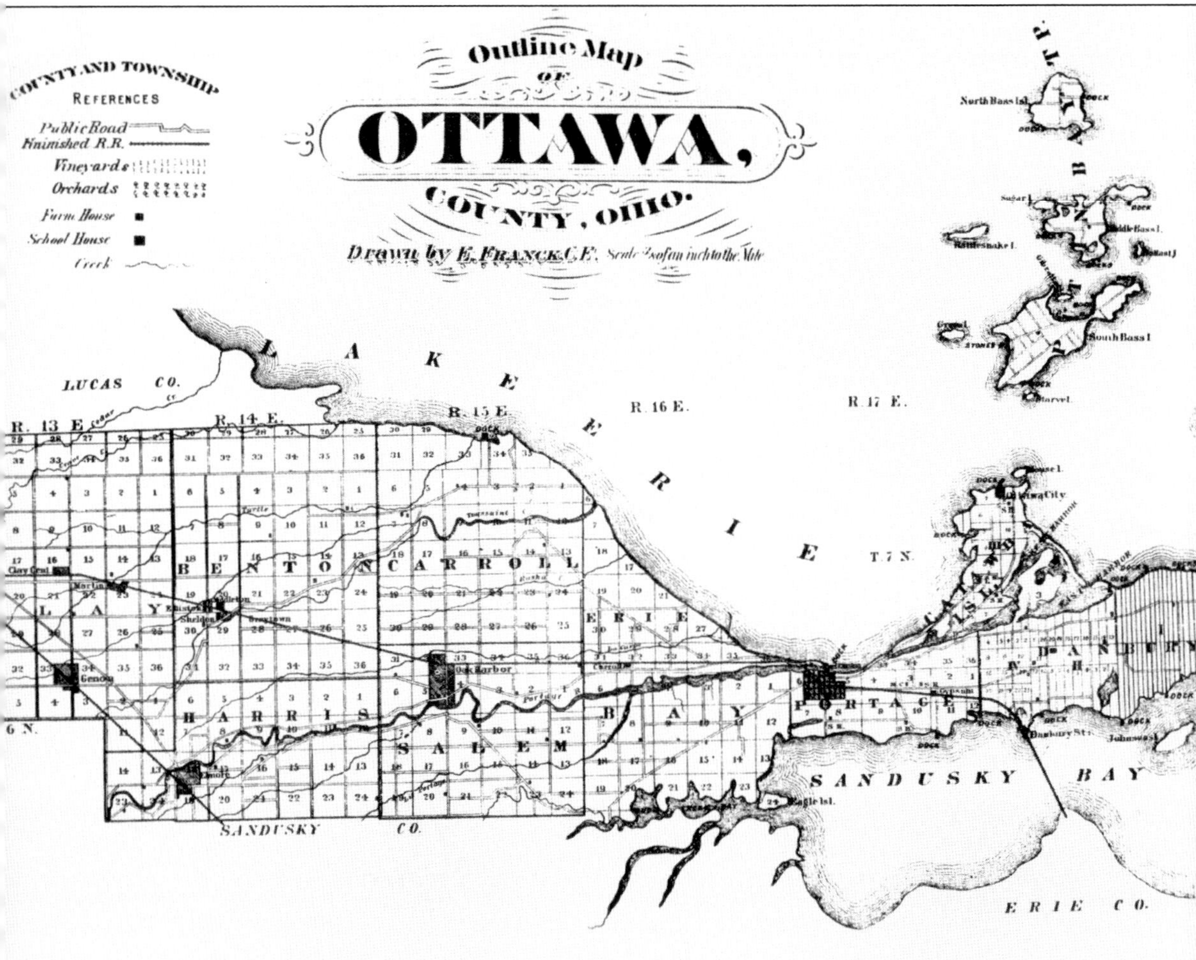

This 1874 map illustrates the borders of Clay and Harris Townships within Ottawa County. (Harris-Elmore Public Library [HEPL].)

ON THE COVER: Families and students who attended Hall Road School just outside of Elmore gather for a picnic near Sugar Creek near the turn of the 20th century. (Susan Trautman, HEPL.)

IMAGES
of America

ELMORE AND GENOA

Jennifer Fording on behalf of
the Harris-Elmore Public Library

ARCADIA
PUBLISHING

ISBN 978-0-7385-8254-2

Published by Arcadia Publishing
Charleston, South Carolina

Printed in the United States of America

Library of Congress Control Number: 2011924849

For all general information, please contact Arcadia Publishing:
Telephone 843-853-2070
Fax 843-853-0044
E-mail sales@arcadiapublishing.com
For customer service and orders:
Toll-Free 1-888-313-2665

Visit us on the Internet at www.arcadiapublishing.com

To my family and friends, your faith in me has made this all possible.

Contents

ACKNOWLEDGMENTS

It was a terrific experience to work with two communities that have such pride and initiative in preserving their village histories. Thank you to all the residents of Elmore and Genoa who contributed photographs and stories that helped to make this wonderful photographic history. I would especially like to thank the efforts of John Jaeger, John Foster, Joe Badger, Eleanor Richards, Eric Hise, Gene Meyers, Ron Cashen, Karen Kruse, Randy Miller, Chris Sheldon, Betty Haar, Dr. Ken Laub, Merlin Lieske, Vera Hille, Donna Schell, Tim Davies, Mary Deno, Garth Reynolds, Lou Herbert, and the Elmore Historical Society for their invaluable time, photographic donations, and assistance.

On behalf of the staff at the Harris-Elmore and Genoa Libraries, I appreciate your support and readiness to help me in my research—both have made this publication possible. The photograph collection at the Genoa Library as well as the extensive archives and photographs at the Grace Luebke Local History Room at the Harris-Elmore Library were invaluable resources.

The following books were helpful in my research: *Elmore, Ohio: A History Preserved*, by Grace Luebke, published in 1975; *Elmore's 100 Years 1851–1951*, written and published by the Elmore Centennial Committee in 1951; the 1968 Genoa Bicentennial Committee publication *Memories of Genoa, Ohio 1868–1968*; and *A History of Genoa*, by the Genoa High School Senior Class of 1928.

Readers who are interested in viewing local digital archives to see more images of life in Ottawa County, Ohio, can access collections at the following sites: http://harriselmore.weebly.com and www.ohiomemory.org.

Unless otherwise stated, the images that appear in this volume are courtesy of the Harris-Elmore Public Library (HEPL), the Genoa Public Library (GPL), and the Elmore Historical Society (EHS).

INTRODUCTION

Shops and eateries on every corner, crowded train stations, busy hotels, and streets full of people might conjure up images of large Ohio cities such as Toledo or Columbus, but these were actually the scenes in the small villages of Elmore and Genoa during their early years. The story of these two Ohio villages is revealed in *Elmore and Genoa*, which portrays two very different places that share a colorful past. Take advantage of seeing time stand still through photographs of two small towns that once took on the personas of bustling cities.

Early pioneers settled this portion of the Black Swamp under horrific conditions that tested any man's endurance. It was these brave families that entered Ottawa County in the 1830s to form two flourishing communities. And it was indeed fortunate for these first settlers that friendly Ottawa tribes were present in the areas to become Clay and Harris Townships. As a result, little resistance was found regarding settlement. The first white man to enter the area near present-day Elmore was Joseph Harris in 1816. The Harris family lived along the Portage River, encountering the John Fletcher family later that year. Harris died in 1820 and was buried near his home, and the present Harris Township was named for him in 1825. Homesteaders slowly trickled in, but it was not until the Rice brothers emerged in Elmore that settlement boomed. Ezekiel and Reuben Rice, along with Bennett Havens, were among the first settlers to come to Elmore in 1824 to take advantage of cheap land offerings. Following them were Israel Harrington, who was a former tavern owner from Lower Sandusky (Oak Harbor), the Luckeys, the Wheelers, and numerous other families. With the draining of the swamp, fertile farming materialized along the serene setting of the Portage River, whose bountiful fishing and boating experiences helped create a desirable way of life in this vicinity.

Elmore was platted in 1851 and owes its existence not only to its determined early settlers but also to the Toledo, Norwalk and Cleveland Railroad (later known as the Lake Shore and Michigan Southern Line). This was especially true after 1858, when the railroad abandoned its northern route that went through Port Clinton, which left those citizens cut off from the world but made Elmore the major transportation center in the area. The railroad brought goods and visitors to this small town, resulting in booming businesses selling not only locally but to larger towns abroad as well. In addition, churches for every denomination, rural and local schools, and an abundance of homes and municipal buildings dotted the city limits and beyond. Up until the 1950s, Elmore was quite self-sufficient, not needing to extend too far for its citizens to enjoy themselves and to create a successful living.

Turning to the establishment of Genoa, 1835 was the year in which the first white man set foot in Clay Township. Timothy Sherman traveled to the Genoa area from Huron County, Ohio, and other ambitious men such as Harvey Warriner, John Packer, Thomas Pitcher, and Martin Follet soon followed suit. Clay Township formed officially in 1840 when Ottawa County finalized its boundaries. At this time, a portion of Allen Township was included within Clay's borders. It was not until 1883, when tensions ran high over the placement of the town hall, Allen split to form its own township. Genoa was called Stony Station before 1857, but inhabitants wanted a more fitting name for their newly platted town. Due to the remnants of the Black Swamp, murky streams and bogs encircled the town, where at times settlers needed rowboats to get around. These features reminded the people of the Italian town of Venice, which they decided to name the former Stony Station. However, a clerical error caused confusion, and the town became known as Genoa, which was formally incorporated in 1868.

In its early days, Genoa's livelihood relied mainly on the fruit and cattle industries. This quickly transitioned to white lime manufacturing as companies such as Wyman and Gregg, Sawyer and Company, and Newman and Ford entered the picture. This industry was so prominent that it was frequently mentioned in the newspapers. Such entries from the 1867 *Ottawa Union* commented on "lime miners blasting day and night, shaking the very core of Genoa village," or that "great fires from the Genoa kilns would light up the ghastly woods, while smoke hung over the earth." The railroad also helped Genoa's businesses thrive, but the introduction of the interurban (streetcars) made it a true transportation hub. Two lines that ran on the quarter hour was a rarity for such a small town. Many can still remember catching the cars on Washington Street for a shopping excursion to Toledo. This was truly a treat for the farmers and villagers who infrequently left home.

Citizens of both villages reminisce about the various church socials, visiting the opera house, strolling through town to peek in the store windows, attending school sports games, homecoming parades, and many other community amusements. Even toward the end of the 20th century, when businesses slowed and inhabitants left to find more opportunity, this way of life from years past was preserved. People have found themselves coming back to these towns to seek out a life that is less complicated and more community oriented.

Small towns have a way of making one feel welcome, of banding people together in times of crisis, of making a good and enjoyable life for their citizens, and of contributing much more to the larger national picture than was thought possible. Elmore and Genoa are no different. For what are now two quiet towns, both have started to successfully reinvent themselves to fit the needs of the 21st century. Next time you pass by a small town, such as these two, slow down and know that they had something to contribute to our past and our futures.

One

Let's Paint the Town Red

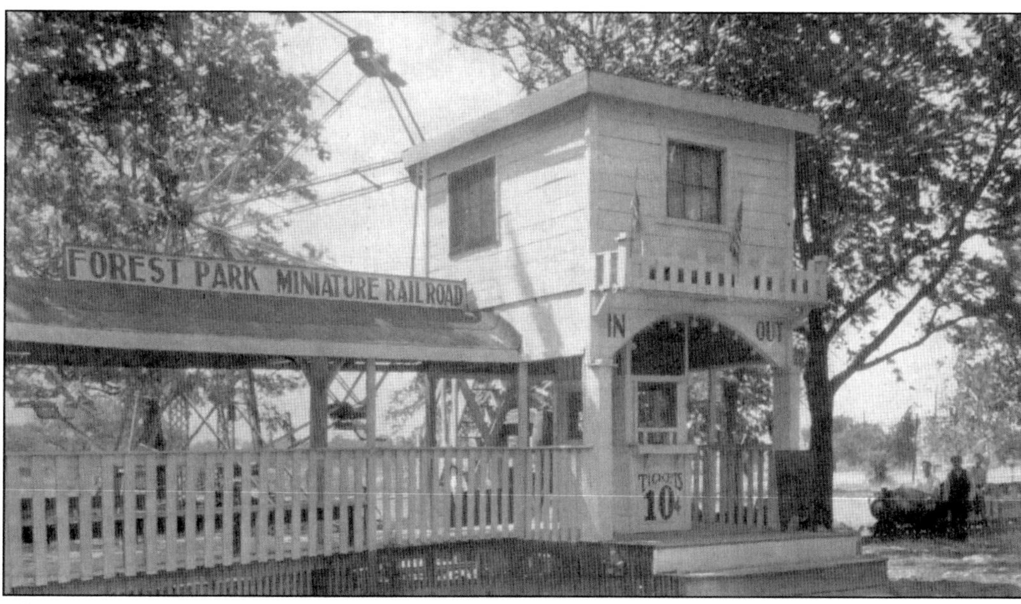

This postcard shows the miniature golf course located at Genoa's Forest Park. The popular amusement park was located on Route 102–Hickory Corners (now Route 51). Forest Park was opened in the early 1920s by Carl Uthoff and was the Cedar Point of its day. The park housed 40 acres, including a skating rink, dance hall, roller coasters, 25 resort cottages, restaurants, movie theaters, circus acts, and carnival games. It closed in 1949 as the war drew patrons away, and the park became part of an unsuccessful attempt at a gambling venue. The dance hall was the site of local auctions until 1967, when it burned down. (Joe Badger.)

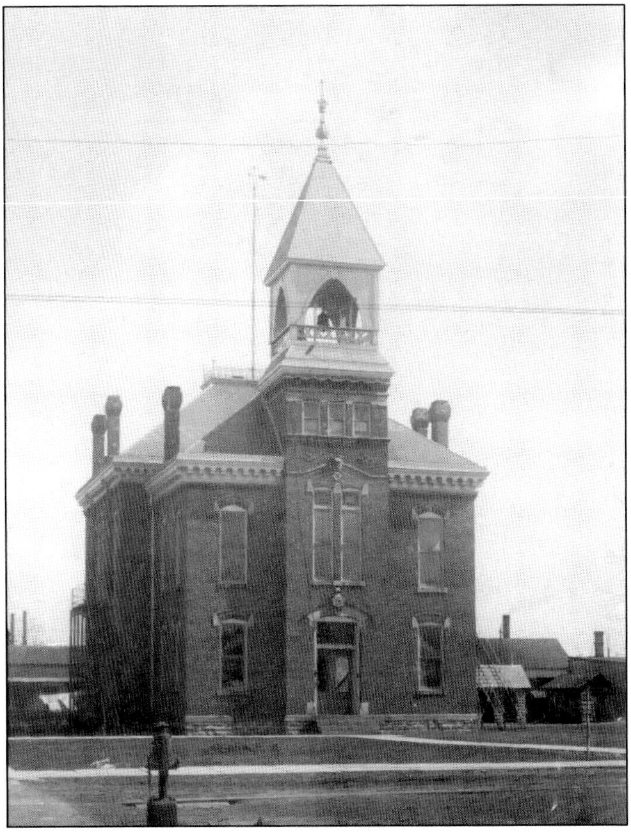

The Genoa Town Hall, pictured here in 1909, is listed in the National Register of Historic Places. It was built in 1883 and featured an opera house. Its first play was *The Three Wise Owls* in 1886, and it was the meeting place for town administrators, organizations, theater, and school commencements. The building fell into disrepair but was renovated in the late 1970s by Tomme Bergman and the Federation of Clubs. (GPL.)

Young Genoans pose at a dress rehearsal for a play they were performing at the town hall. (Kirk Hise collection, via Eric Hise.)

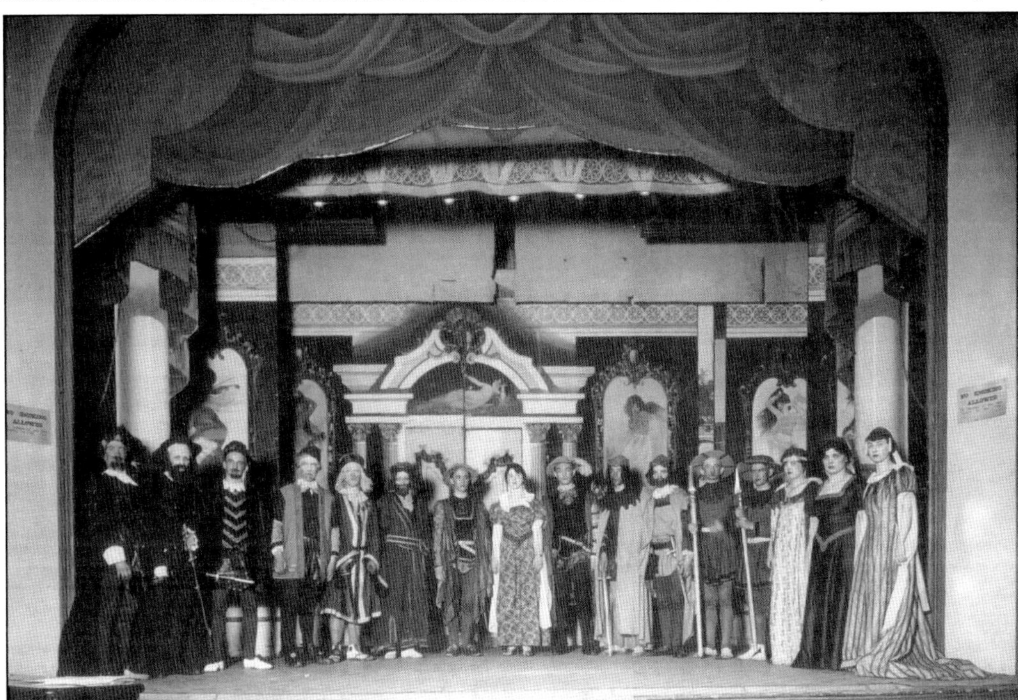

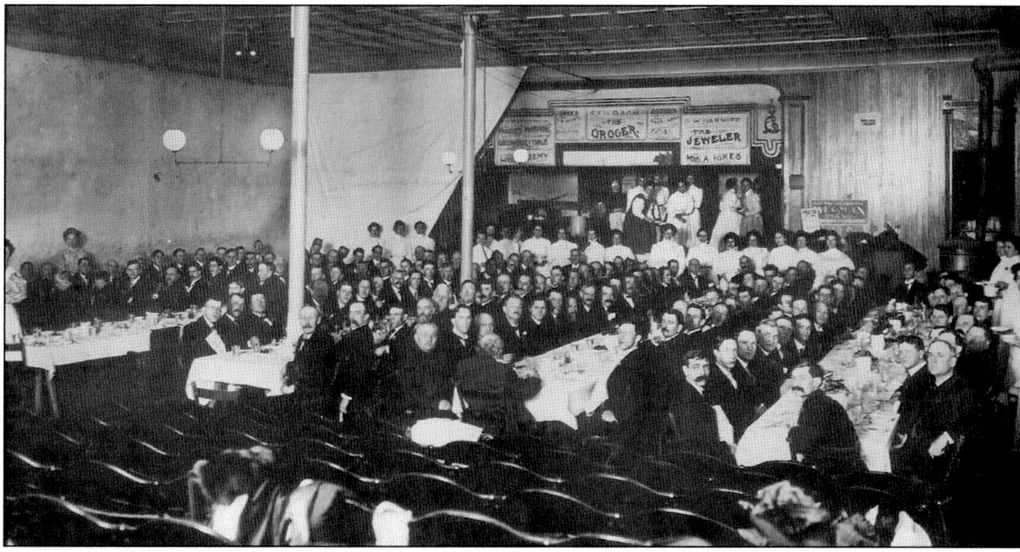

The Elmore Masons of the Portage Lodge are pictured holding a dedication dinner in the facility to celebrate their new lodge location on the second floor of the opera house in 1909. The Elmore Opera House was host to traveling theatrical groups, minstrel shows, dancing, basketball games, and school commencements. The first opera house was destroyed in the fire of 1895, but it was rebuilt the following year by Louis Jeremy. (HEPL.)

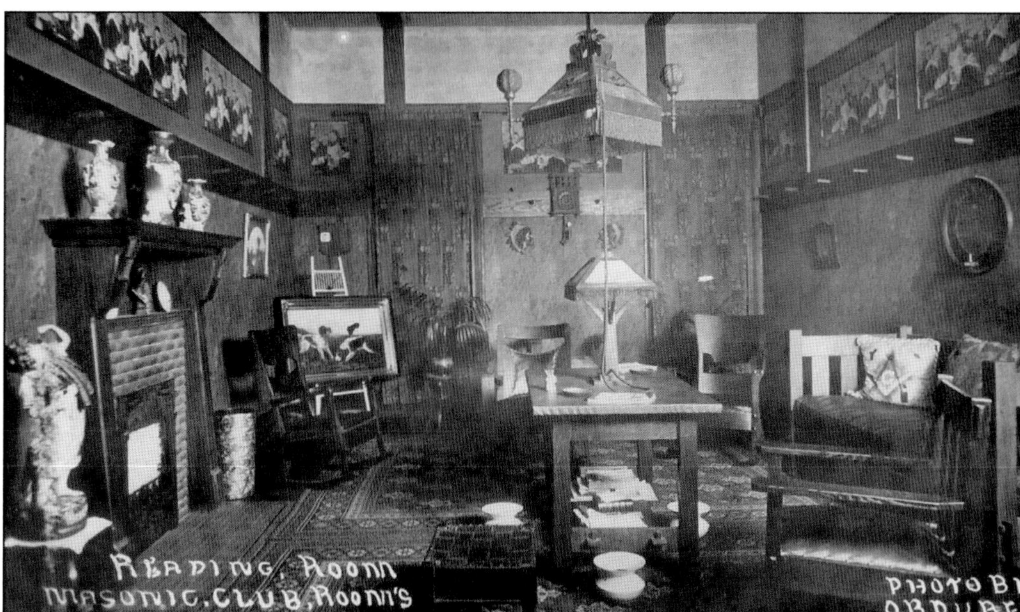

The Masonic reading room was on the second floor of the Elmore Opera House until 1925, when the lodge was moved to the old Brethren Church. The reading room contained several paintings from local artist and brother Mason Henry Dischinger. This room and the billiard and card rooms were places where fellow Masons could relax when not performing other civic duties. (Charles Dibert, HEPL.)

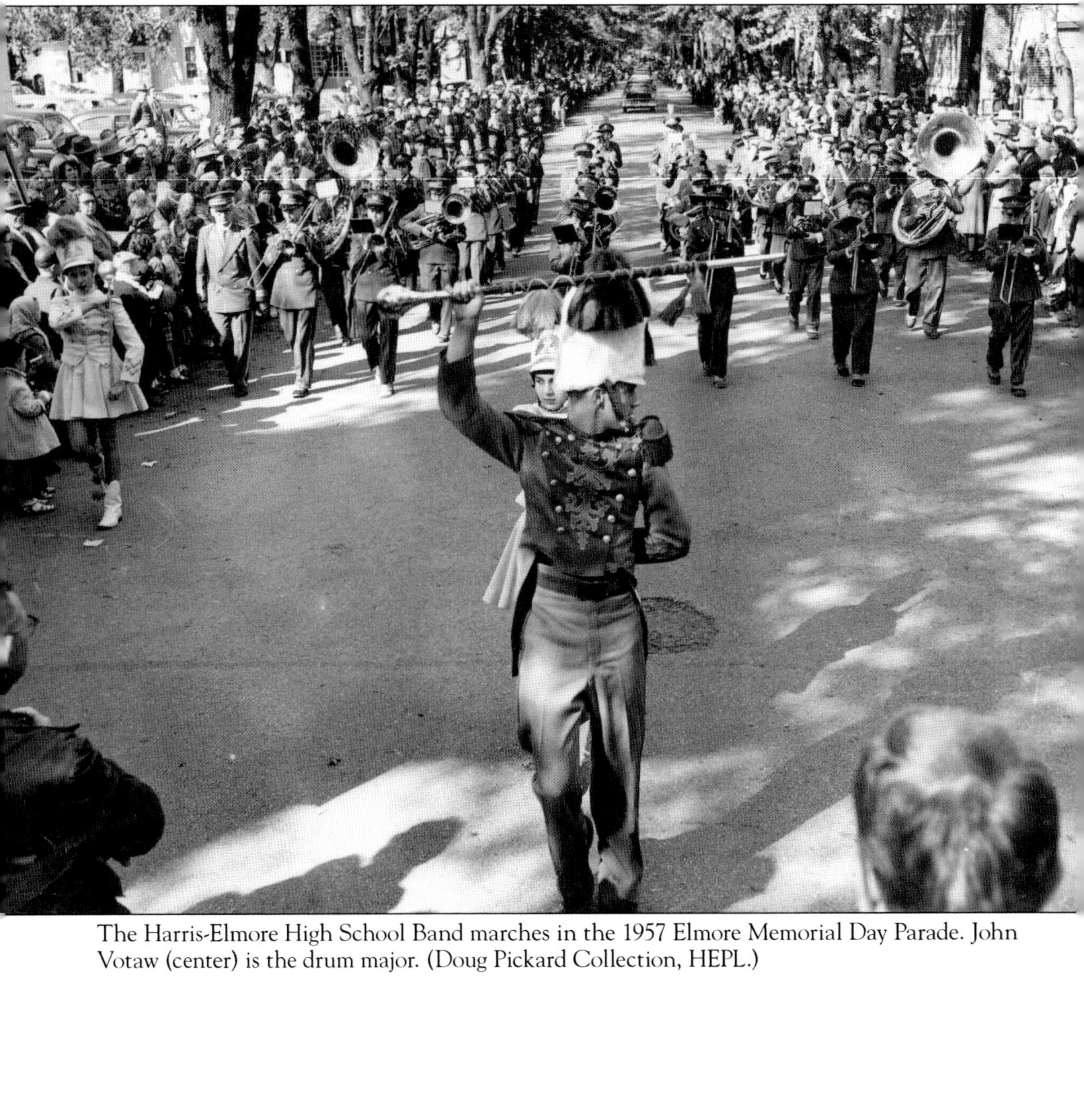

The Harris-Elmore High School Band marches in the 1957 Elmore Memorial Day Parade. John Votaw (center) is the drum major. (Doug Pickard Collection, HEPL.)

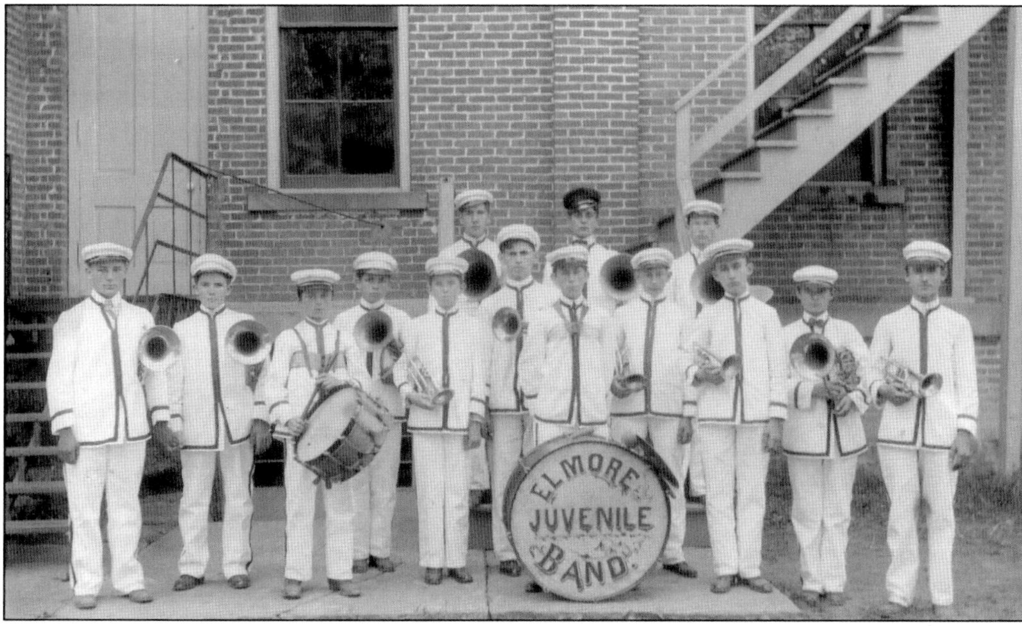

The popular entertainment in 1906 was the Elmore Juvenile Band. The band played many brass marches at places such as Wheeler's Grove. Members are, from left to right, (front row) B. Hilganeck, J. Melms, C. Wainwright, H. Hyatt, P. Shoenfeldt, W. Rozine, W. Schott, L. Strick, C. Weis, J. Hess, and B. Hess; (back row) C. Melms, N. Wainwright, and E. Hilgeneck. (HEPL.)

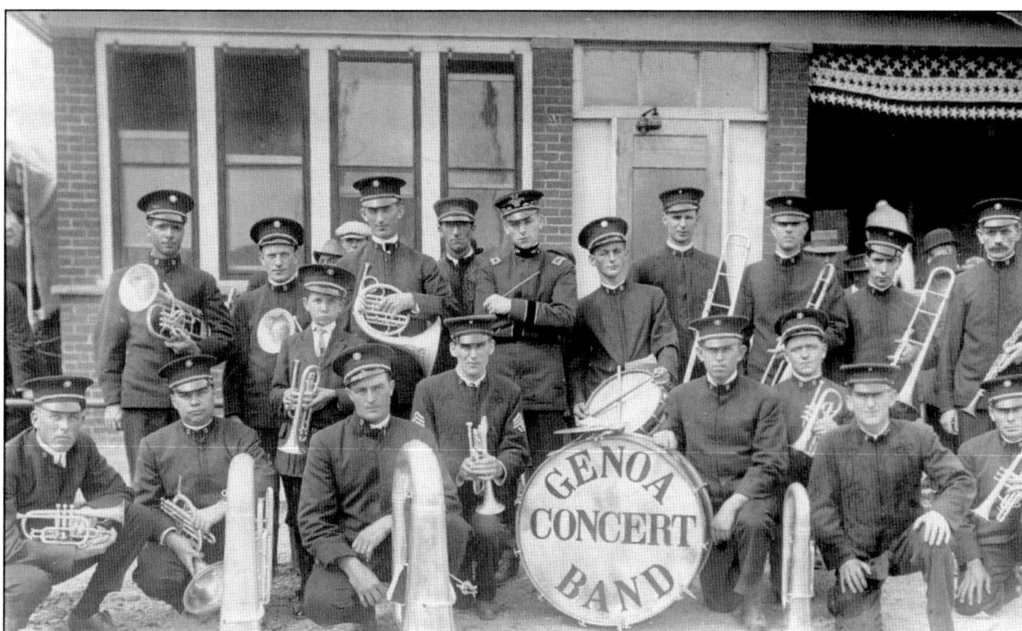

Genoa Concert Band members pose together before a Memorial Day or Fourth of July celebration around 1910 to 1912. The child at left in the second row is Arnold Berndt, who holds a cornet. (Ron Berndt, through the collection of the Birmingham Historical Museum, Birmingham, Michigan.)

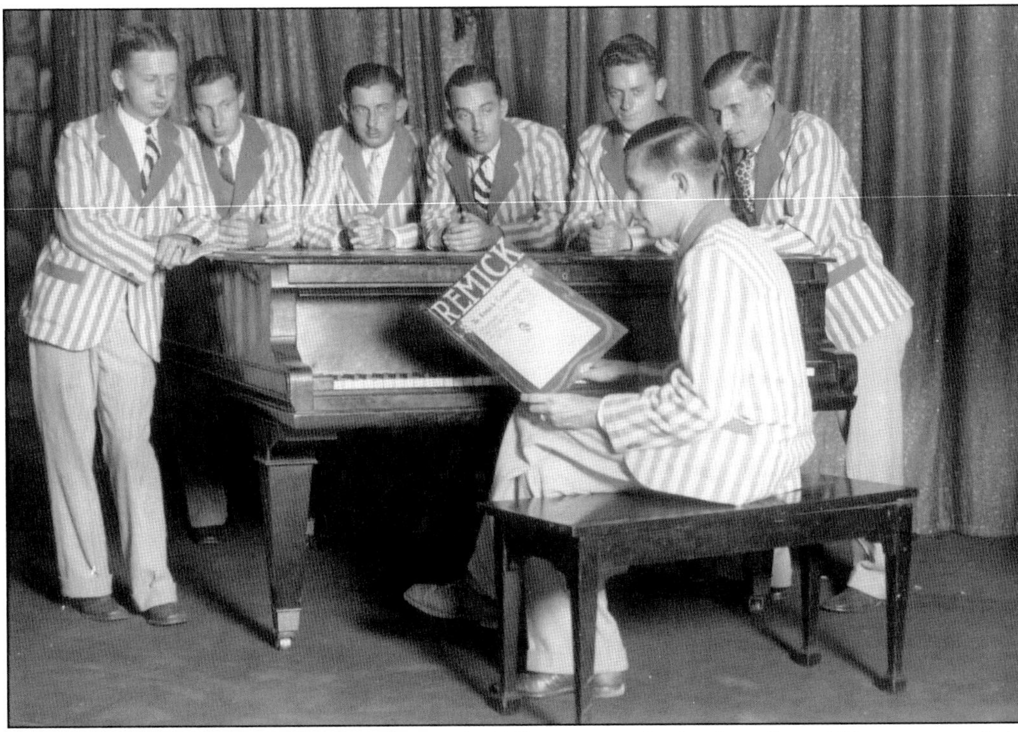

For over 40 years, Lewis Waterman (sitting) of Elmore was the leader of Lew Waterman and the Oriole Orchestra. During the big-band heyday in the 1940s and 1950s, the band had regular gigs at Gem Beach in Catawba, Ohio, and at the Rainbow Gardens in Fremont, Ohio. Waterman also had a radio broadcast on Toledo, Ohio, radio station WSPD and was featured bimonthly on Detroit, Michigan, station WJR. (EHS.)

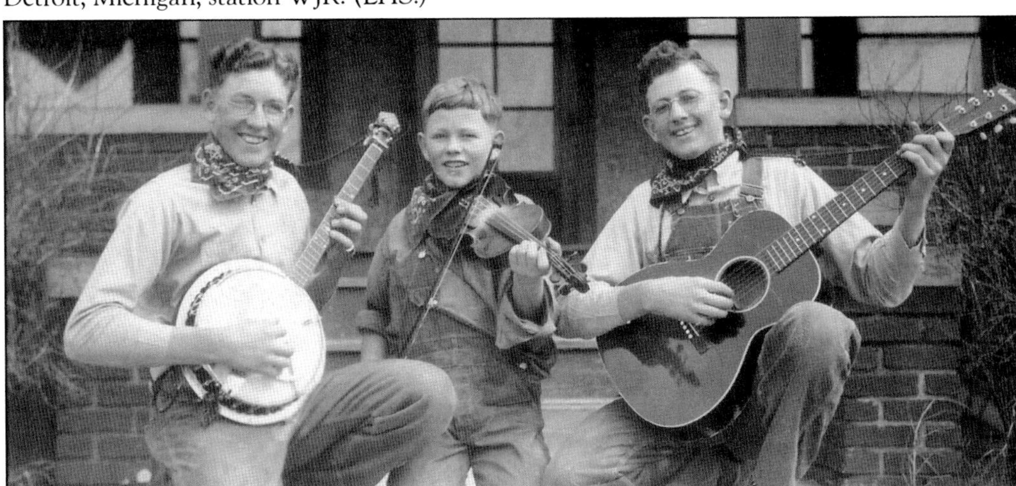

A local bluegrass/folk group called the Ohio Corncrackers was made up of members of the Damschroder family from Elmore. In this 1936 photograph are, from left to right, Wilson, Gene, and Forest Damschroder. (Damschroder Collection, HEPL.)

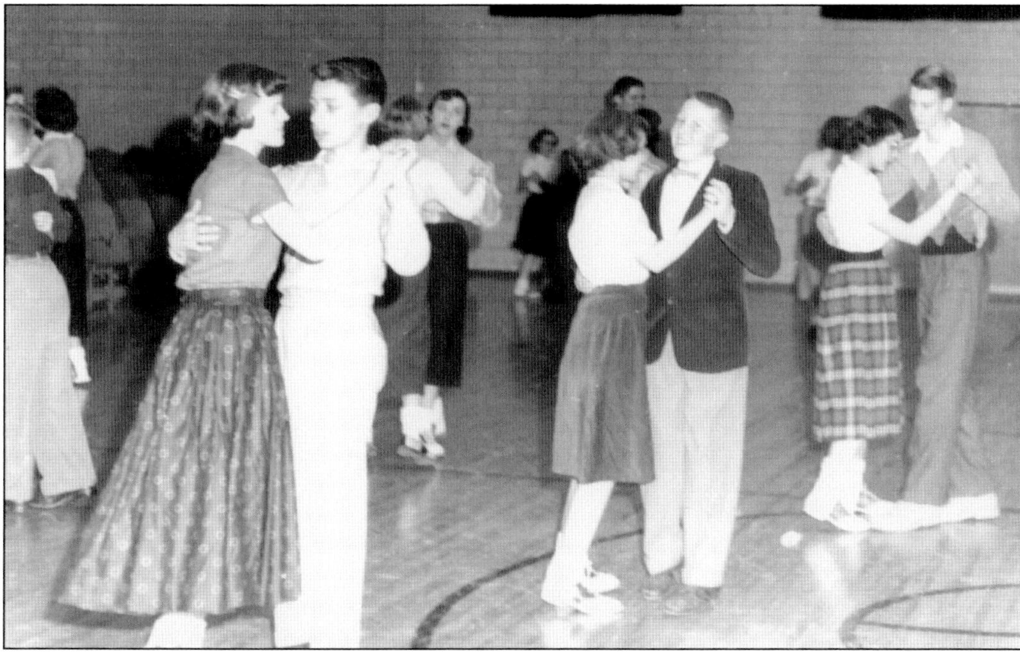

Pictured is a dance at the Harris-Elmore High School gymnasium during the early 1950s. From left to right are Beth Brandes, Jerry Krueger, Joanne Roepke, Dale Klingbiel, Nancy Haar, and John Votaw. (Doug Pickard Collection, HEPL.)

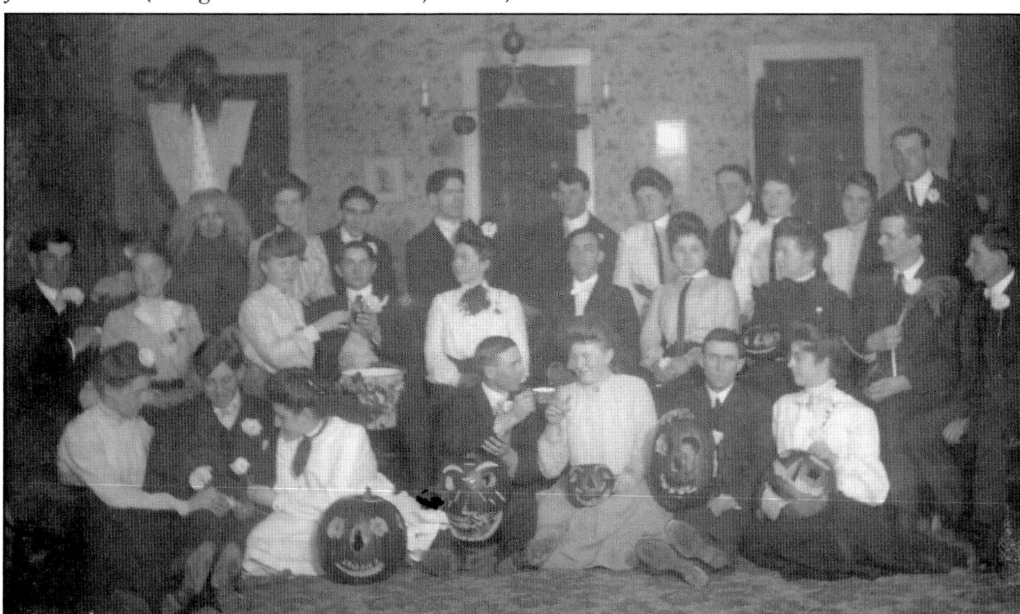

At a Genoa Halloween party are, from left to right (first row) Lucy Dolph, unidentified, Helen Powers, Clarence LaVigne, Edith Bittinger, John Gregg, and Carrie Camper; (second row) Clark Armstrong, Alma Armstrong, Leone Beam, Ray Dolph, Ida Gallup, Hattie Whitney, Nelle Frutton, Ralph Uthoff, and Wallace Gregg; (third row) Frances Doty, Alice Hassan, Walter Hassan, Lyman Chambers, Ralph Chambers, Ralph Welch, Elsie Camper Werner, Harmon Faber, Mabel Schessler, Blanche Bowland, and Emmett Bowland. (GPL.)

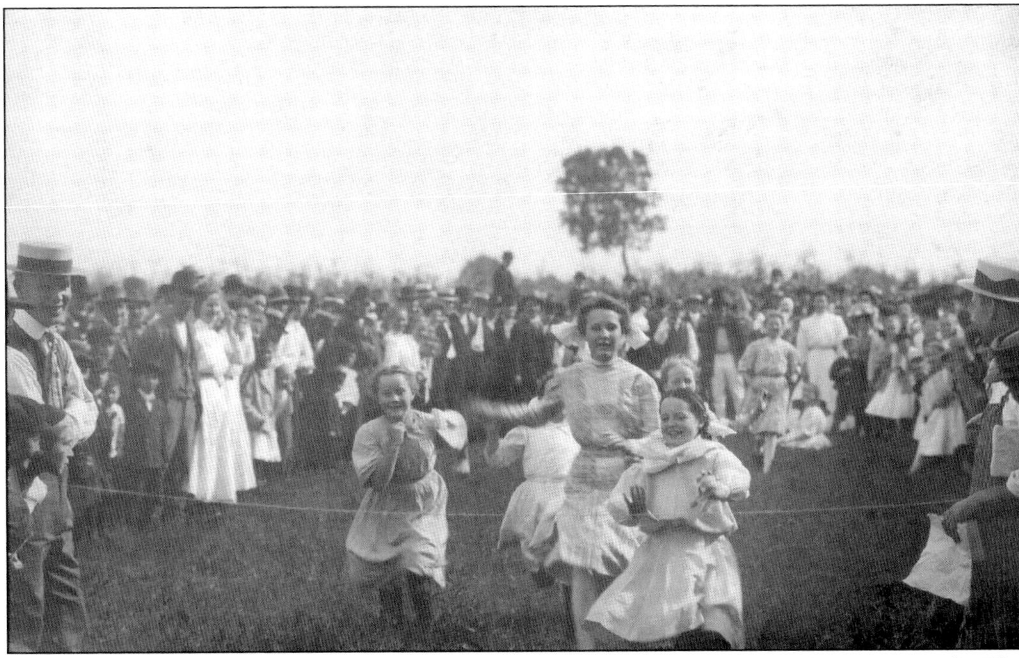

Elmore children race to the finish line at a community picnic in the Ernsthausen Woods. This photograph was taken around the turn of the 20th century. (Nellie Linker Collection, HEPL.)

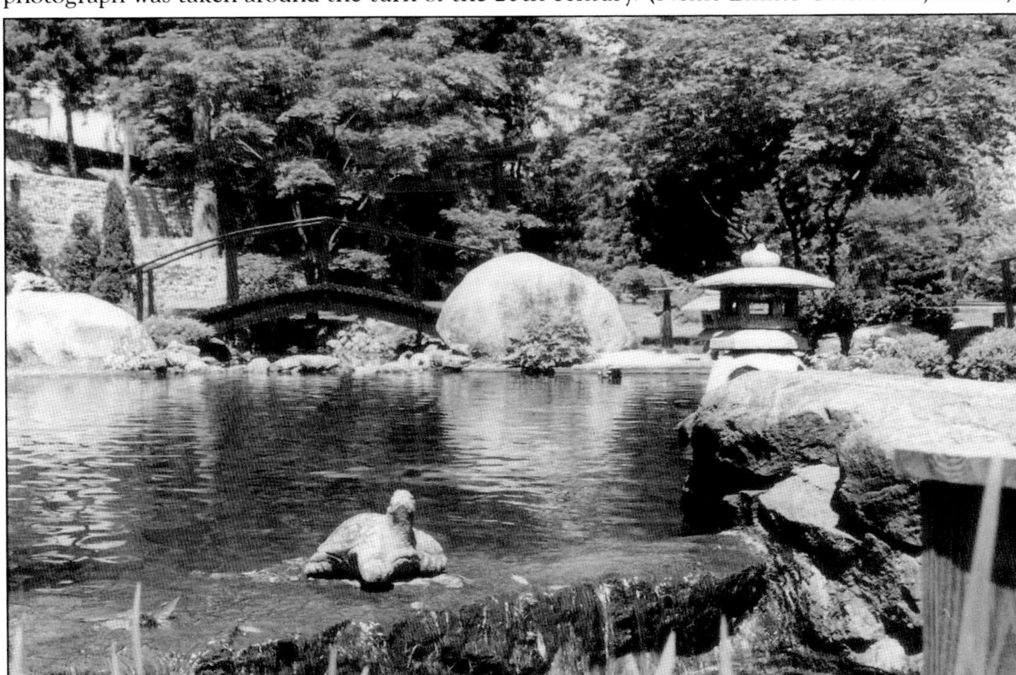

The Japanese Gardens at the Schedel Arboretum and Gardens were opened to the public by the Schedel Foundation in 1991. Previously, the garden was privately tended by Joe and Marie Schedel on their estate. The Schedels had traveled to Asia and embraced the culture. The Schedel estate is a popular tourist destination in Elmore and showcases four gardens, a manor house, a banquet hall, meeting facilities, and a trellis gallery featuring local artwork. (HEPL.)

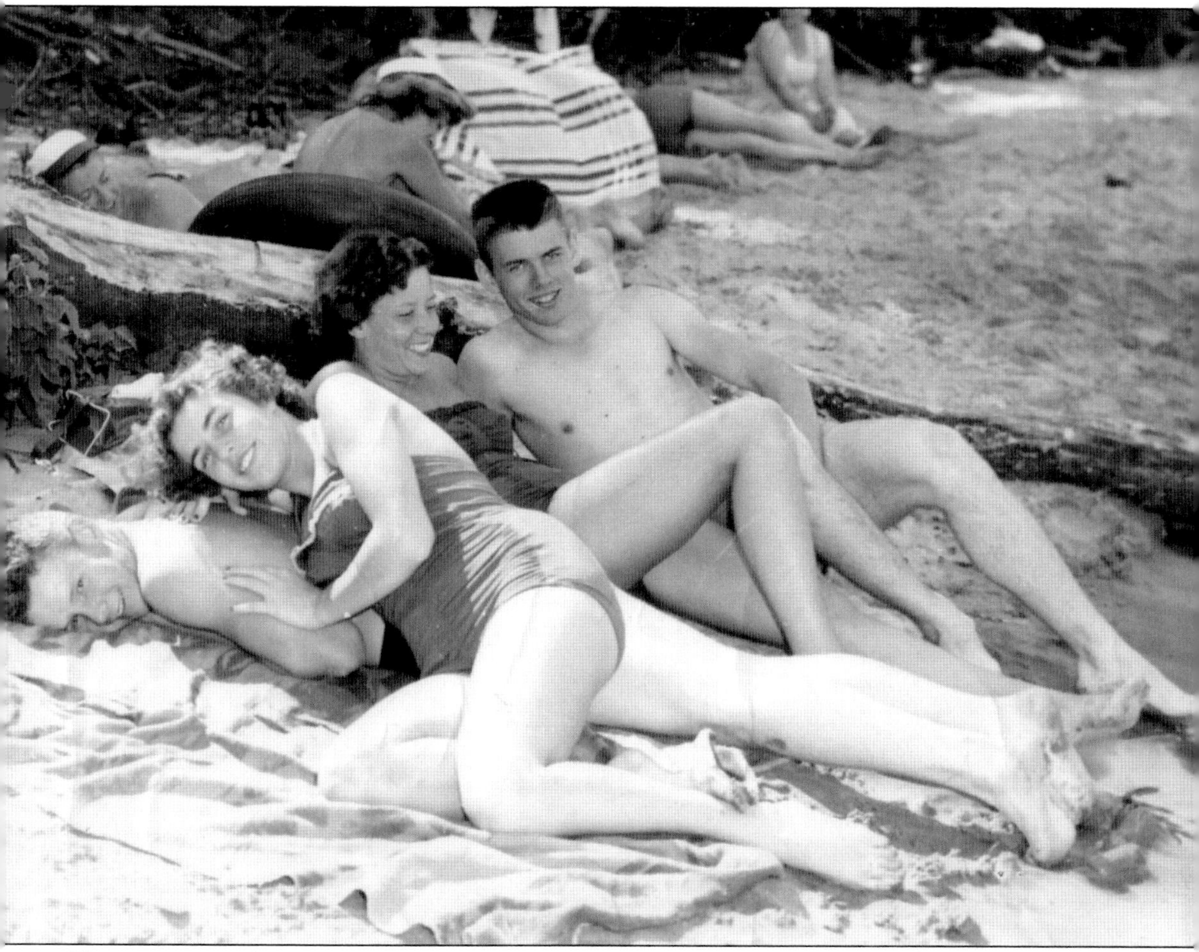

Elmore teens soak up some sun at one of the nearby beaches in the summer of 1954. From left to right are Red Lemke, Marlene Sondergeld, Barbara Summers, and Dick Manzeck. (Doug Pickard Collection, HEPL.)

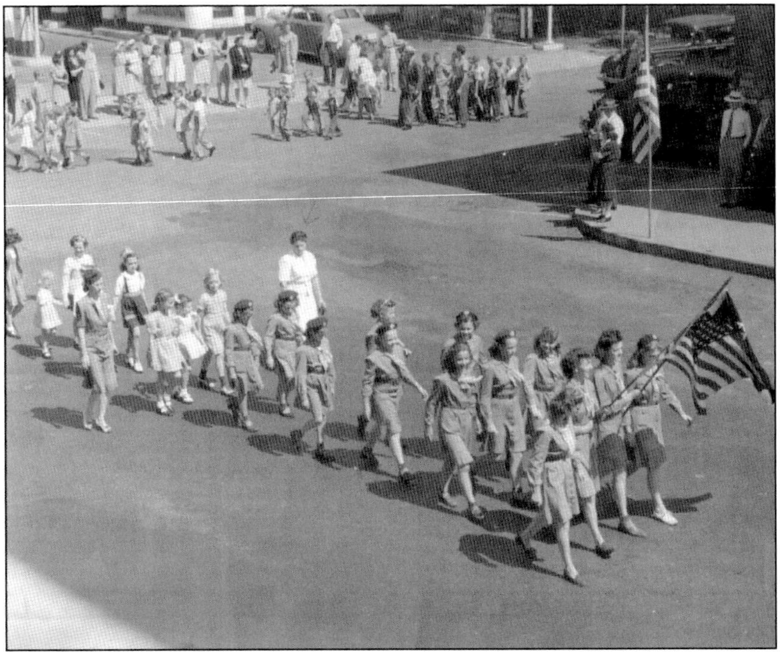

Margaret "Ma" Willett walks with her Elmore Girl Scouts in a homecoming parade during the early 1950s. Willett formed a Brownie troop for her daughter when there was none available in town and ultimately became the driving force for Scouting in the community. Willett and her husband have also put on the Elmore fireworks show each year since the 1980s. (Pete Willett, HEPL.)

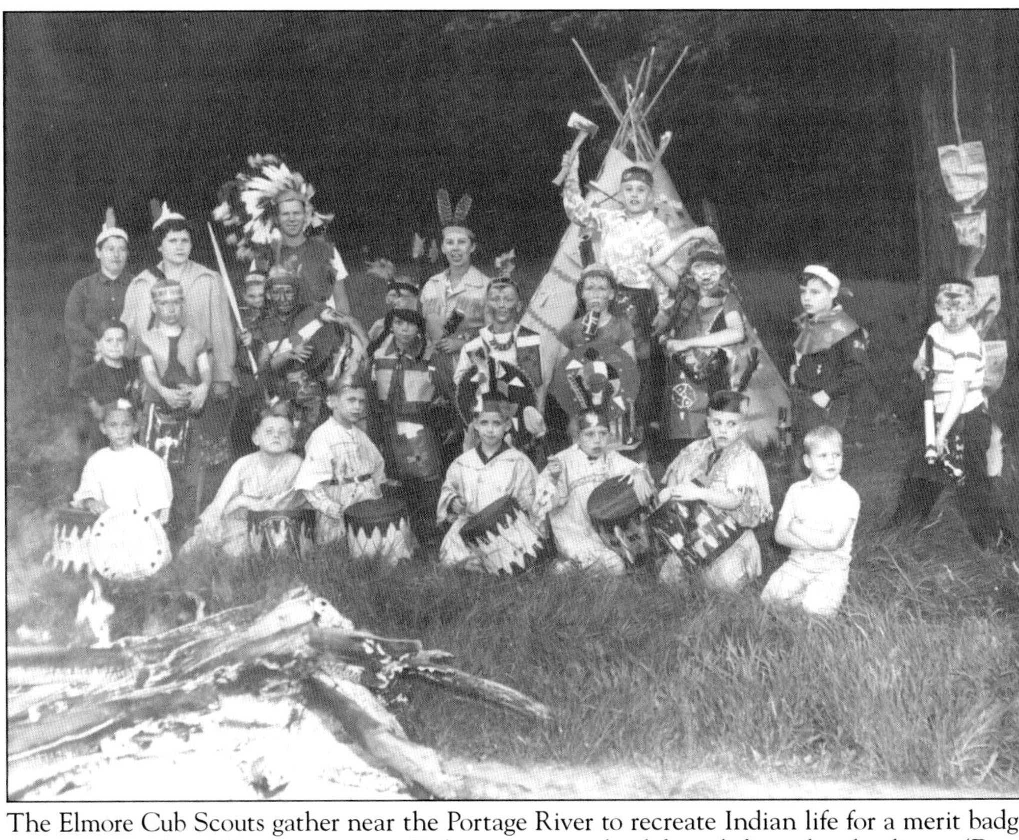

The Elmore Cub Scouts gather near the Portage River to recreate Indian life for a merit badge during the early 1950s. Scoutmaster Robert Avers is third from left in the third row. (Doug Pickard Collection, HEPL.)

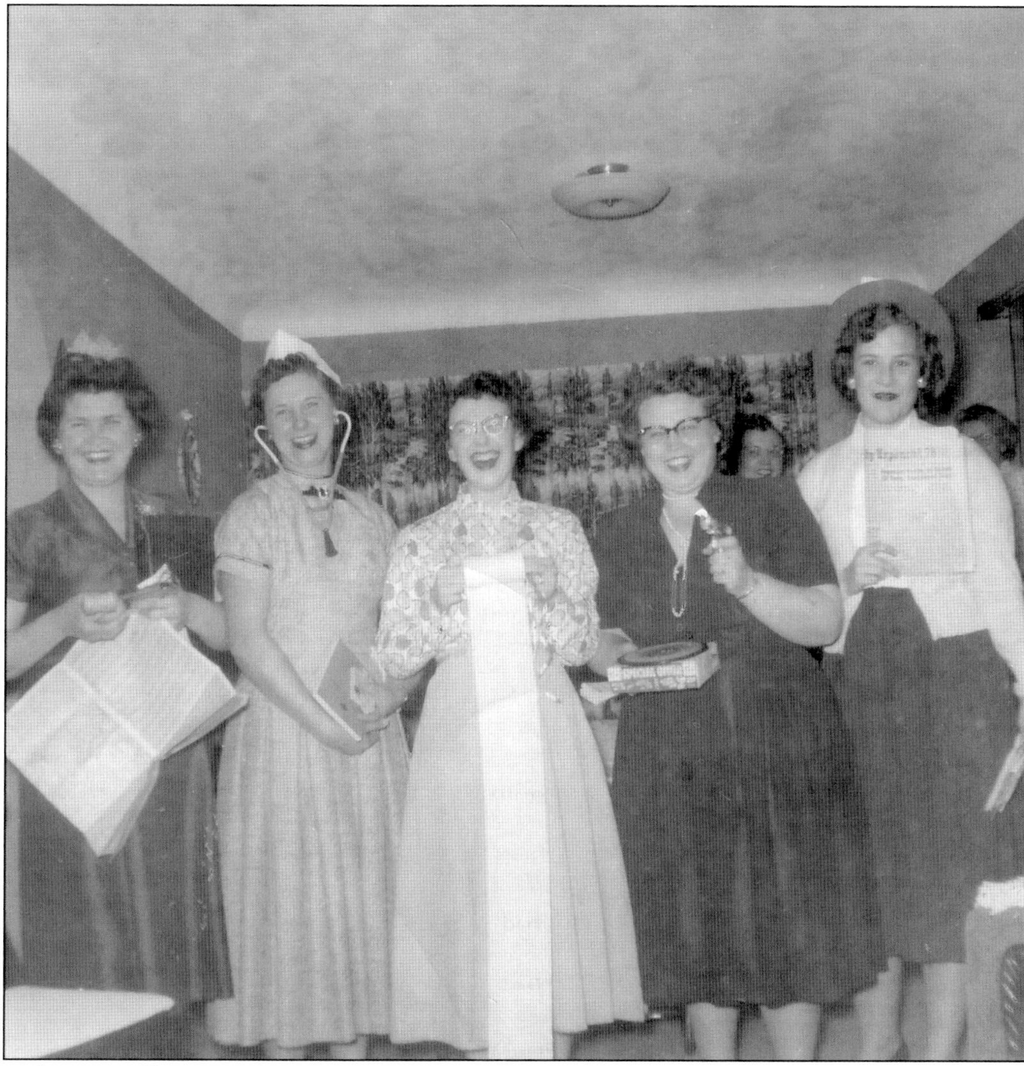

Ladies win silly prizes after a game played at a 1959 Modern Mothers Club meeting in Elmore. These types of organizations were formed by young mothers to discuss issues and events within the community that would have an affect on their children. From left to right are Betty Haar, Donna Dittman, Vera Hille, Elizabeth Ory, and Mitzy Paule. (Vera Hille.)

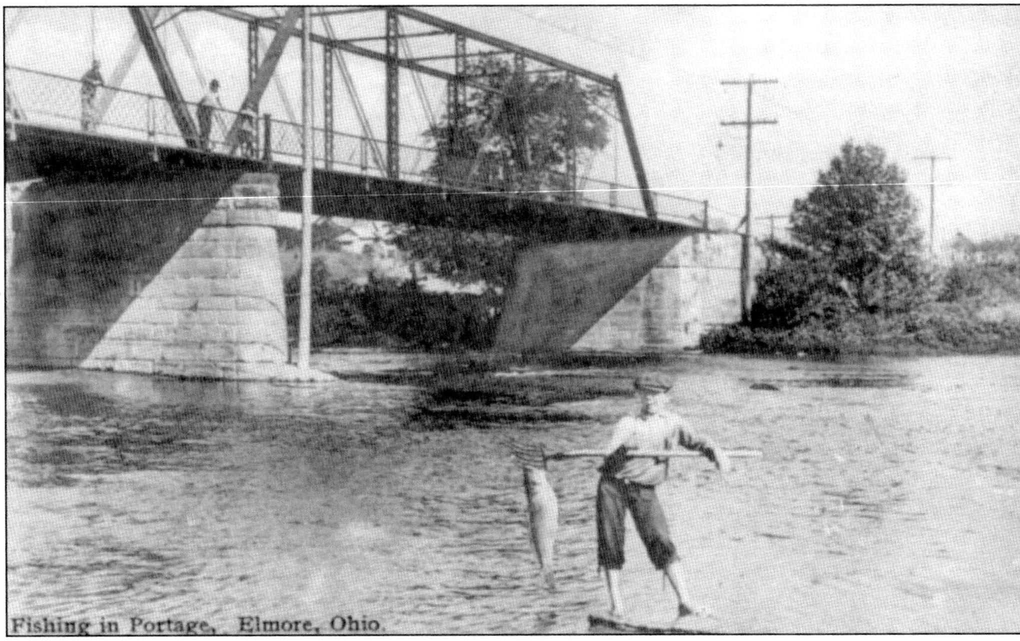

A 1917 Elmore postcard shows a boy spearing a fish in the Portage River with a pitchfork. Fishing was a popular pastime, as the fish were plentiful, especially underneath the wagon bridge. (HEPL.)

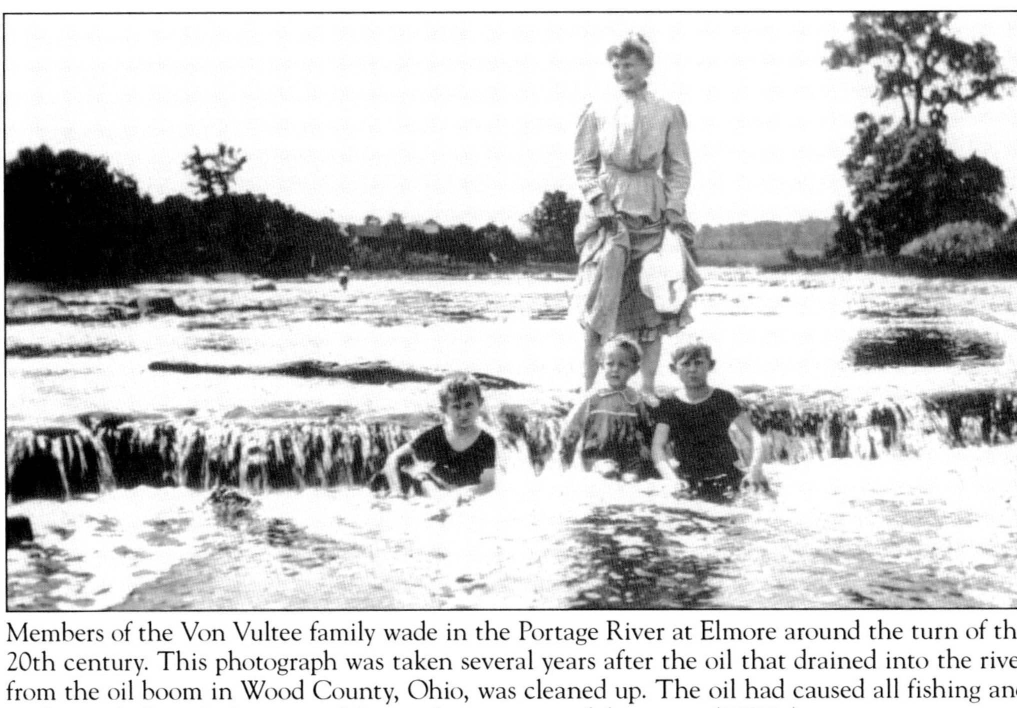

Members of the Von Vultee family wade in the Portage River at Elmore around the turn of the 20th century. This photograph was taken several years after the oil that drained into the river from the oil boom in Wood County, Ohio, was cleaned up. The oil had caused all fishing and wading to halt and often caused fires to burn on top of the water. (HEPL.)

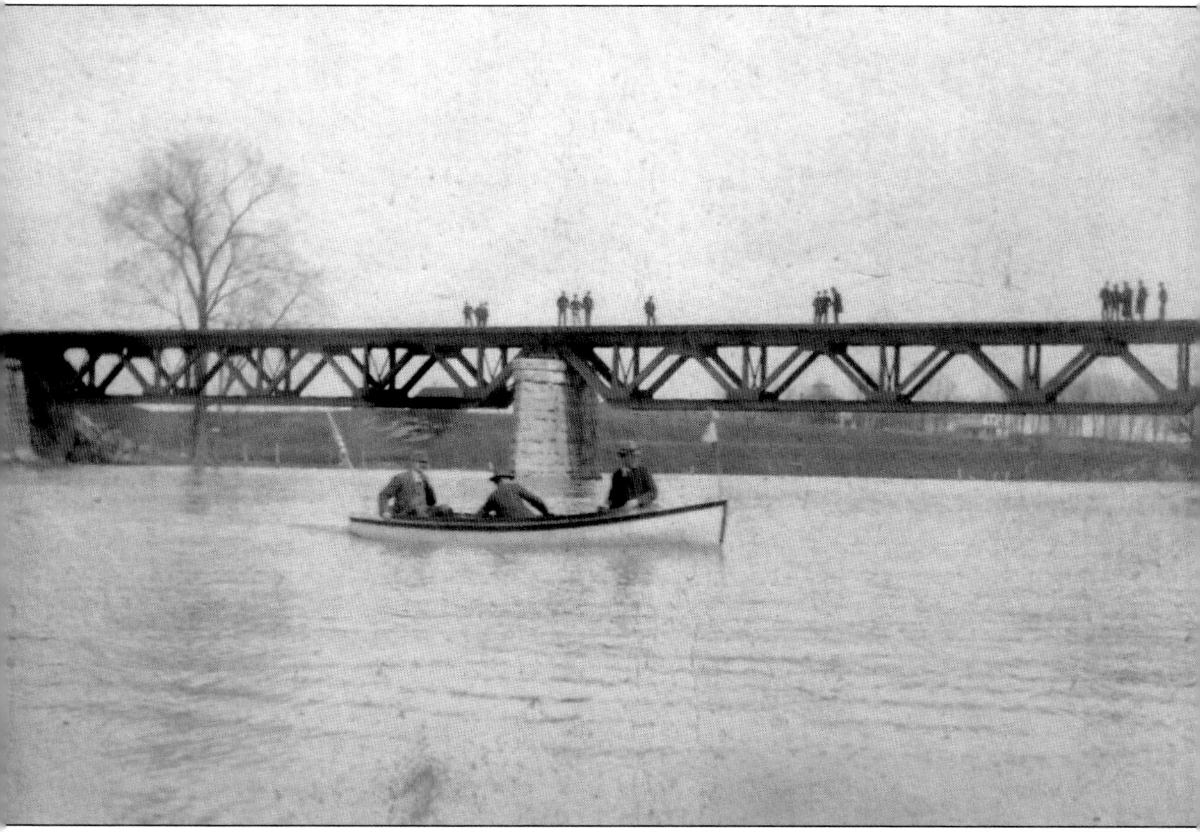

Viewing the people on the wagon bridge that enters town, three unidentified men canoe along the Portage River in Elmore. (HEPL.)

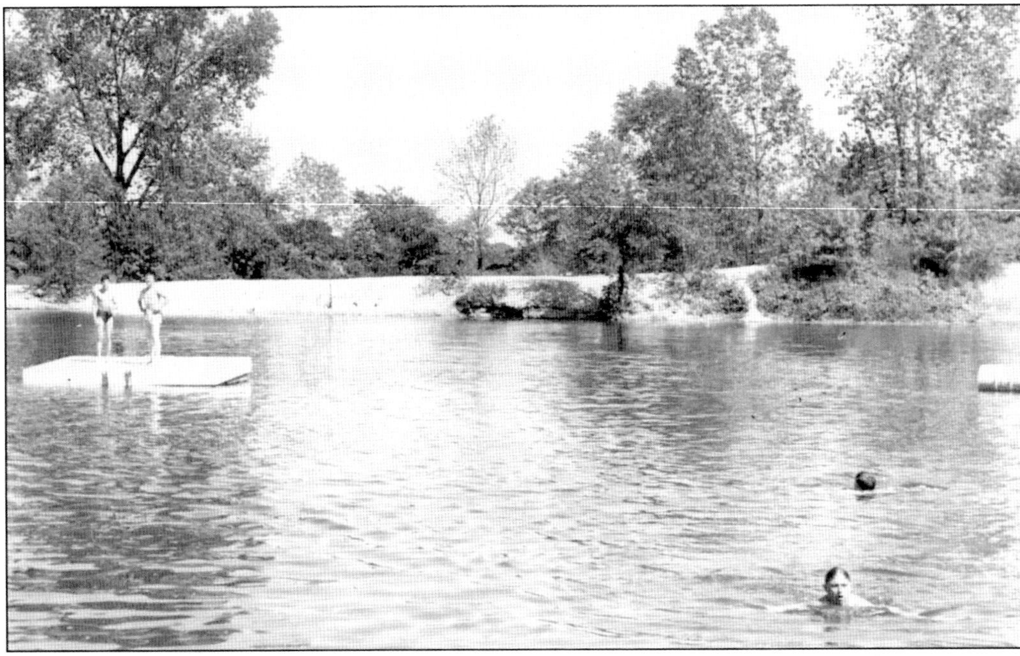

This beautiful swimming area in Veterans Memorial Park was once home to the Big Quarry and the Wyman and Gregg Quarry. In 1944, Bob Skilliter Sr., Bernard Huss, and Jack Boyson thought to fill in the quarry previously consumed with trash from the Kelly Lime and Transport Company and create a park. It opened the following year at a water carnival. (Doug Pickard Collection, HEPL.)

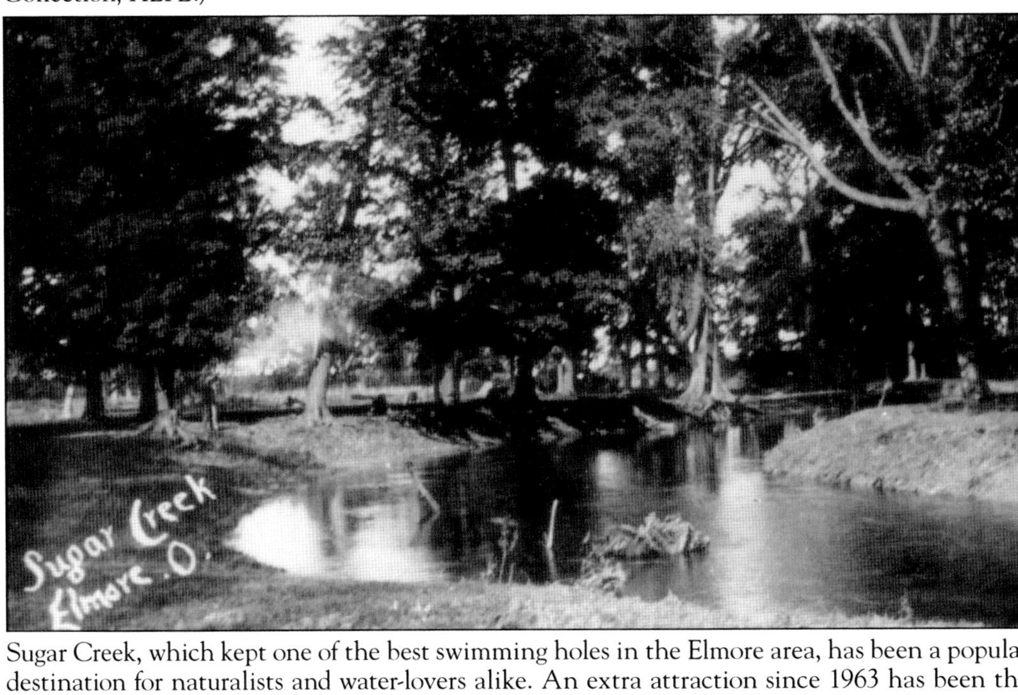

Sugar Creek, which kept one of the best swimming holes in the Elmore area, has been a popular destination for naturalists and water-lovers alike. An extra attraction since 1963 has been the Sugar Creek Golf Course, which has picturesque scenery. The course was developed by Stanley and Marylene Neeb at Sugar Creek near the site of the family's former meat market. (HEPL.)

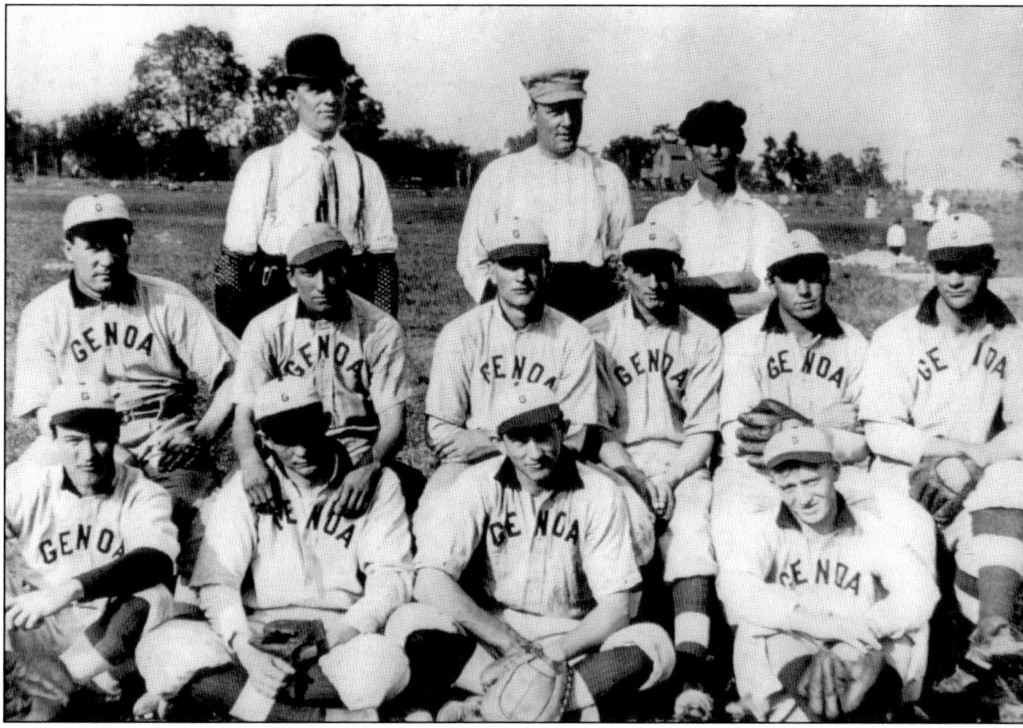

After slaughtering local foes, the amateur Genoa baseball team was the area champion in 1912. The team included, from left to right, (first row) Casey Burhett, Merrill Rudes, Henry (Heine) Bergman, and Carl Widmer; (second row) George Dunn, unidentified, Bill Peiffer, unidentified, Joe Vogel, and Ralph Welch; (third row) Henry Satoris, John Werner, and Clyde (Babe) Doty. (Dr. Kenneth Laub.)

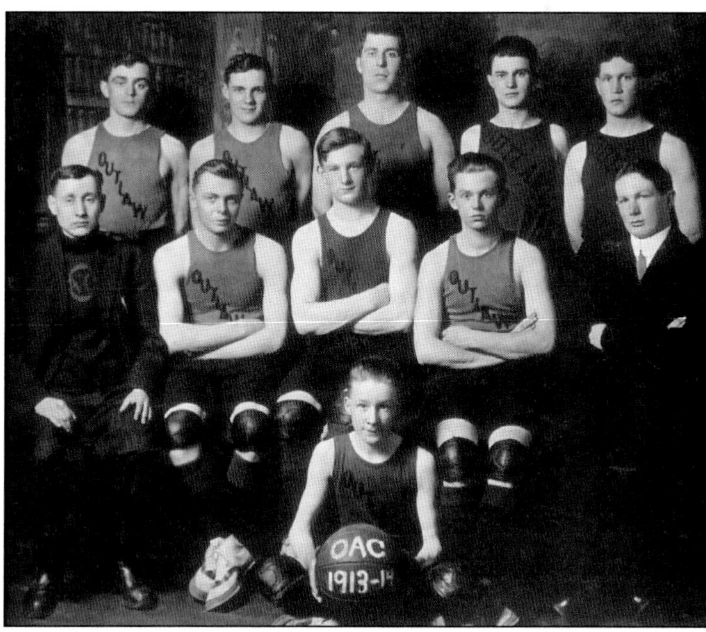

Pictured is the semiprofessional Elmore Outlaw basketball team during the 1913–1914 season. The team played home games at the Jeremy Opera House in town. In this photograph are, from left to right, (first row) Elmore Damschroder; (second row) Karl Witte, Otto Meyer, Clayton (Brownie) Weis, Russell Vining, and the unidentified superintendent of Elmore schools; (third row) Carl (Sox) Wainwright, Ed Dischinger, Lyle Baldwin, Karl Reed, and George Avers. (HEPL.)

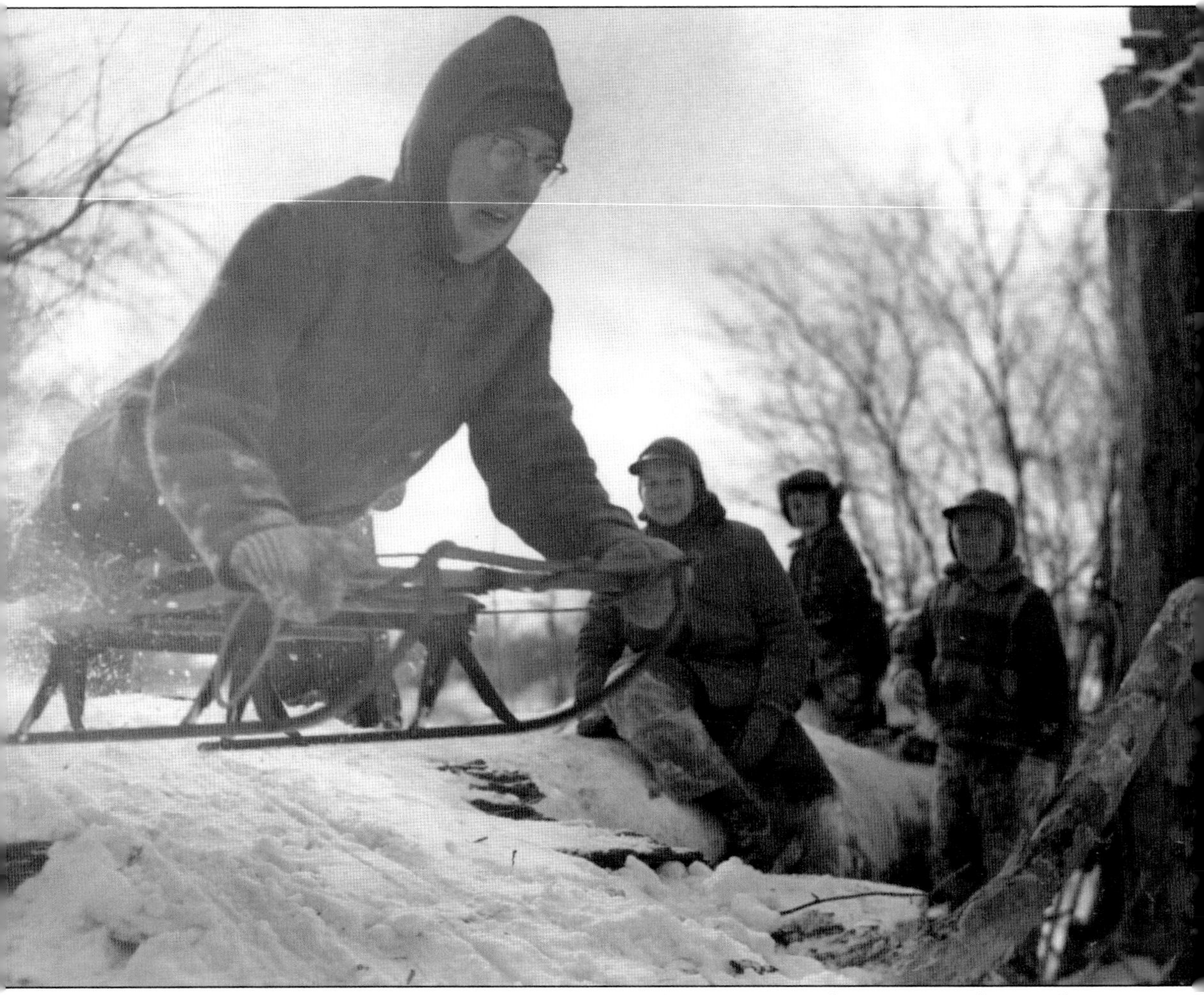

Nelson Henry sleds down Reed's Hill in Elmore around 1953. Waiting their turns on the treacherous slope, local children watch in the background. (Doug Pickard Collection, HEPL.)

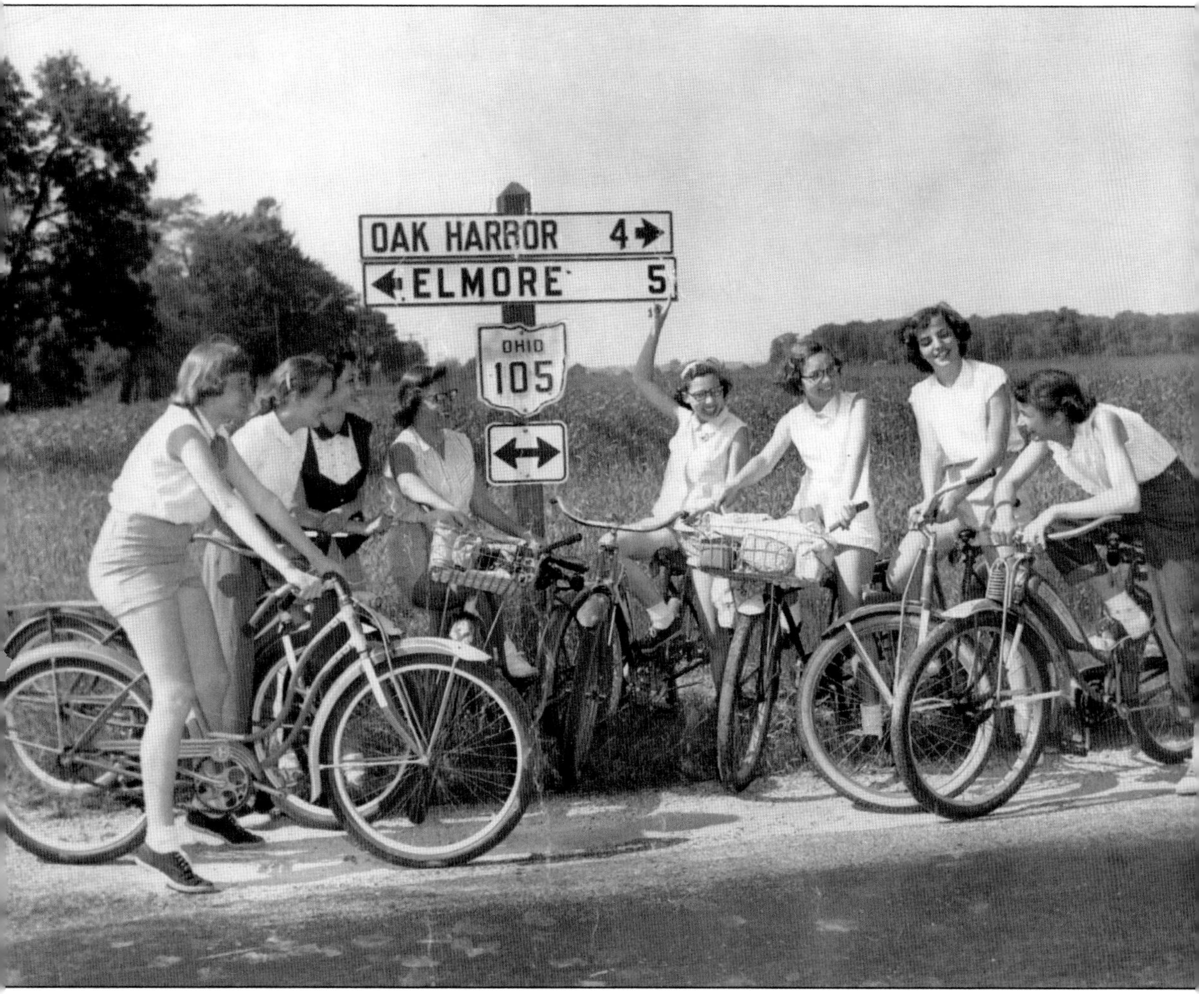

While riding their bikes on Route 105 in 1954, Elmore girls point to road signs and try to decide on a path. They are, from left to right, Patty James, unidentified, Karen Hetrick, Karen Jacobs, Judy Owen, Joanne Frania, Joanne Chio, and Shirley Griffin. (Doug Pickard Collection, HEPL.)

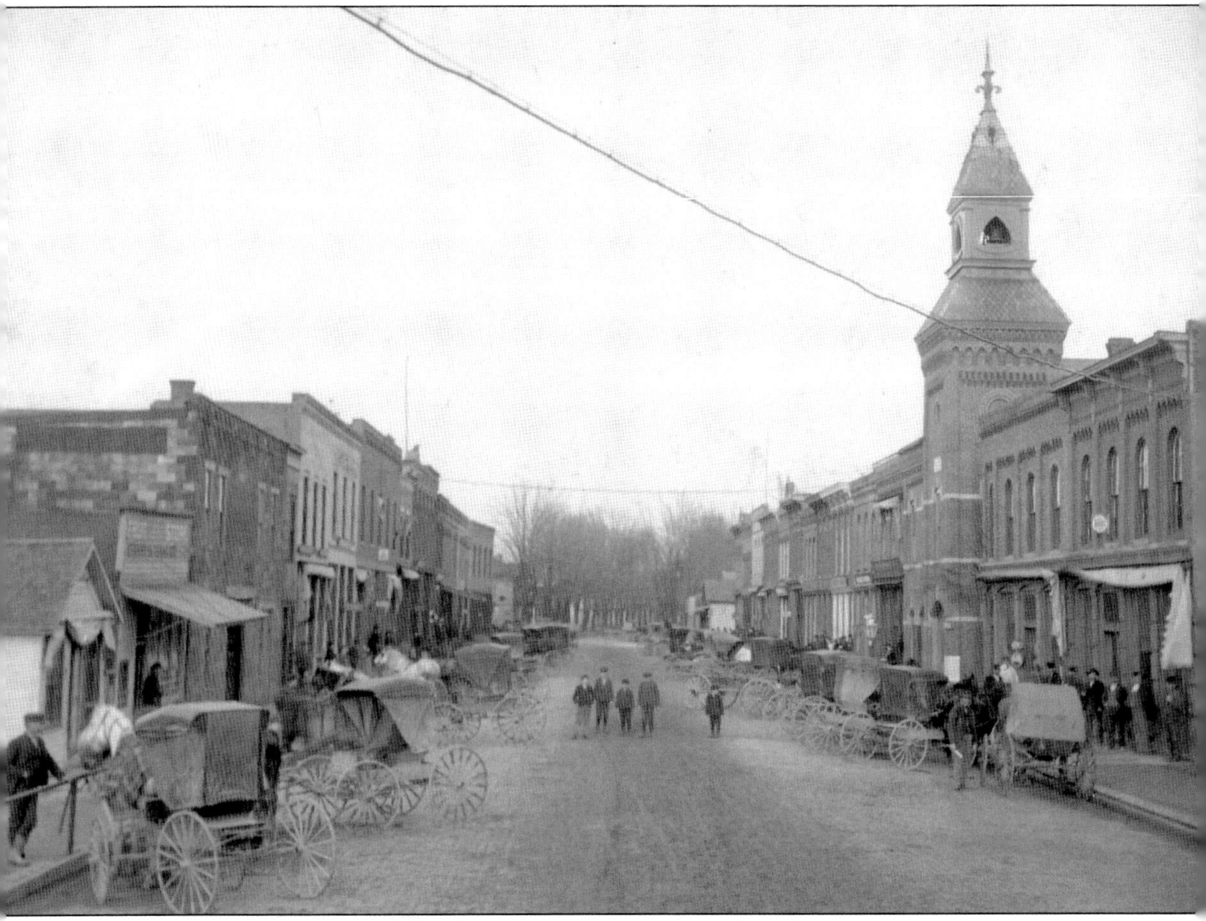

Local boys stand in the middle of Elmore's Rice Street in 1906. Boys often met up in the middle of the street to enter the local stores or to play a game of football. A lot of the games took place right on Main Street, much to the chagrin of business owners and shoppers. (HEPL.)

Two

The Customer is Always Right

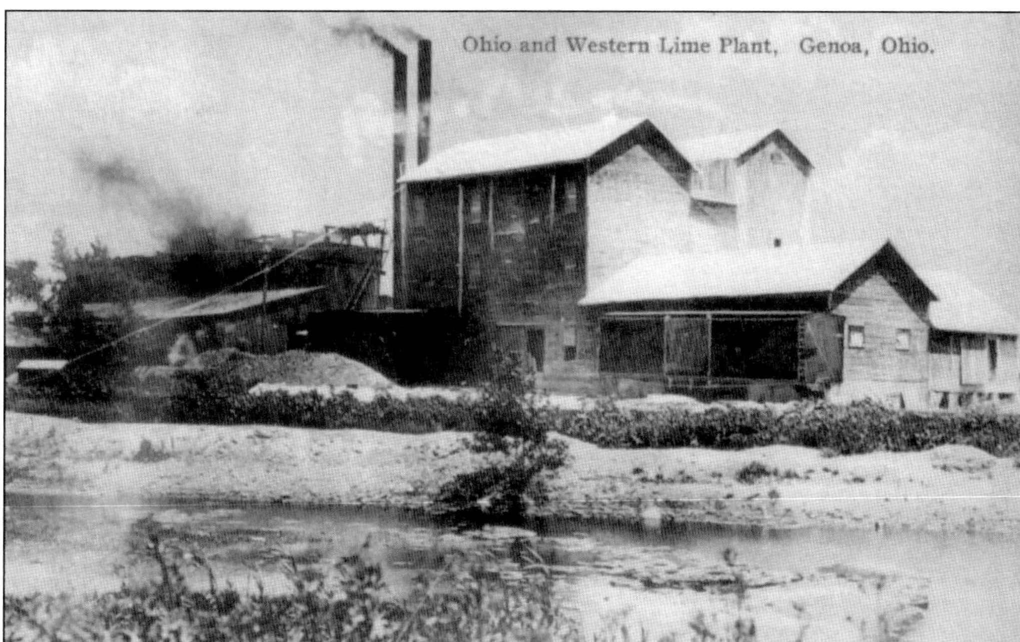

Featured on this postcard is the Ohio and Western Lime Plant in Genoa. This photograph was taken between 1904, when the company began, and 1917, when it merged with the Kelly Island Lime and Transport Company. The US Gypsum Company took over the local lime industry in the 1920s. Genoa still continues to be one of the biggest lime manufacturers in the country. (Kirk Hise collection, via Eric Hise.)

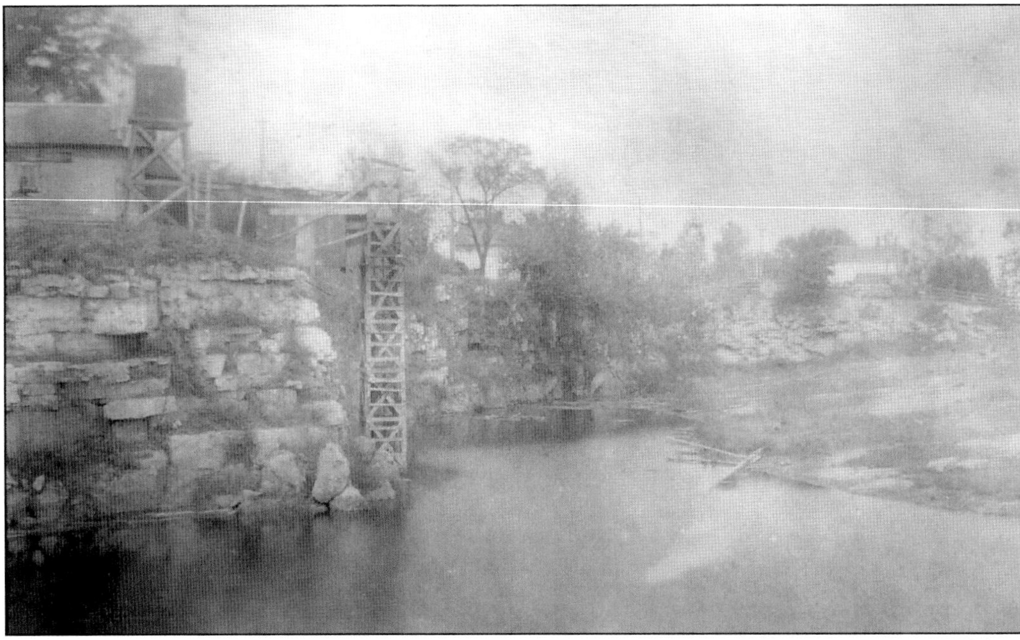

The Wyman and Gregg Quarry is pictured prior to 1900. Albert Wyman manufactured lime with Leander Gregg from the 1850s to the 1890s. They produced some of the first pot limekilns in Genoa, dating back to 1855. The quarry has been filled in and is part of the Veterans Park parking area and playing fields. (Edna Turner Collection, GPL.)

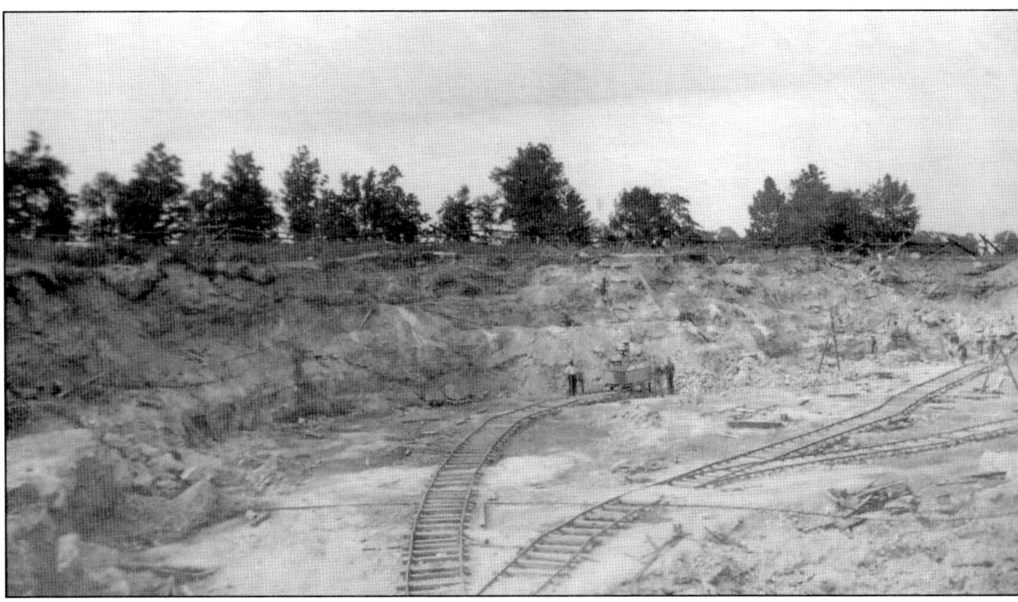

The Big Quarry is now filled with water and used for swimming in Veterans Park in Genoa. Shown here in the 1880s, the men are hauling white limestone along the tracks to be crushed and placed into kilns. (Edna Turner Collection, GPL.)

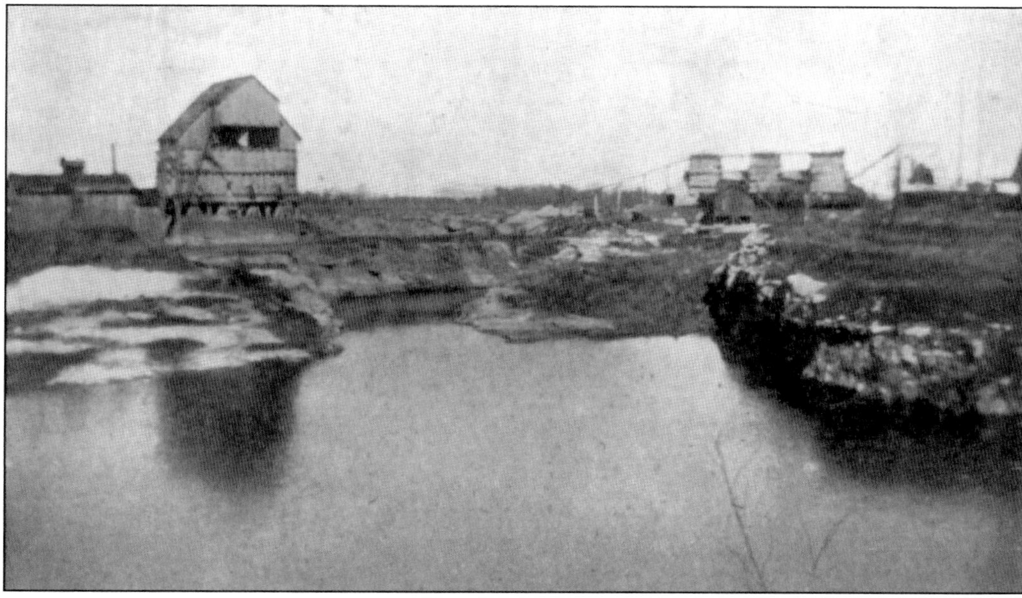

The limekilns and stone crushers in this 1903 image are at one of the quarries east of Washington Street in Genoa. When US Gypsum took over the quarries in the area in the 1920s, it was common to see small frame homes that belonged to the immigrant lime workers on the banks. (Kirk Hise collection, via Eric Hise.)

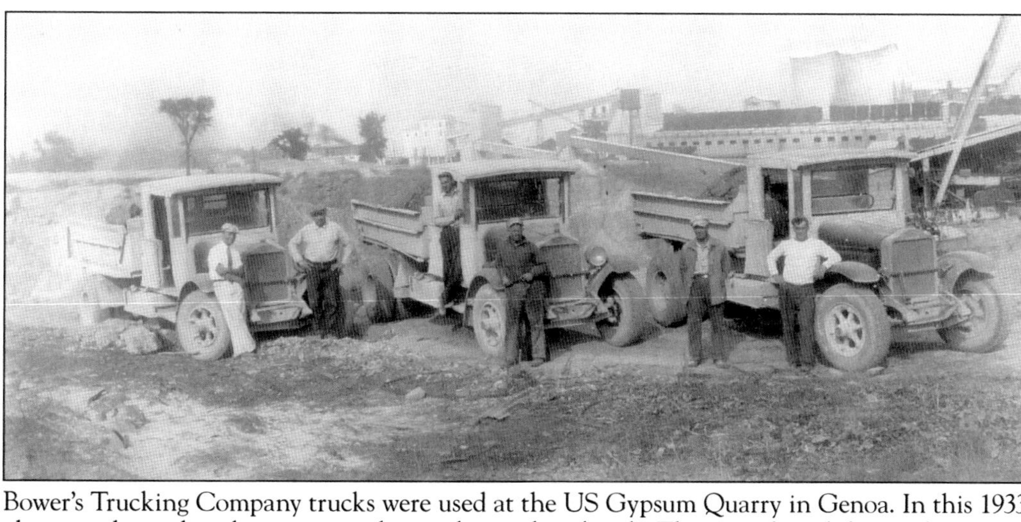

Bower's Trucking Company trucks were used at the US Gypsum Quarry in Genoa. In this 1933 photograph, workers lean against the trucks on their break. They are, from left to right, Rich ? (quarry boss), Harold Bower, Larry Welch, Clarence Kramer, Henry Dates, and Peter Holcomb. (Lamar Bowers, via Gene Meyers.)

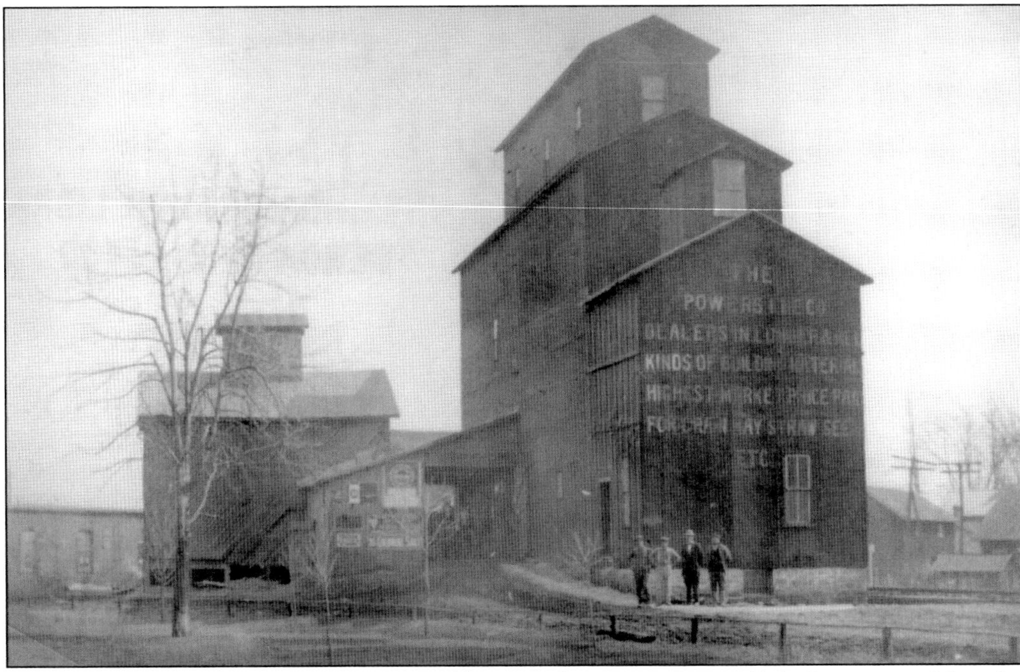

The Powers Elevator Company is pictured here in the 1890s. Owner E.A. Powers would get his logs out at Webb's Station, where he also had a side grocery business that later moved to Genoa. The elevator bore Powers's name from 1883 until 1913, when he died. His sons Charles and George took over the business. (GPL.)

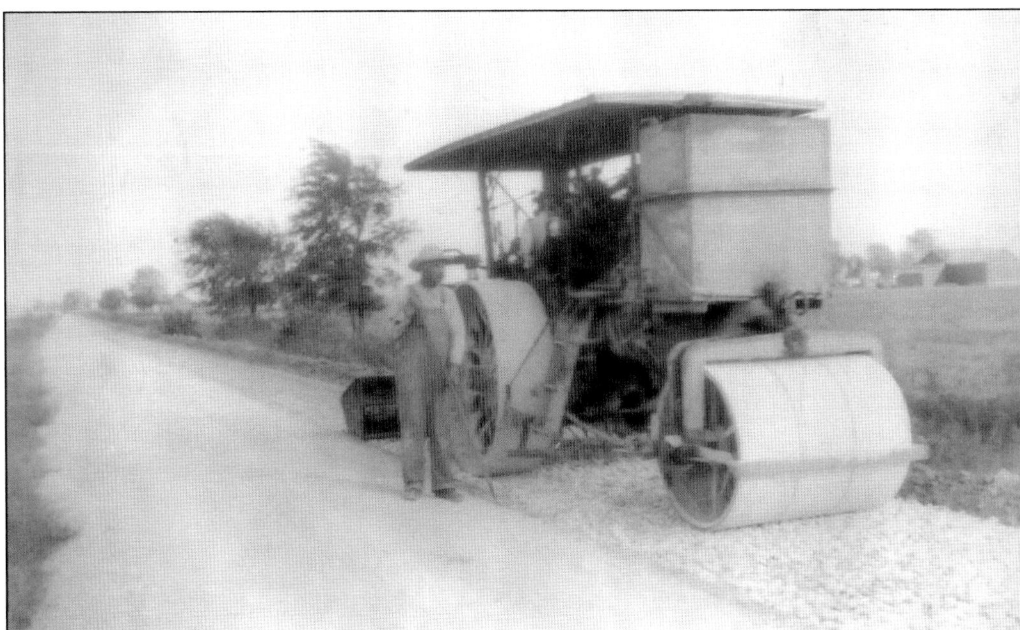

Country roads such as Holt-Harrigan in Genoa were being paved in 1929. A roller from the Bower Trucking Company is pictured here. (Lamar Bowers, via Gene Meyers.)

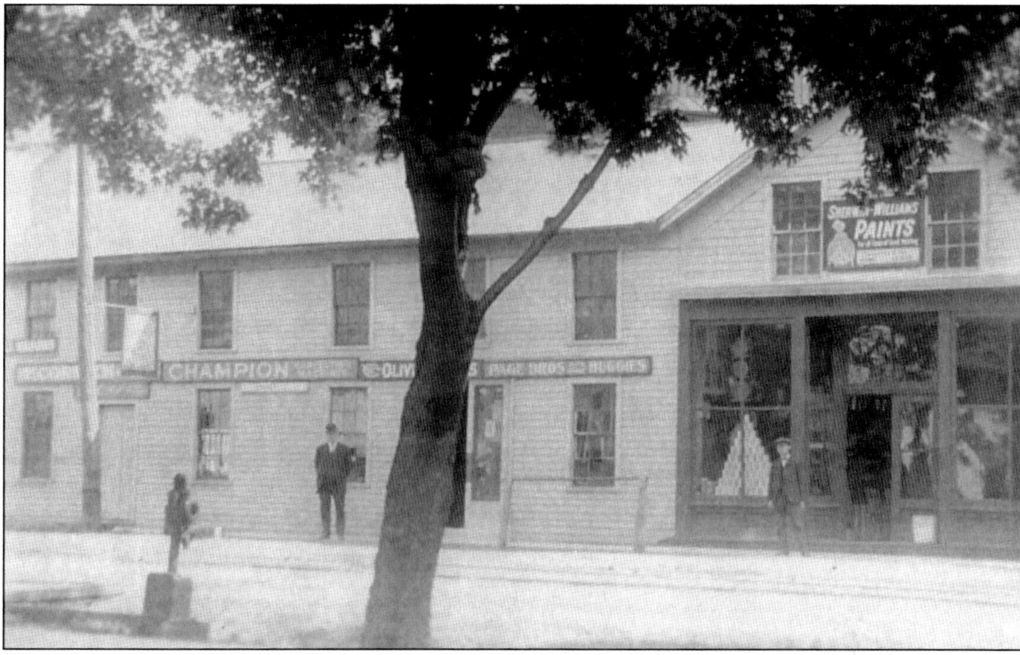

The business district on Main Street in Genoa in 1911 featured Page Brothers Buggies and Skilliter & Son Hardware. Note the dwarf block signal for the Lakeshore Electric Railway in the foreground. (Courtesy of Eric Hise.)

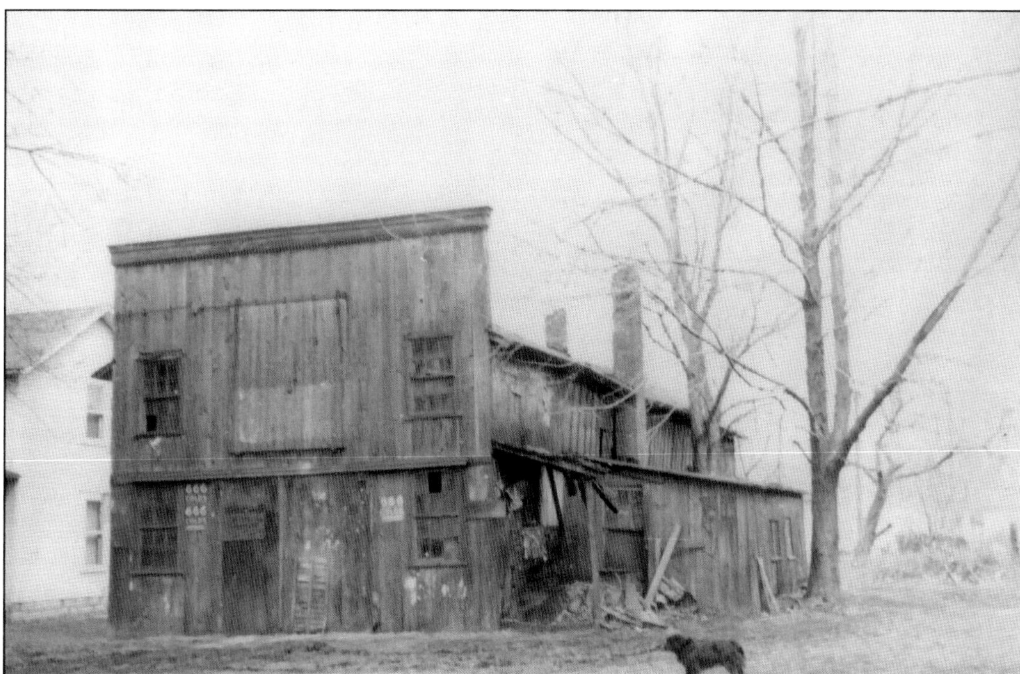

A 1939 shot shows the remains of a Genoa blacksmith shop at 917 Main Street. It was run by Dave Jensen before it fell into disrepair. (GPL.)

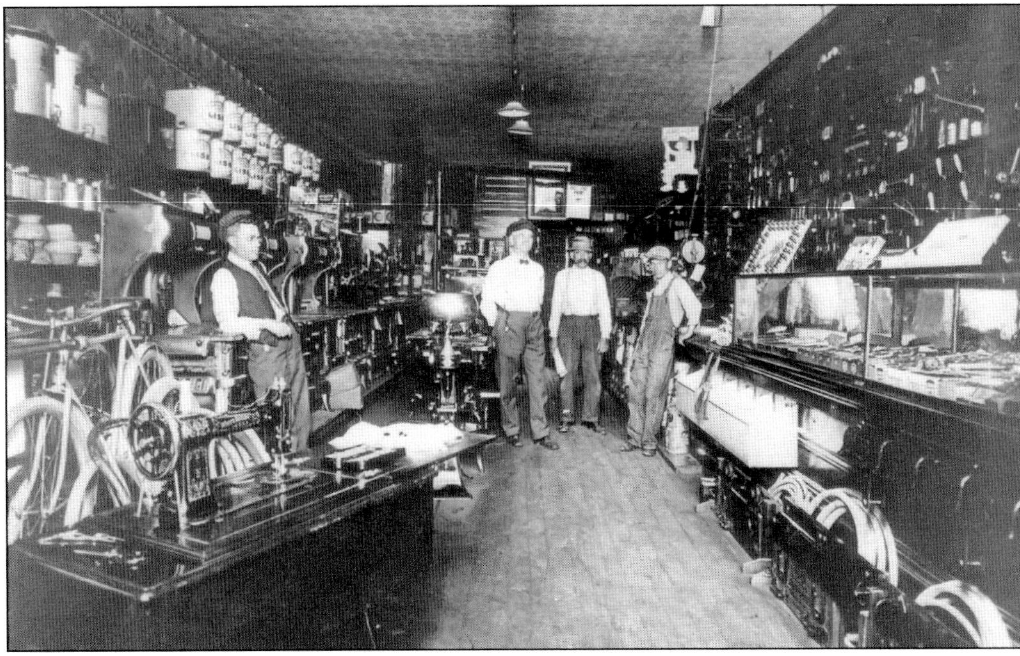

This is the interior of Skilliter and Son Hardware in December 1917. This store offered a variety of home products in the Habbler Block of Genoa from 1890 until 1960, when a fire claimed the store. Pictured are, from left to right, Walter D. Skilliter, Harry Skilliter, Tom Skilliter, and Robert Skilliter Sr. (Kirk Hise Collection, via Eric Hise.)

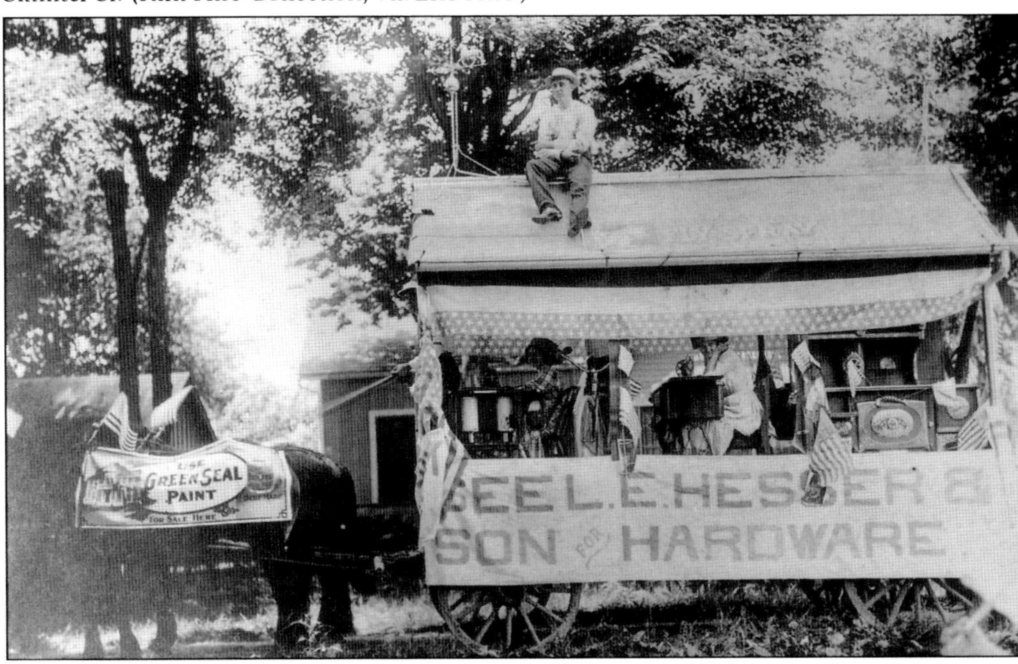

The Hesser Hardware Company of Genoa used advertisement wagons such as this to travel around the area to showcase and demonstrate store items. The Hessers began the business by taking over the firm of Jaeger and Bryant in 1911. James Hesser sits atop this wagon waiting for customers. (GPL.)

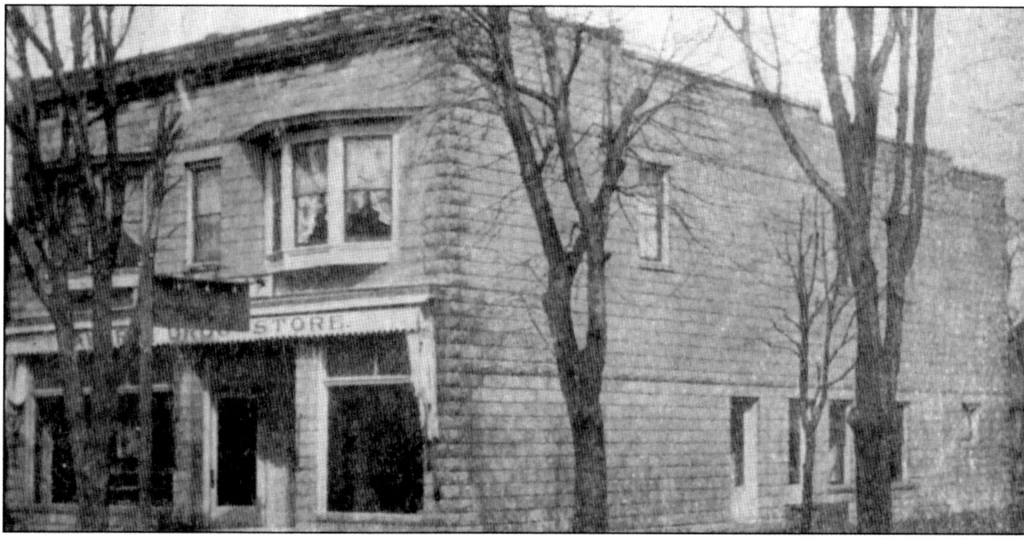

The pharmacy on Genoa's Main Street was built sometime between 1905 and 1910 by Dr. C.E. Baker. A former assistant of Baker, Charles Steincamp, bought the building in 1922 and continued to run a drugstore until 1946. The structure underwent several venue changes through the years and houses Bharmacy, a local bar, in 2010. (Joe Badger.)

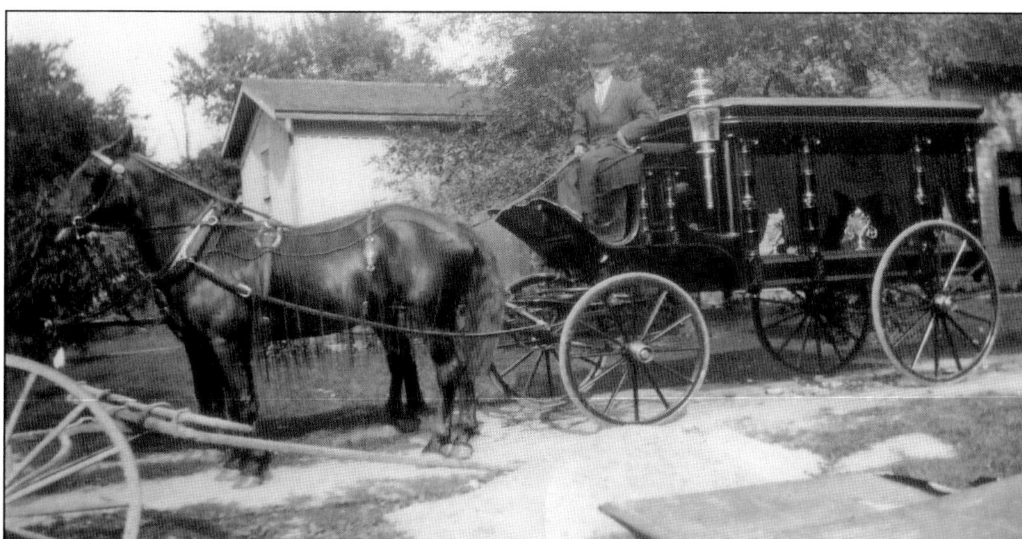

A hearse from the Burman Funeral Home is parked on Main Street in Genoa in 1906. The owners, Henry and George Burman, opened locations in both Elmore and Genoa. Genoa's Burman's Furniture was formerly Wesley Shaner's Furniture, and a separate building was constructed for the funeral home. As former cabinetmakers often built coffins, it was common for funeral home owners to run furniture stores. (GPL.)

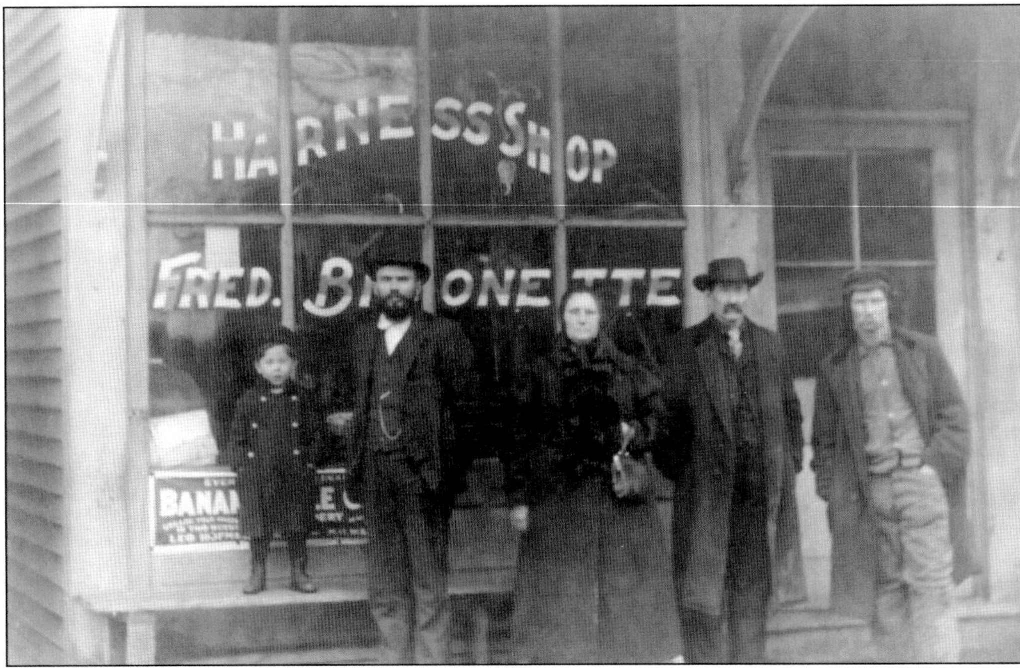

Genoans stand in front of the Fred Bisonette Harness Shop and shoe store on Main Street in the late 1800s. (GPL.)

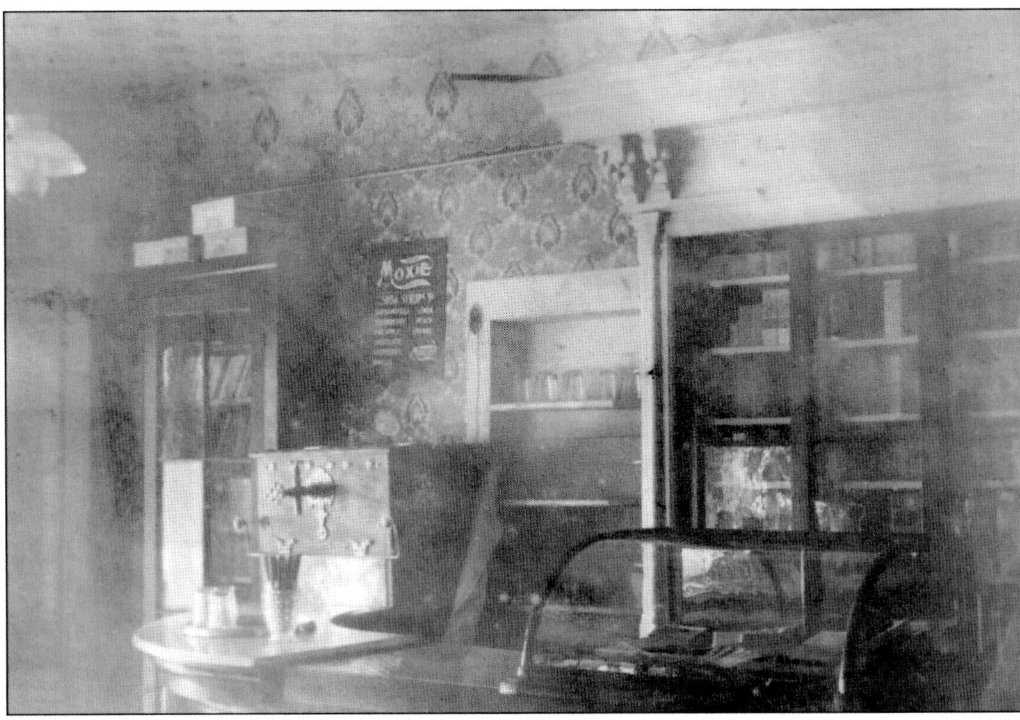

Mina Uthoff, daughter of J.H.H. Uthoff, an early settler, ran this millinery shop in Genoa from the early 1900s until the 1930s. The building also served as her home. The millinery was previously owned by Meltha Shaner. (GPL.)

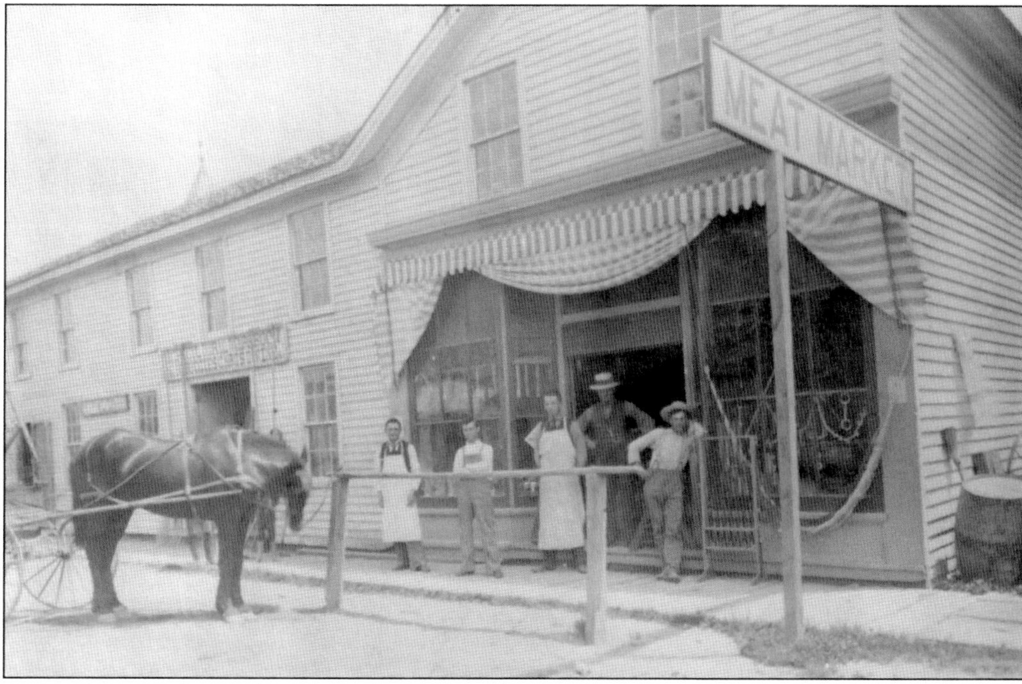

Pictured is one of several Genoa meat markets that appeared on Main Street. Due to the existence of the canopy, this is most likely the Gallup Meat Market. The Gallup market was bought out by the Growegs in 1928. Other meat markets in town included William Herman's (1911) and Nick Cashen's (1926). (Kirk Hise Collection, via Eric Hise.)

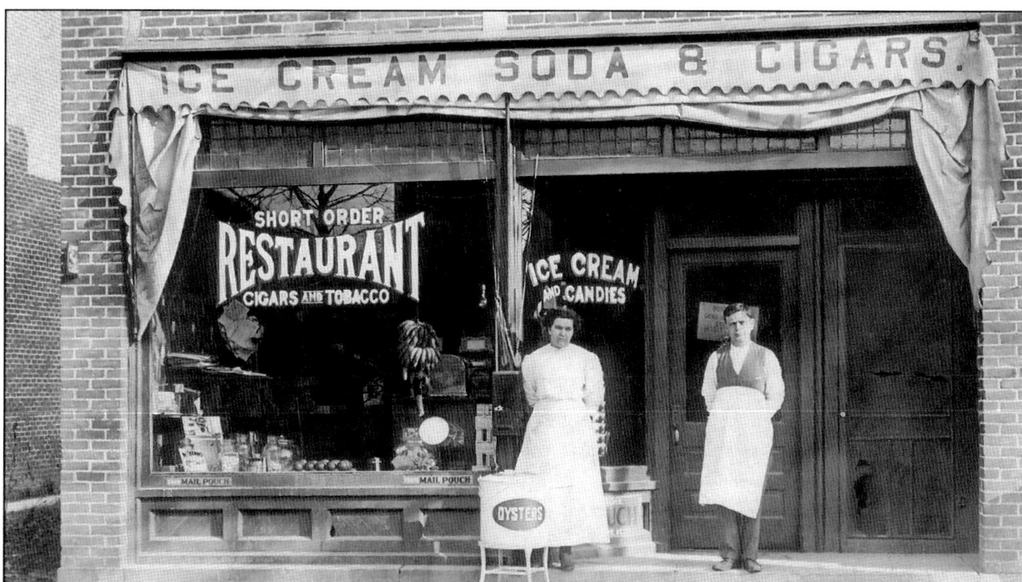

Mary (left) and Abadia Johnson stand in front of Genoa's Short Order Restaurant on Main Street in 1905. At some point, the eatery was also known as the O.J. Johnson Restaurant. In 1890, there was a telephone office above the restaurant, and Johnson's daughters Eva and Ruth worked the lines. They were known as the "Hello" girls. (HEPL.)

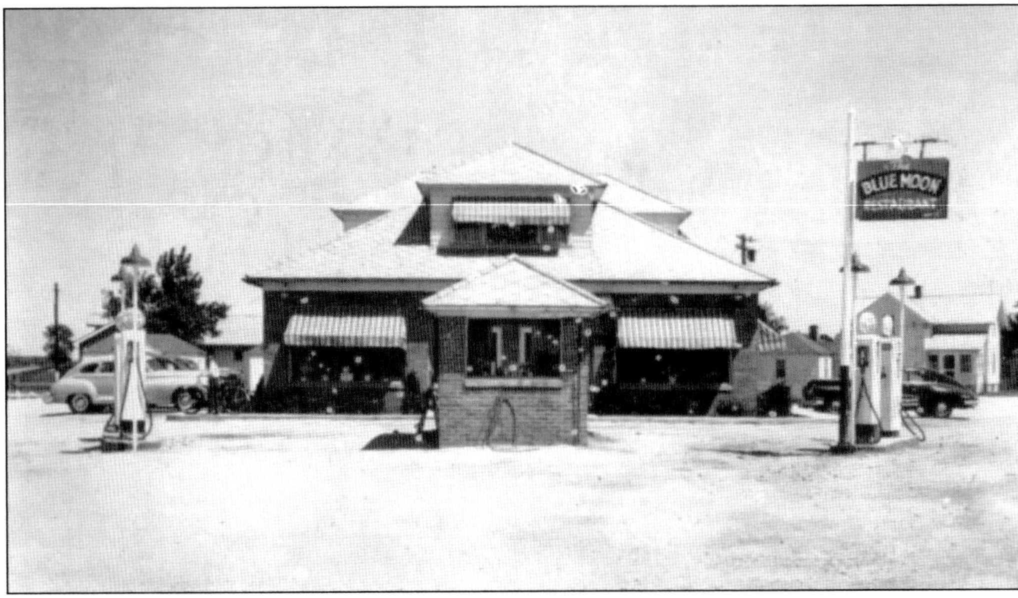

Opening in the 1950s, the Blue Moon Restaurant (above) and Motel (below) were located at the junction of Routes 63 and 51 in Genoa. Owners Carl and Myrtle Widmer offered 24-hour service, good food, heat, showers, and six double cabins. The business was sold in 1964 to Joe Latham, who turned it into Latham's Country House. Ernesto's Mexican Restaurant inhabits the building above in 2011. (Courtesy of Joe Badger.)

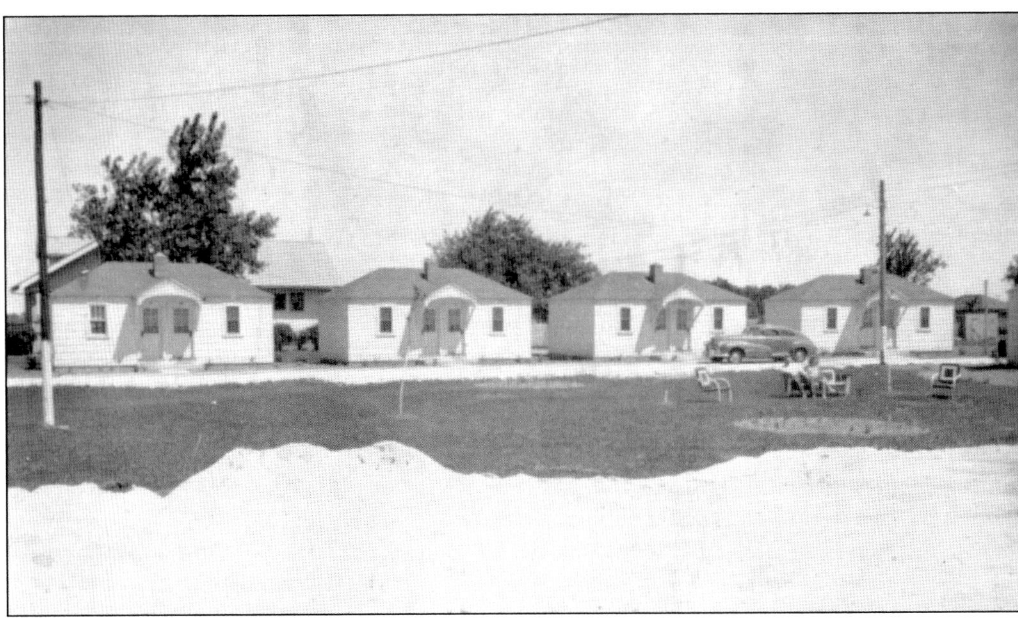

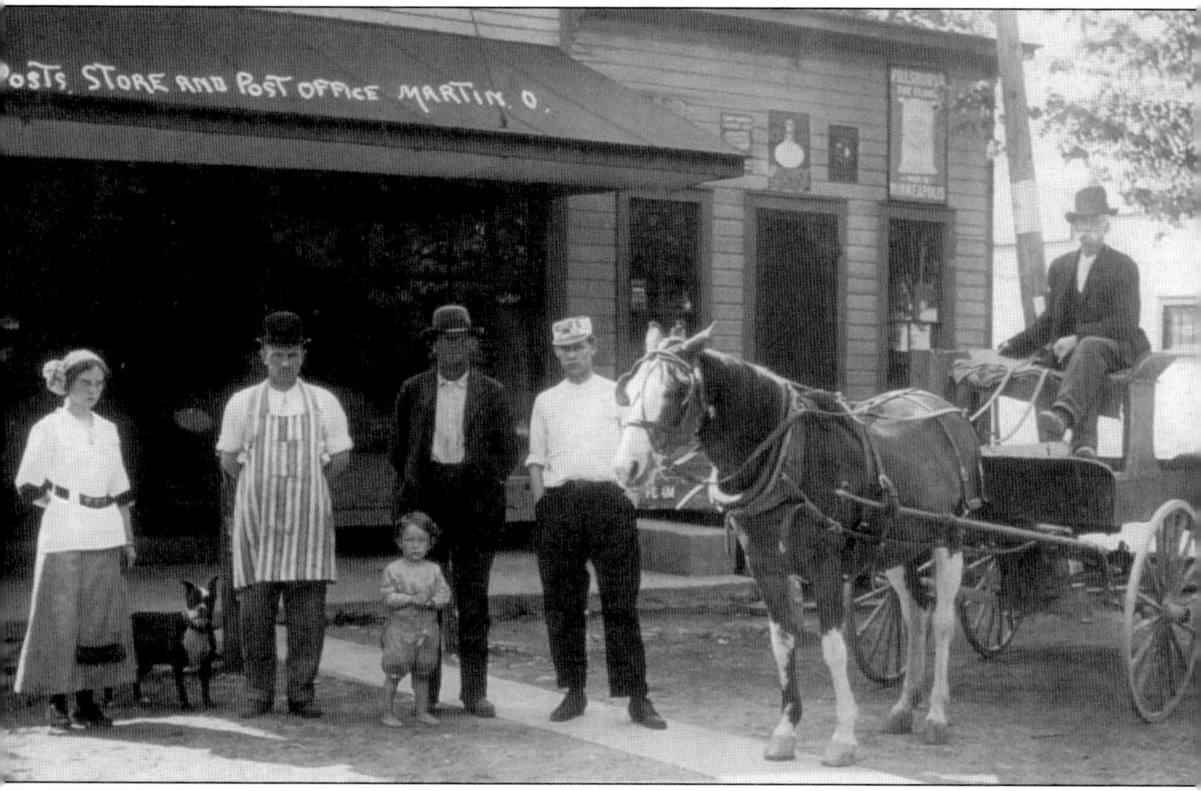

The Post's General Store and post office of Martin, Ohio, is seen after 1908. Clarence Post bought this former school building in 1900. On Saturday nights, dances were held on a platform between the store and loading dock. The wagon in front was used to deliver groceries to people in rural areas. The business was later owned by the Witts. It was then transferred to the Yackees, who ran the store until it closed in 1987. (GPL.)

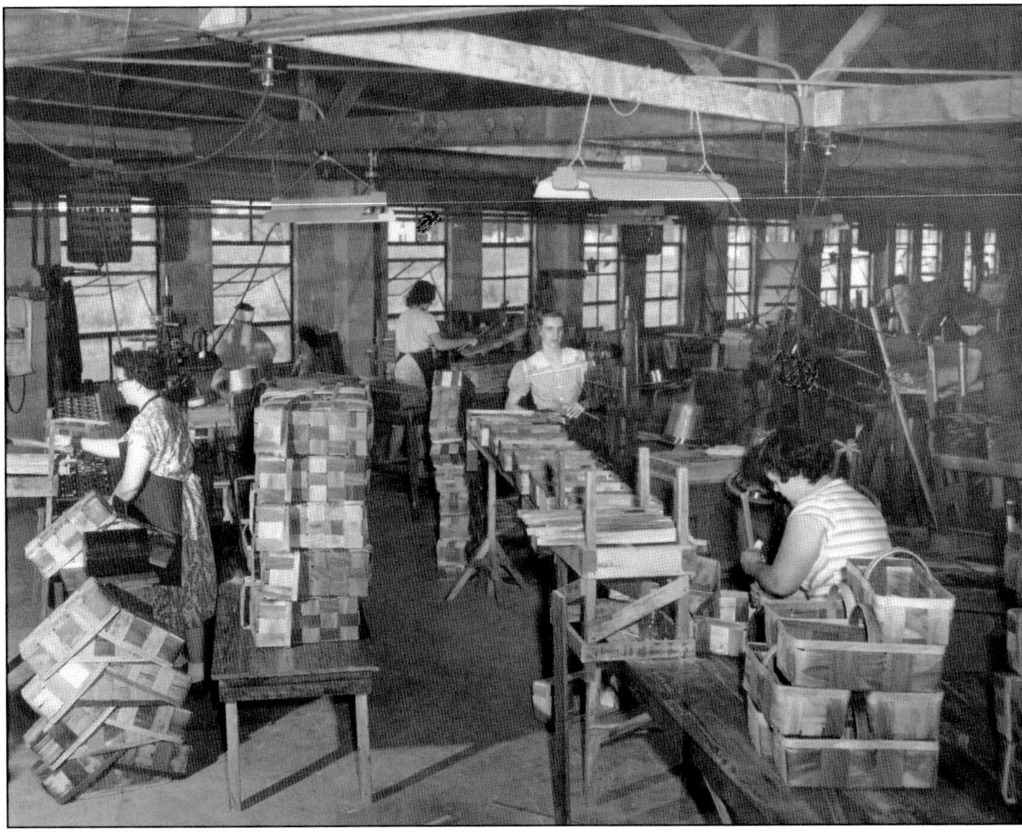

Employees of the Ottawa Basket Company work in the Elmore factory in 1949. The company opened in 1895 in Oak Harbor, Ohio, and had branches in Port Clinton and Elmore. The business produced baskets of various sizes for the farming and greenhouse industries. The Elmore branch experienced a fire in 1946 but rebuilt the following year. The Oak Harbor factory closed in 1952, but the Elmore division thrived well into the 1970s. (HEPL.)

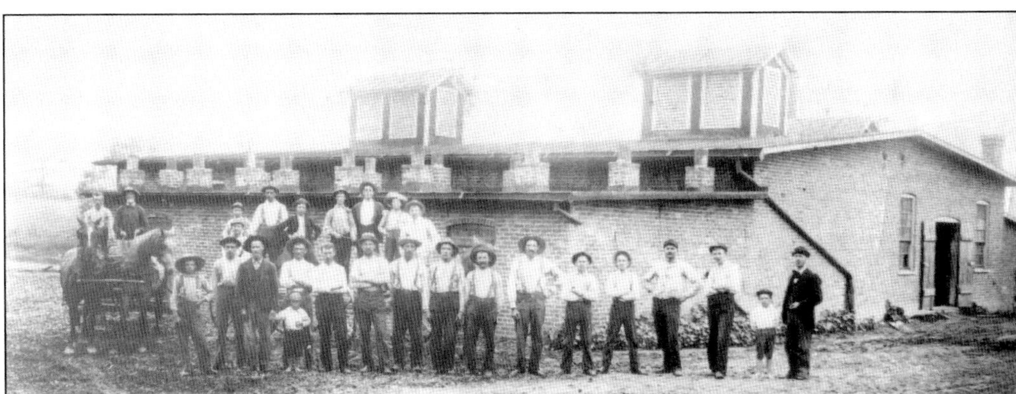

The Becker Stave Factory was located at the bottom of the Toledo Street hill in Elmore. The company had produced staves since the 1870s and did well financially despite a fire and having to close a few weeks each spring due to high water in the river. This photograph was taken in the summer of 1889, a few weeks before the fire on August 2. (HEPL.)

Elmore native Loren Hall perches on an Elmore-made bicycle in 1892. Starting in 1892, the Elmore Manufacturing Company, headed by Harmon Becker and sons, made these bicycles in a foundry building on Ottawa Street in Elmore. Popular nationwide, the bikes, called Elmore Roadsters, sold for $100 each. The Beckers ceased bicycle production in 1899 as interest waned and turned their focus to the Elmore car. (Loren Hall Collection, HEPL.)

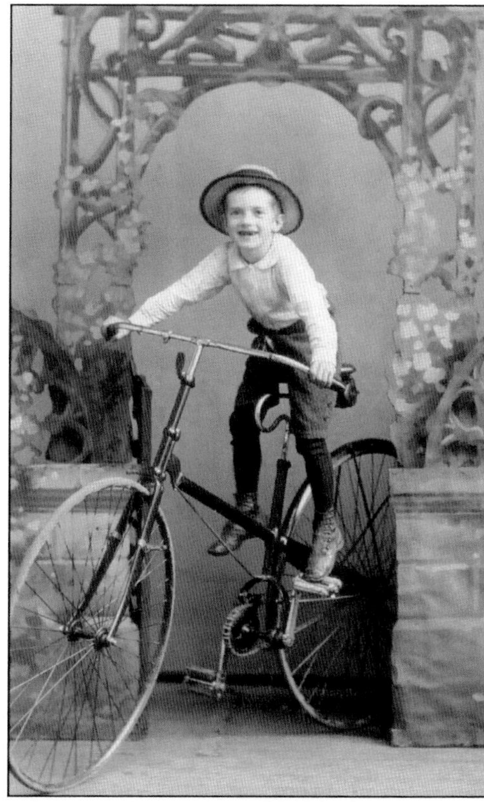

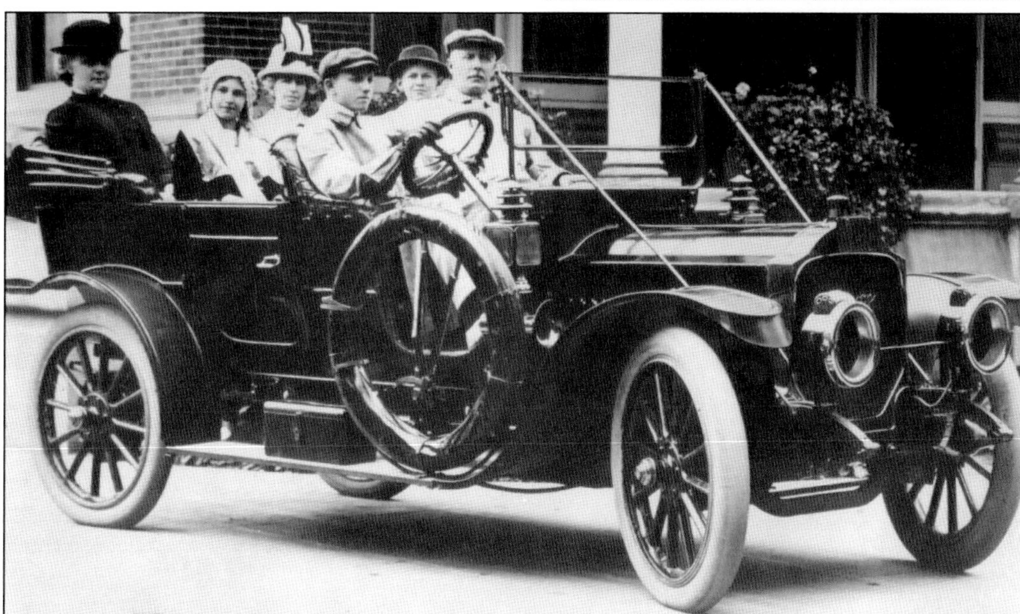

Though Elmore cars were manufactured in Clyde, Ohio, the village of Elmore is proud to be named for these vehicles that were purchased across the country. Elmore cars were also used as the official taxis in Washington, DC, around the turn of the century. In this photograph, a 1910 Elmore car is being driven in Michigan. (John A. Conde Collection, HEPL.)

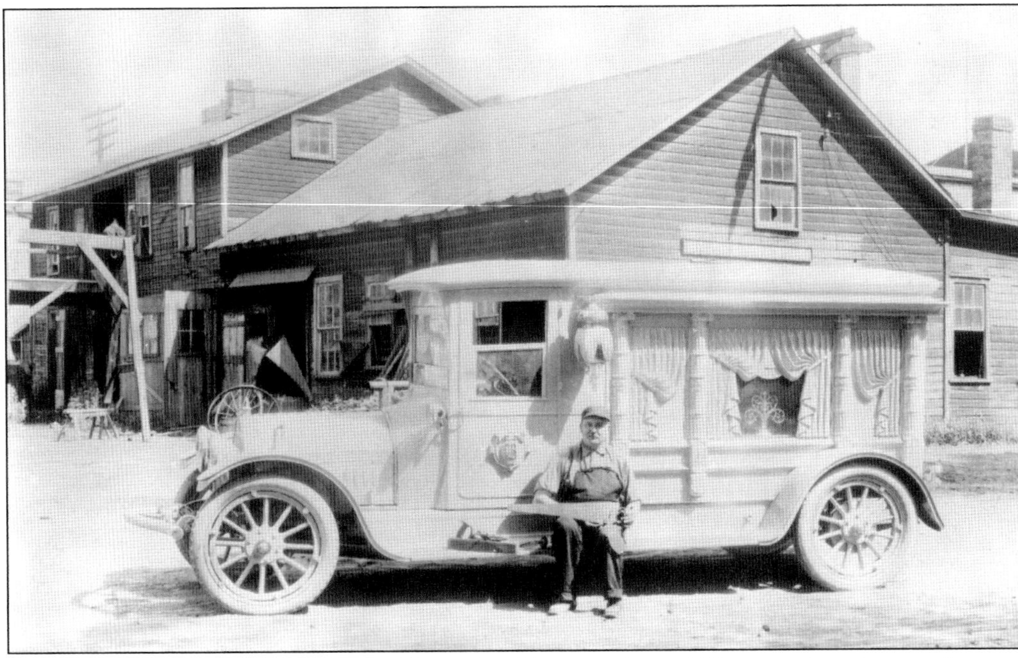

Henry Brandes of the firm Hahn and Brandes, Blacksmiths and Wagonmakers is seated on one of the Burman Funeral Home's newly motorized hearses around 1908 to 1910. Brandes's shop is shown in the background. Wagons were made on the second floor and then taken down the inclined ramp when they were completed. The shop was in business in Elmore from 1892 until 1931, though the two partners had been in the trade since 1871. (HEPL.)

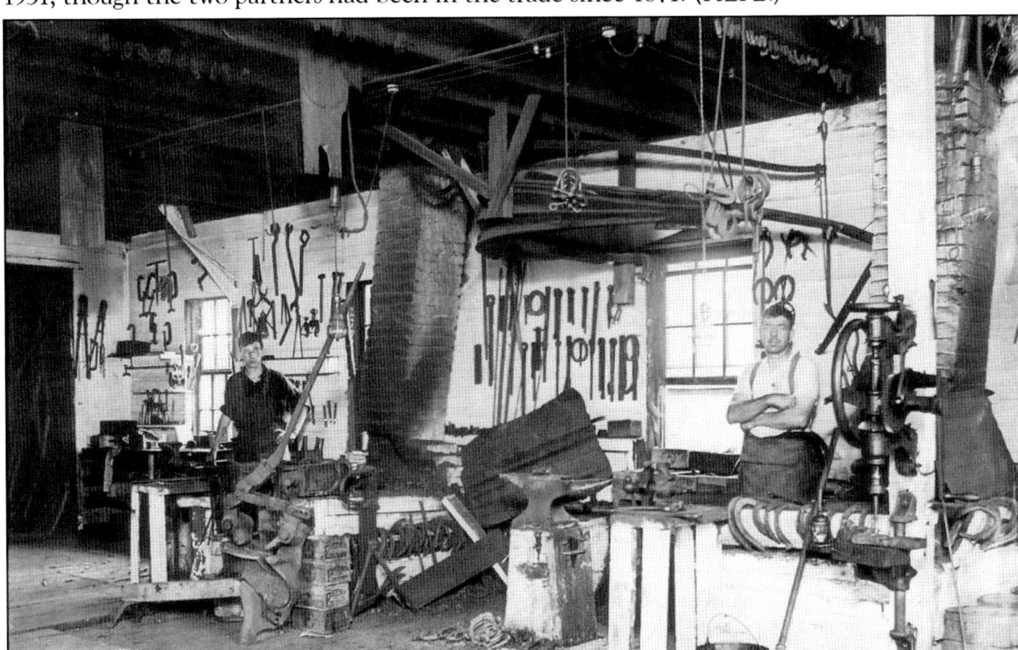

The inner workings of an Elmore blacksmith shop are shown around the turn of the 20th century. The man on the left is apprentice George McGowin. (HEPL.)

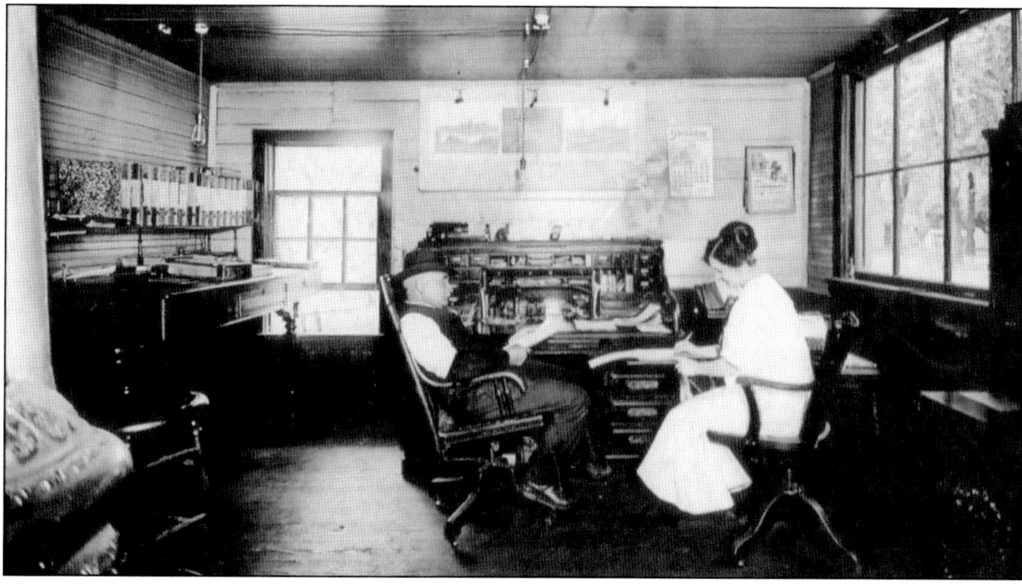

This is the office of the Multiplex Concrete Block Machine Company in 1915. Seated are general manager Andrew Feilbach (left) and his secretary, Amanda Breslau. The office was located on the corner of the railroad in Elmore. The company began in 1905 as a furnace foundry and transformed into a fabrication plant. (HEPL.)

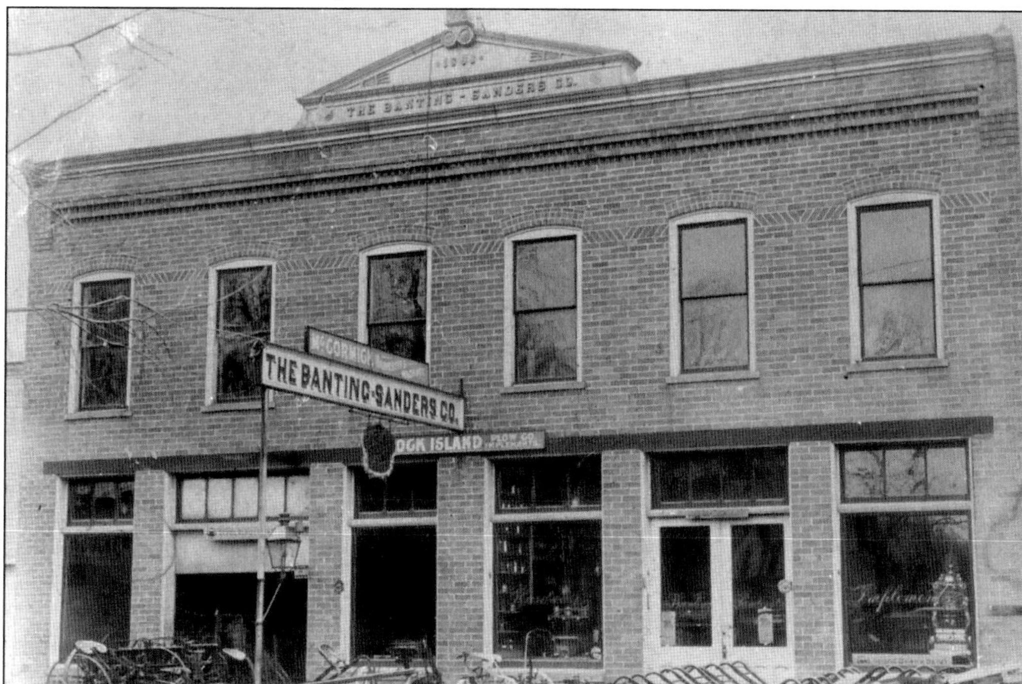

John Banting and J.F. Sanders opened the Banting Sanders Hardware in Elmore in 1882 for the sale of hardware and farm implements. After an 1889 fire, the partners moved to a new building on Toledo Street. The old Rice Street location was rebuilt and used for showrooms and storage. The Bantings moved the business to Toledo in 1901, but the building remained the Elmore Hardware Company under new ownership. (HEPL.)

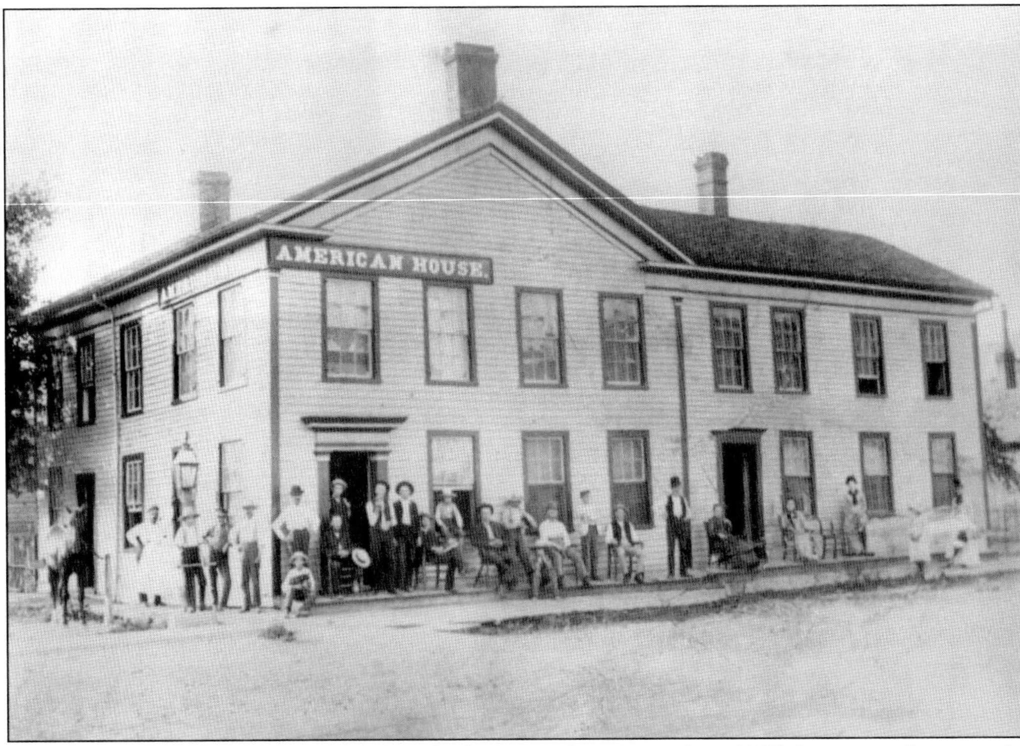

American House Hotel was built by Ezekiel Rice and Jesse Cook in 1855, but it was later run by Charles Hineline. Like most hotels, it had sample rooms where drummers (traveling salesmen) displayed trade items to solicit customers. Local businesses would come to the sample rooms to decide which items to order from the wholesale houses. The hotel burned down in 1902. (HEPL.)

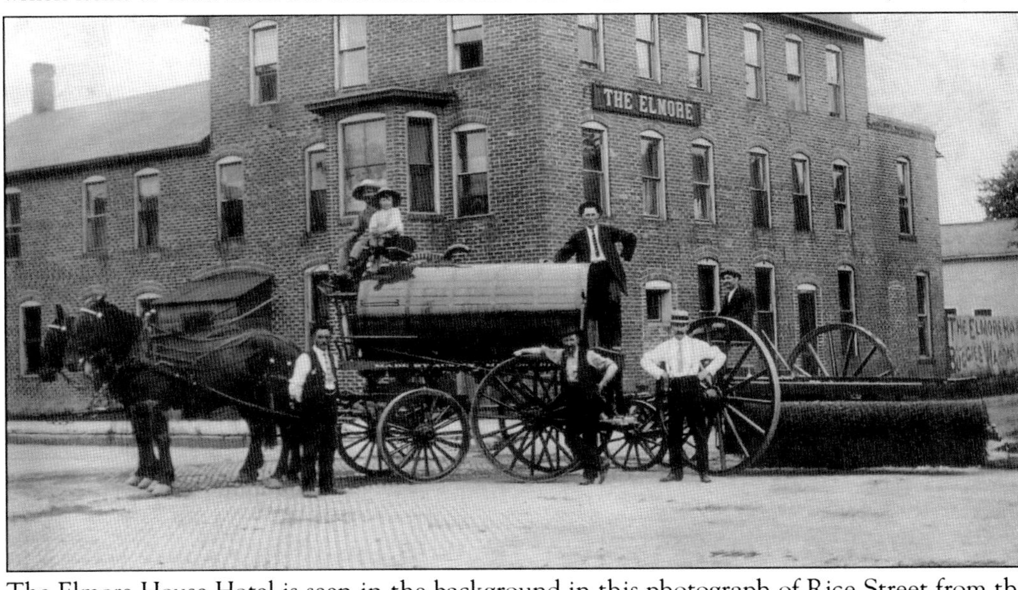

The Elmore House Hotel is seen in the background in this photograph of Rice Street from the 1890s. The lodging was built in 1853 by D.M. Day. The hotel had in its possession the Spafford Bell, made by Ohio pioneer Jarvis Spafford in 1834 out of 36 Spanish silver dollars and other metals. Also pictured here is one of Elmore's first street-cleaning crews using automated equipment. (HEPL.)

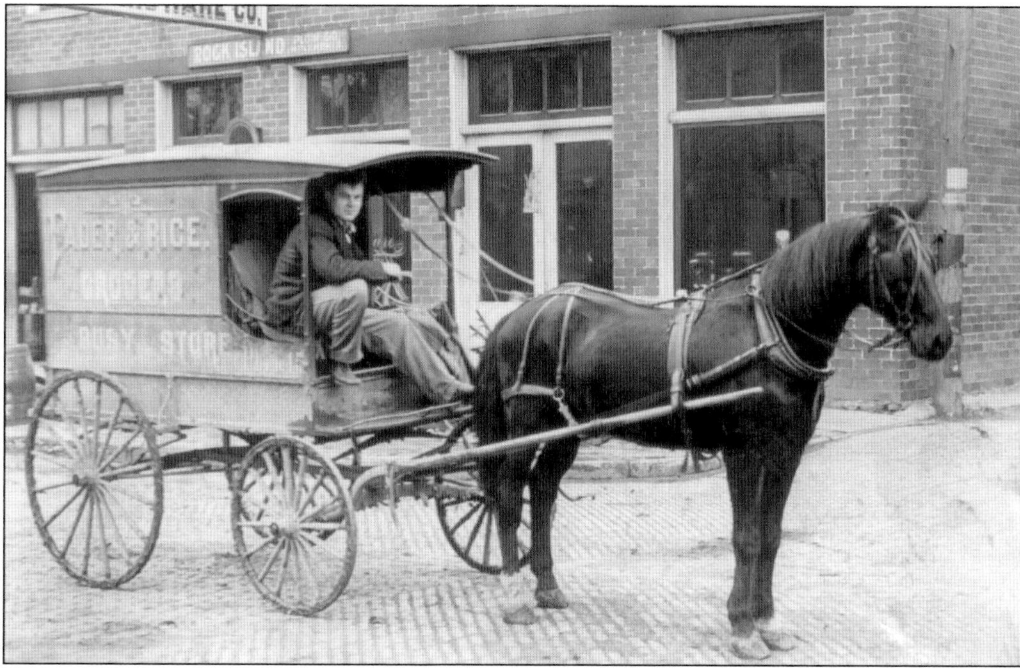

The Fader and Rice Grocery wagon is parked for a delivery in front of the Elmore Hardware Company in the early 1900s. (John Jaeger.)

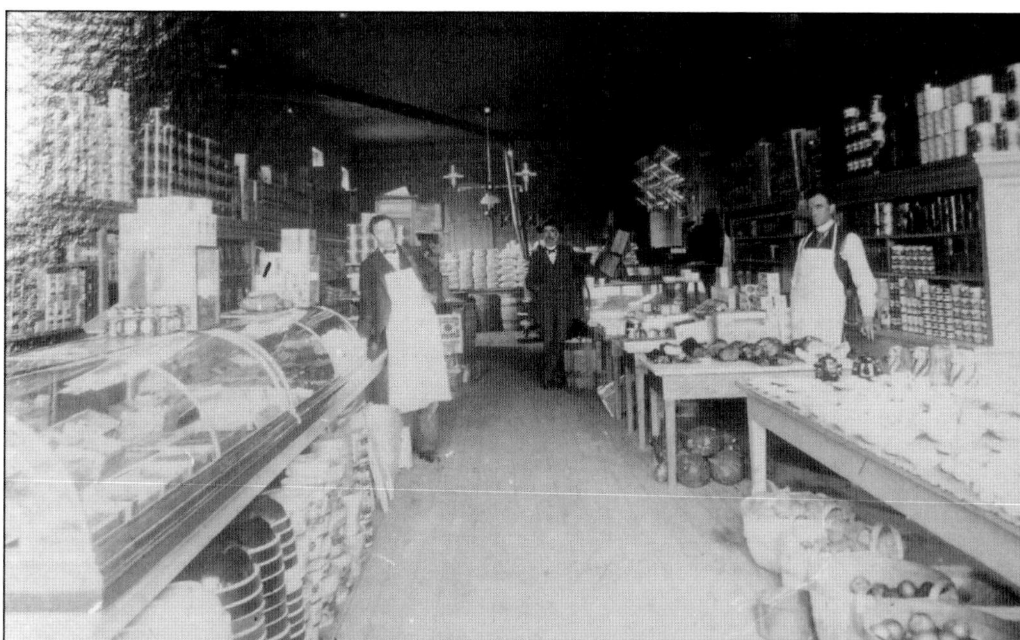

Feilbach Brothers Grocery was situated in the Shaenfeld Building in Elmore in 1889. The grocery was known for its brightly colored window displays featuring exotic products. It later moved to the Anderson Building in 1894, and Shaenfeld returned to the grocery business in his former building. George A. Feilbach (left) and Philip W. Feilbach (right) stand with an unidentified man inside the store in 1892. (HEPL.)

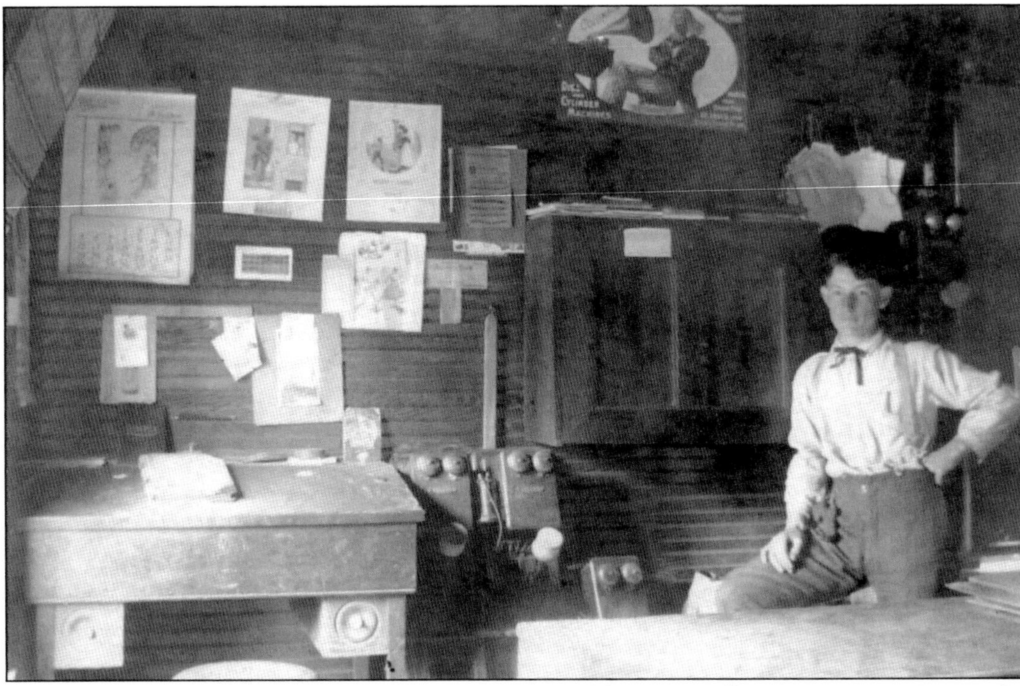

In 1898, Shaenfeld tired of his grocery business and sold out to William Waterman. Pictured is Charles Henry, the bookkeeper for the grocery store in 1907. In later years, the grocery was owned by the "Corner Grocery Man," Albert Weis. (Alberta Hennessey, HEPL.)

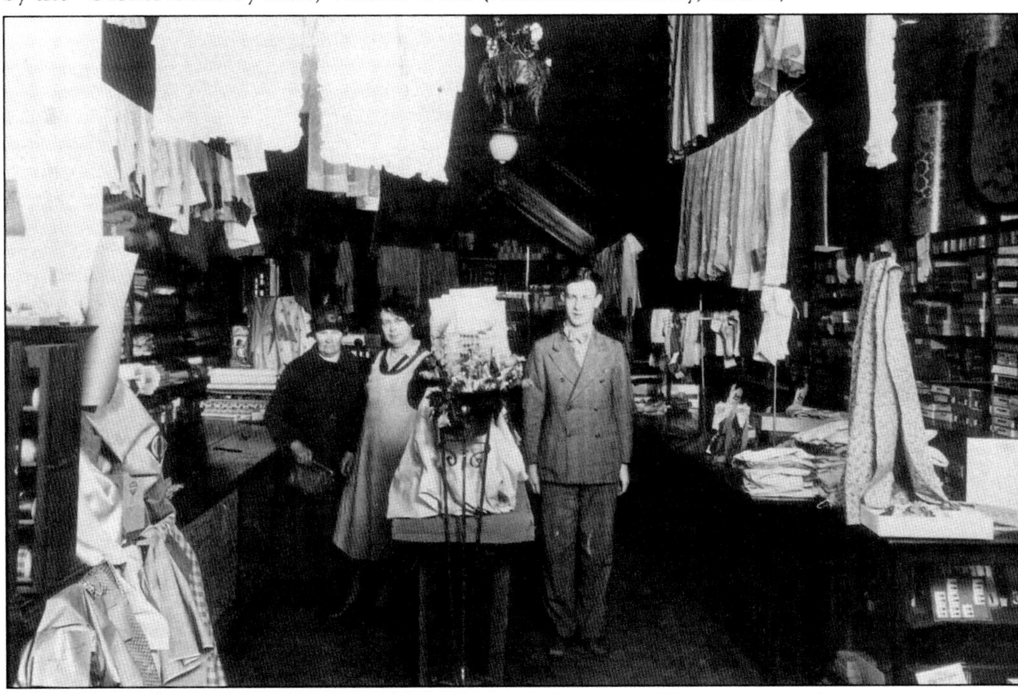

This shot of the interior of Henry House's general store in Elmore was taken sometime after the shop opened in 1907. Pictured from left to right are Mrs. Semrock, Mrs. Henry House, and Bernard House. (Bernard House Collection, HEPL.)

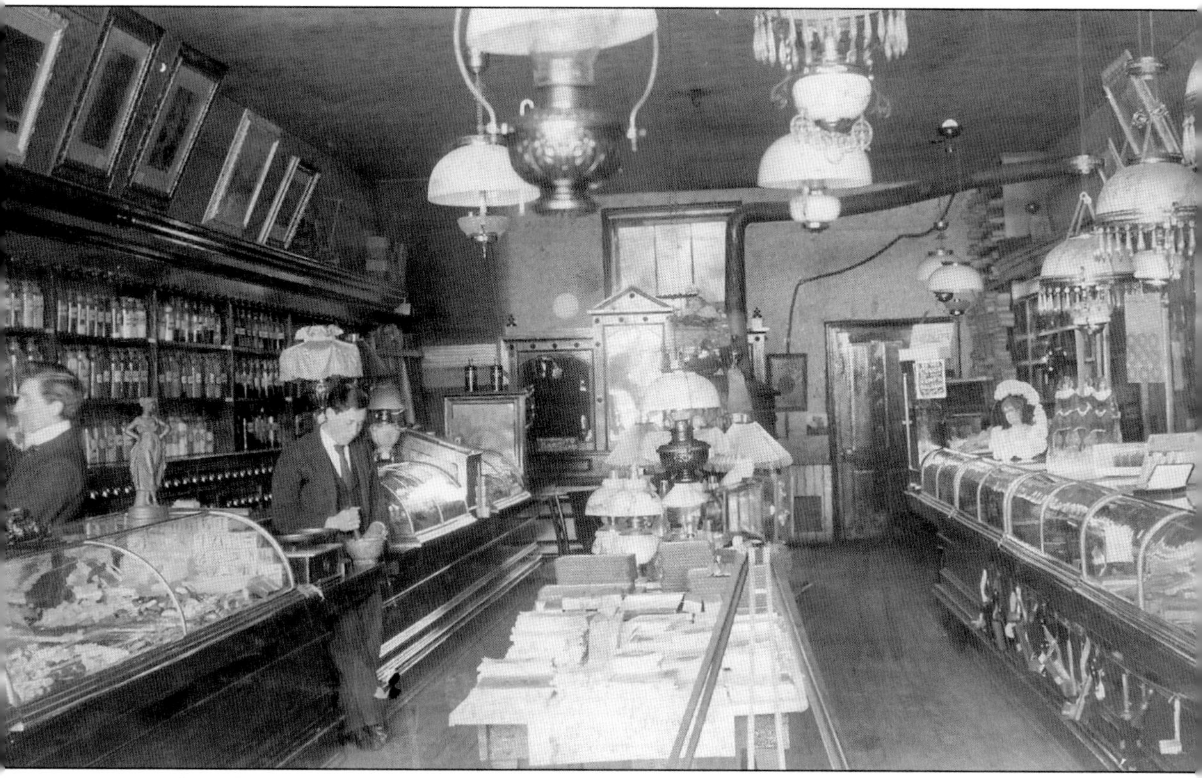

W.C. Fink and M.D. Brown, pharmacists from Wauseon, Ohio, opened the Fink and Brown drugstore in Elmore in 1894. They were known for their "Hot Soda Water Fountain" and for introducing the healthful remedy of Coca-Cola to the town in 1897. They were bought out by the Gehring Brothers in 1901. (HEPL.)

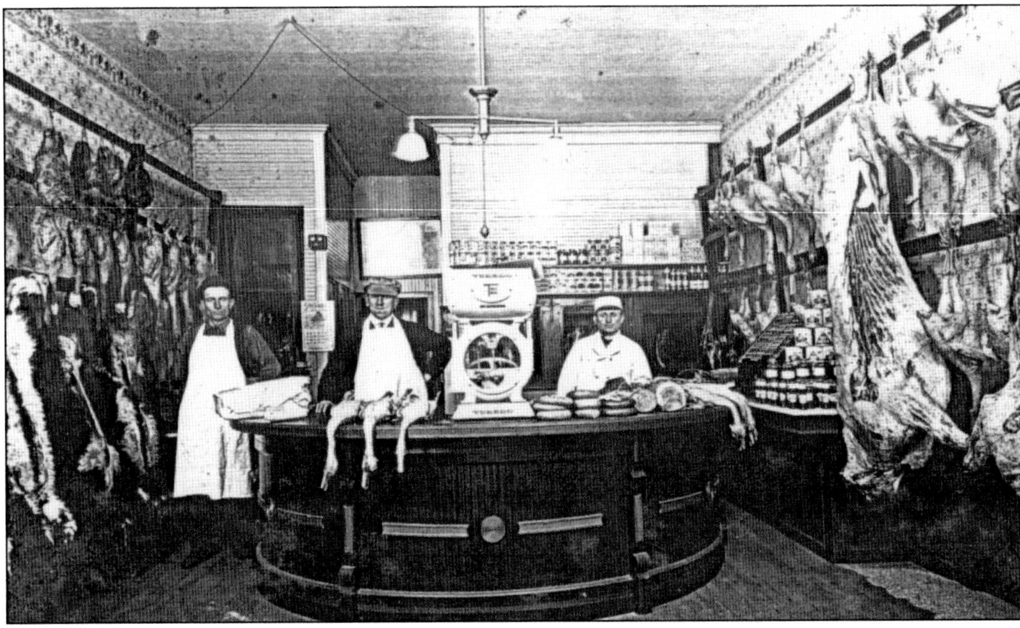

This photograph of Tank's Meat Market in Elmore was taken on December 22, 1909. From left to right are Earl "Speeder" Dean, Fred J. Tank, and Julius Damschroder. Tank bought the meat market and slaughterhouse from Al Witte in 1907 and provided his own market on Rice Street. The store later moved to the site of the slaughterhouse on Route 51 just south of Elmore in 1958. (HEPL.)

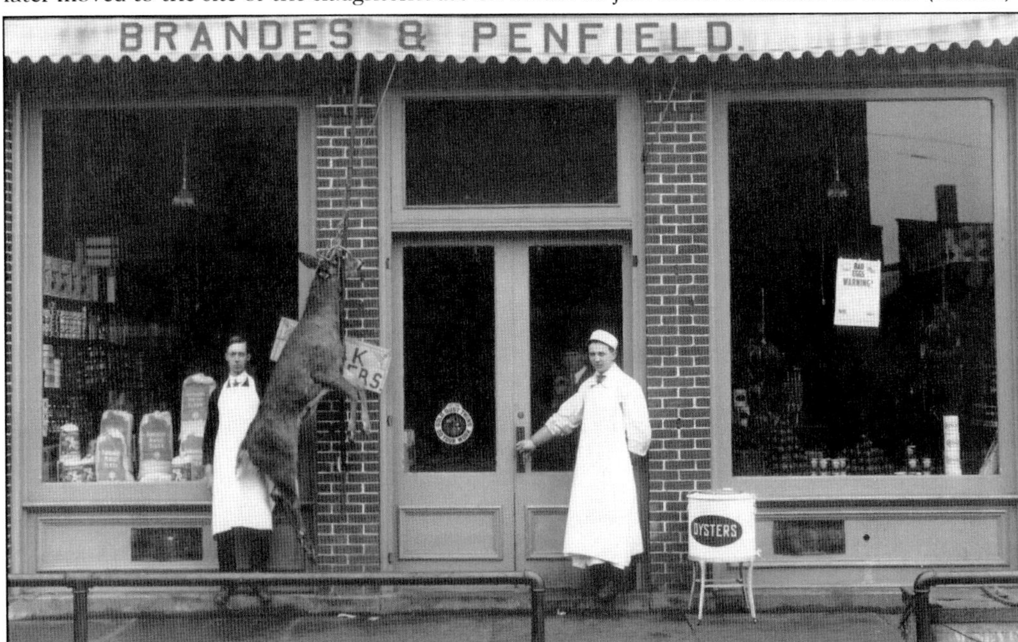

The men standing in front of the Penfield and Brandes grocery and meat market are Charles Brandes (left) and Harry Trautman. This was taken in 1913 when Penfield had sold his interests to Edward Avers, making the store Brandes and Company. This particular business was sold to Rudolph and Richard Sauer in 1925, and Brandes and Trautman established their own meat market outside of town. (HEPL.)

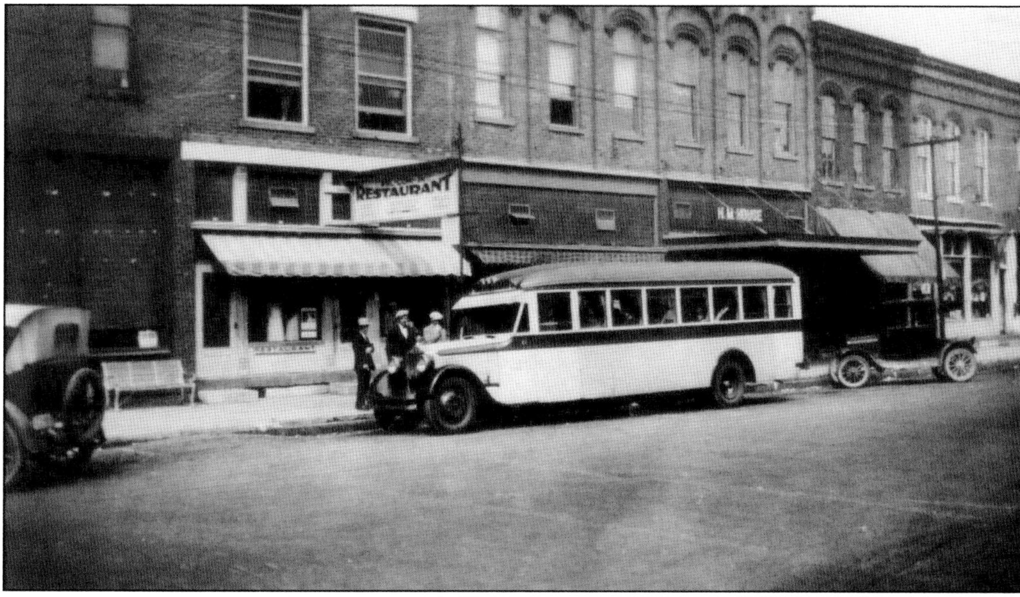

The Wel-Com-In Restaurant was owned by Elmer Damschroder and was a popular spot for the high school crowd in the 1920s and 1930s. Henry Ford was a regular customer; he often ate here when passing through town on business. (HEPL.)

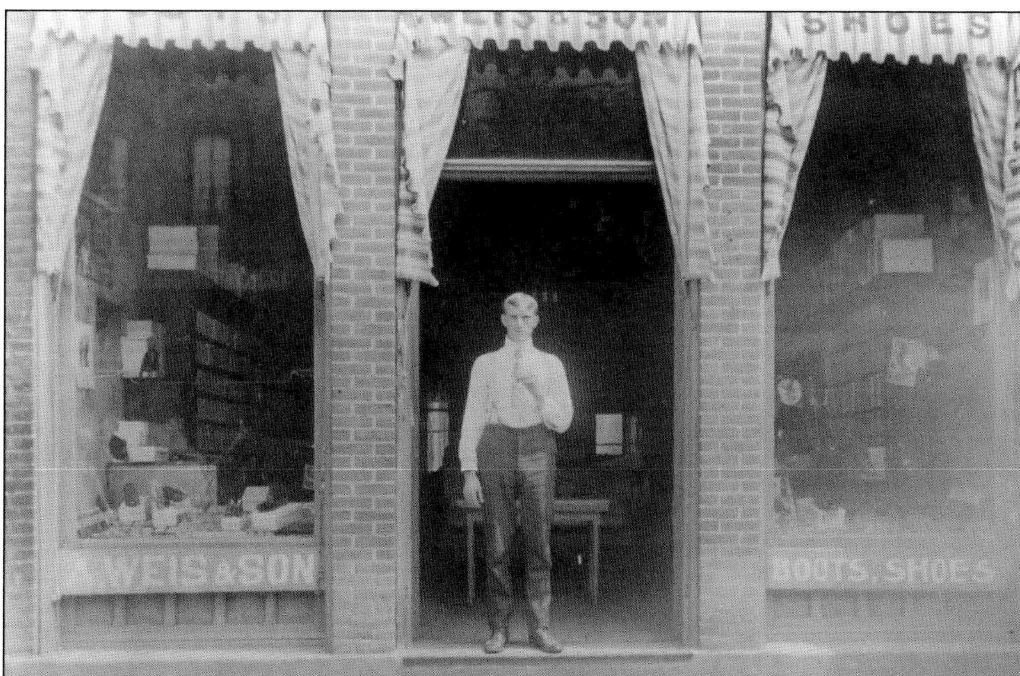

The Weis and Son shoe store in Elmore was opened in 1903 by Andrew and George Weis. It was operated by George (pictured) until his death in 1970. (HEPL.)

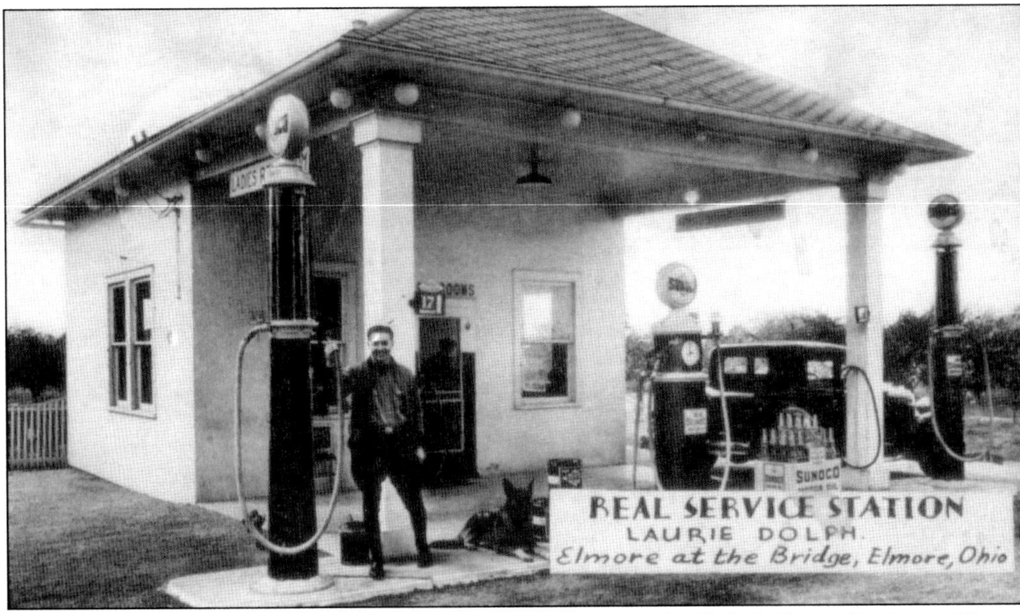

Laurie Dolph stands in front of his Sunoco service station at the Toledo Street Bridge in Elmore in 1922. (HEPL.)

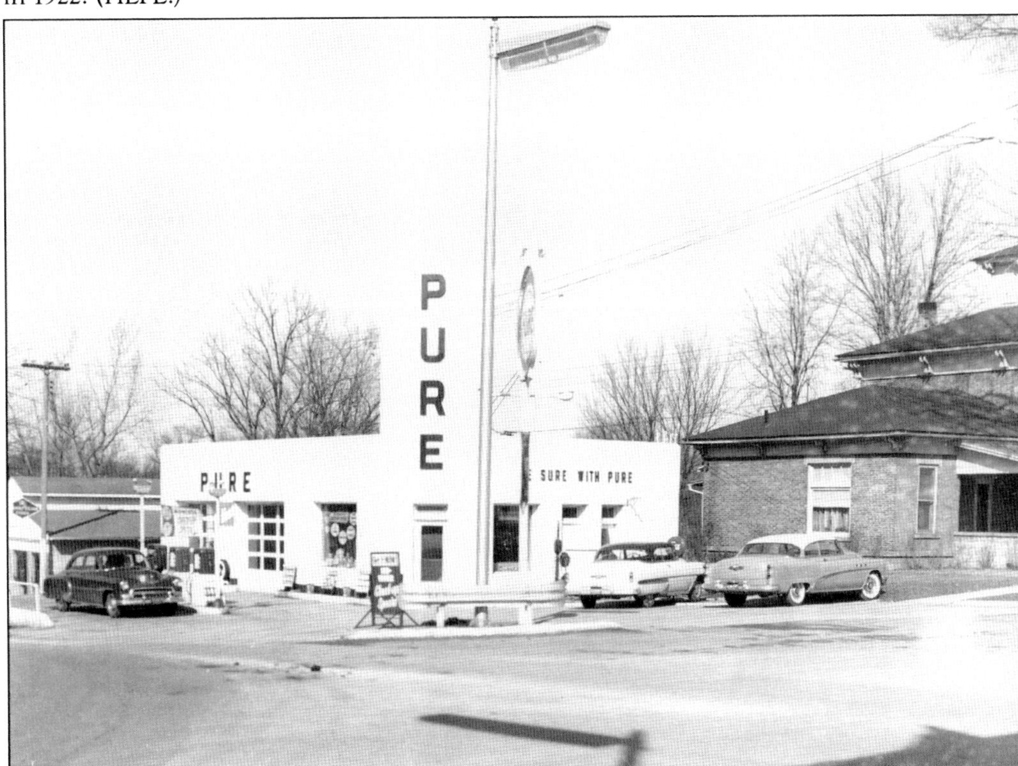

The Pure Oil gas station, pictured here in 1953, was located on the corner of Toledo and Rice Streets in Elmore. When the Anderson building was razed in 1935, a Hi-Speed gas station was constructed in its place. The Pure Oil station replaced it years later. (HEPL.)

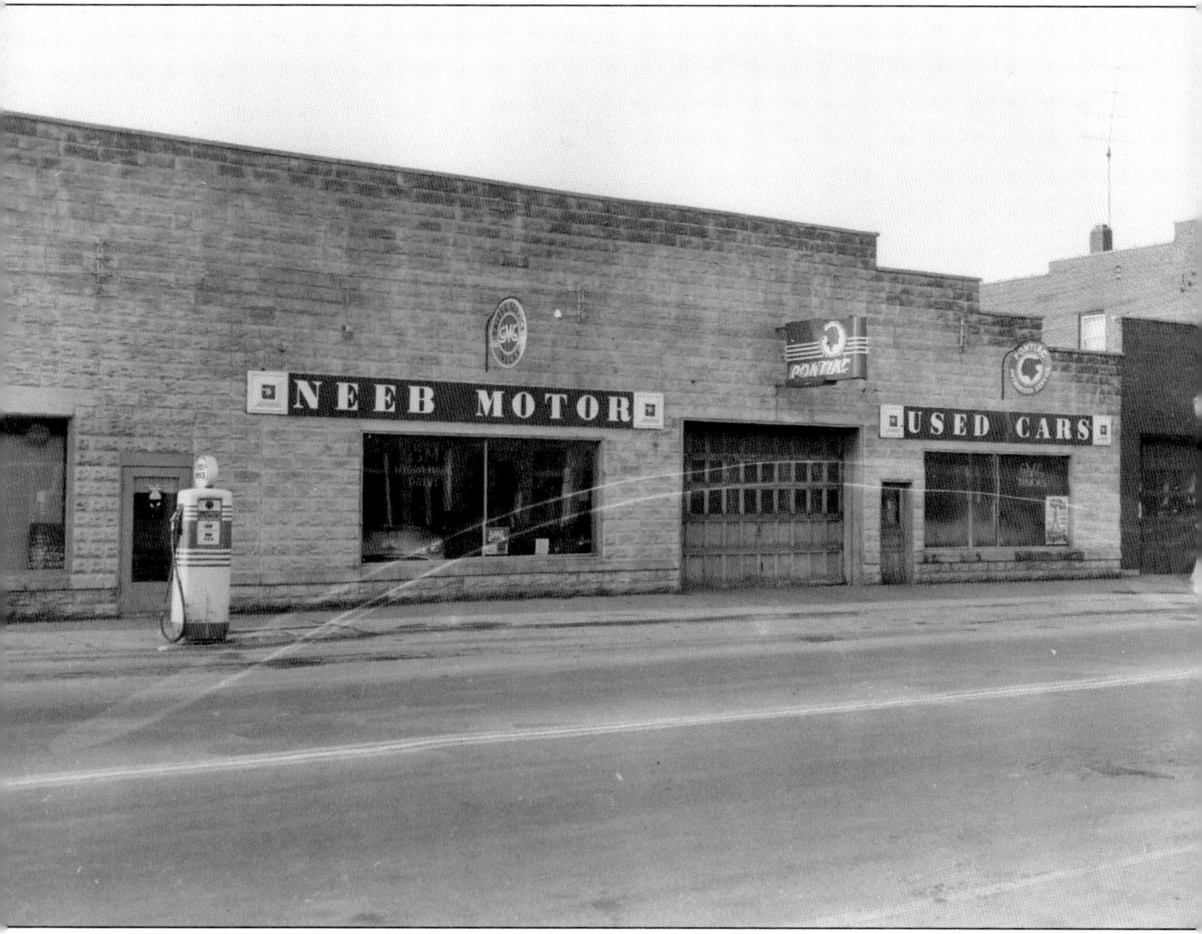

Howard Neeb bought the Peterson Garage in 1936, moving his garage from a previous location on Clinton Street. It was a mainstay in Elmore until the 1980s. (HEPL).

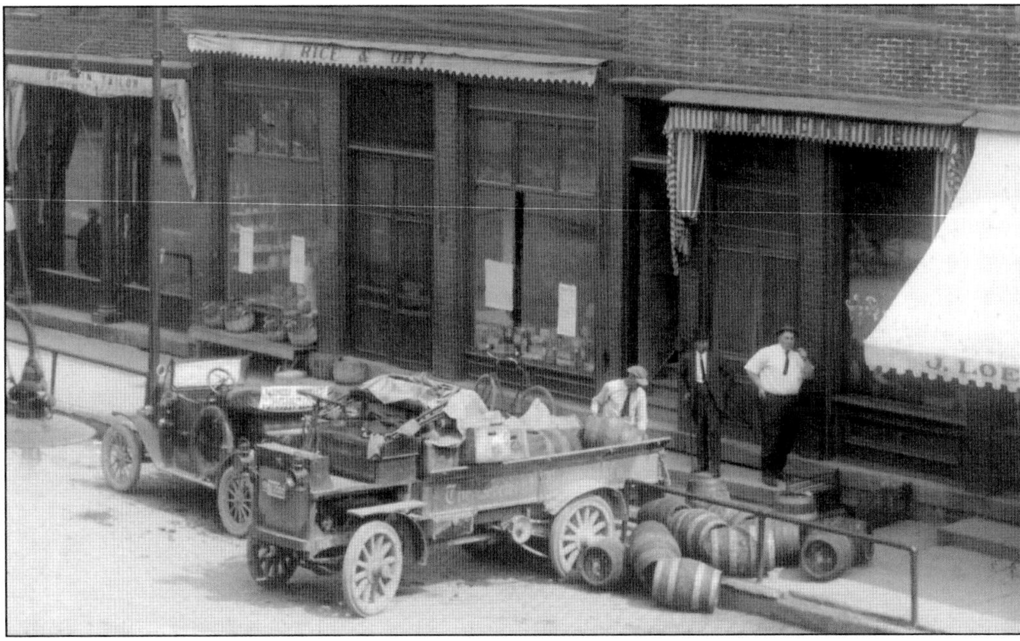

Pictured are workmen from the Fremont Brewing Company unloading kegs of beer into the basement of the J.P. McIntire Saloon in Elmore through an opening in the sidewalk. (HEPL.)

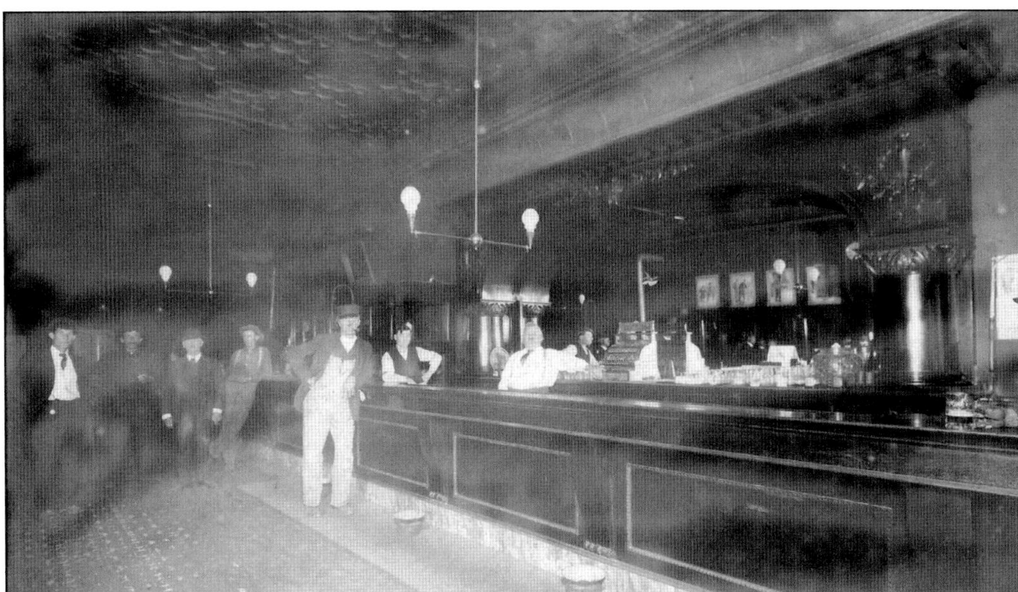

The Peter Keil Saloon opened in the Damschroder Building in 1889. After it burned down in the great Elmore Fire of 1895, it was lavishly rebuilt. Seen as the best of seven saloons in town, it advertised a restaurant, a marble bar, modern furniture, improved refrigerators, and expensive wallpaper. The bar closed upon Keil's death in 1922. (HEPL.)

Elmore barber Alton "Jake" Eoff cuts the hair of Ronald Witte, son of Newell and Frances Witte. Eoff kept the shop from 1915 until his death in 1958. (HEPL.)

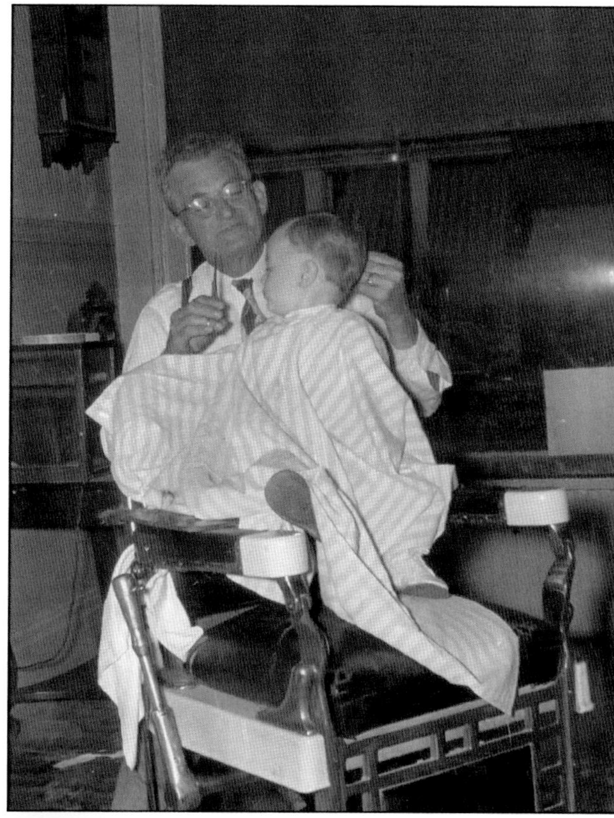

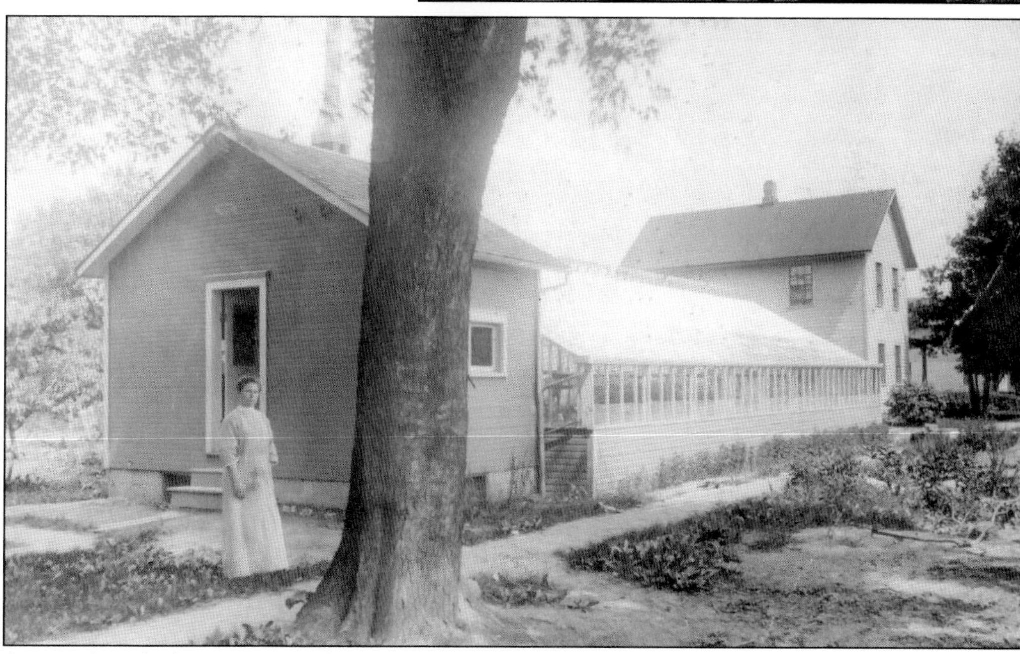

An unidentified woman stands in front of the old greenhouse on Augusta Street in Elmore. It was owned by Blanche and Emmett Hilganeck from 1914 to 1935. In 1945, it became the Pickard Greenhouse. (Alta Pickard, HEPL.)

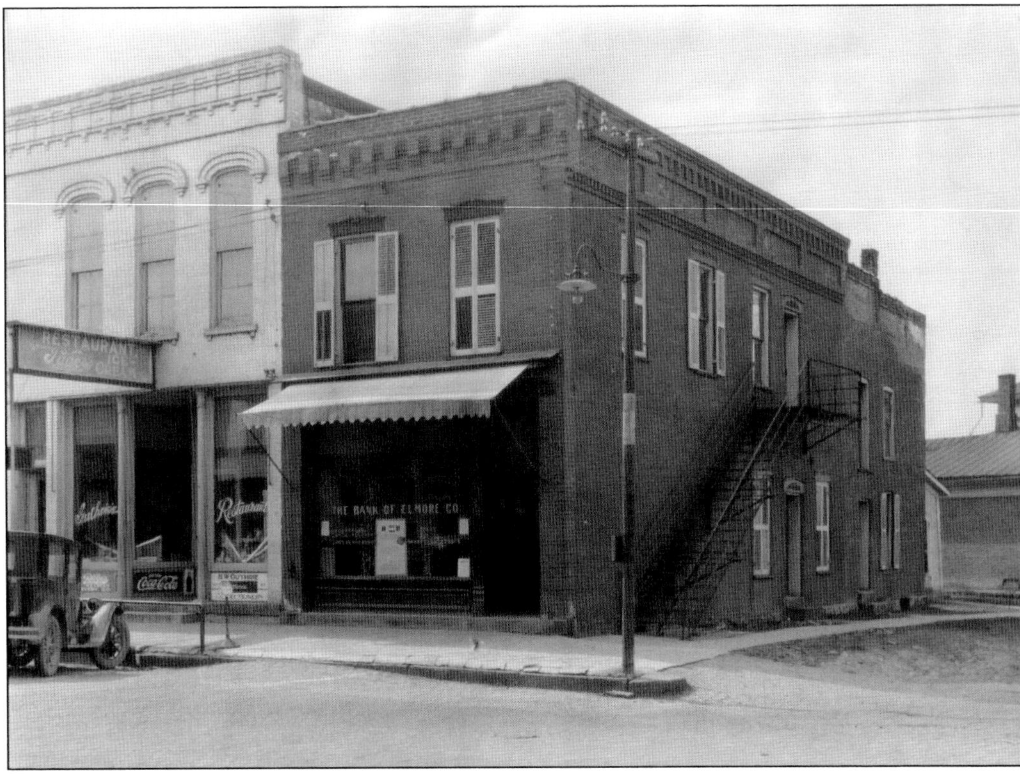

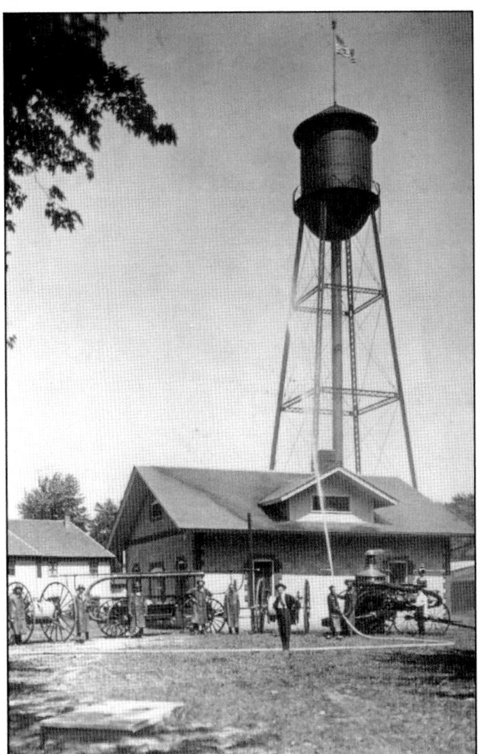

The Elmore Bank Company was established in 1873 with John H. Magee as president. This building on Rice Street was occupied by the Ottawa County Bank in 1892, but it sold out to Magee and the Bank of Elmore two years later. The Elmore Bank Company building in the photograph was torn down in 1926, and a new structure was erected. (HEPL.)

The Elmore waterworks plant was erected in 1910. In previous years, water was taken from a town well located at the top of the Toledo Street hill. This photograph shows the fire department trying out hoses with the new hydrant just after the building was erected. (HEPL.)

Three

All Aboard!

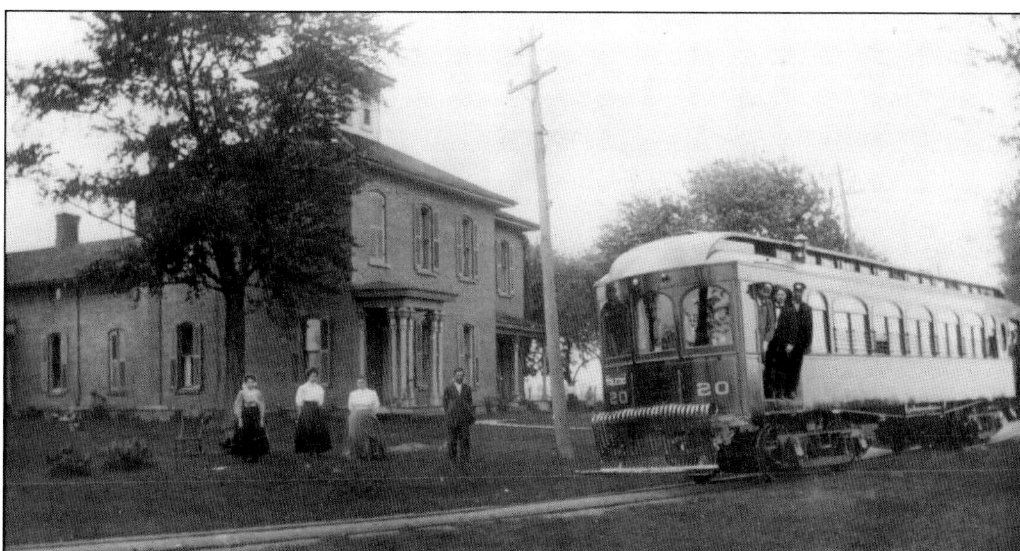

A Toledo, Port Clinton and Lakeside (TPCL) interurban coming from Oak Harbor, Ohio, makes a stop at the John Luckey homestead in Elmore to pick up passengers. This stop was at the corner of the present State Route 51 and State Route 105. A depot was located just across the road. From Elmore, these electric streetcars traveled north up Route 51 to Genoa and Toledo and also could go west on Route 105 into Woodville. The TPCL Railway was incorporated in 1902 and began routing passengers to Elmore in 1903. This photograph was taken the day after passenger service began near Elmore. (HEPL.)

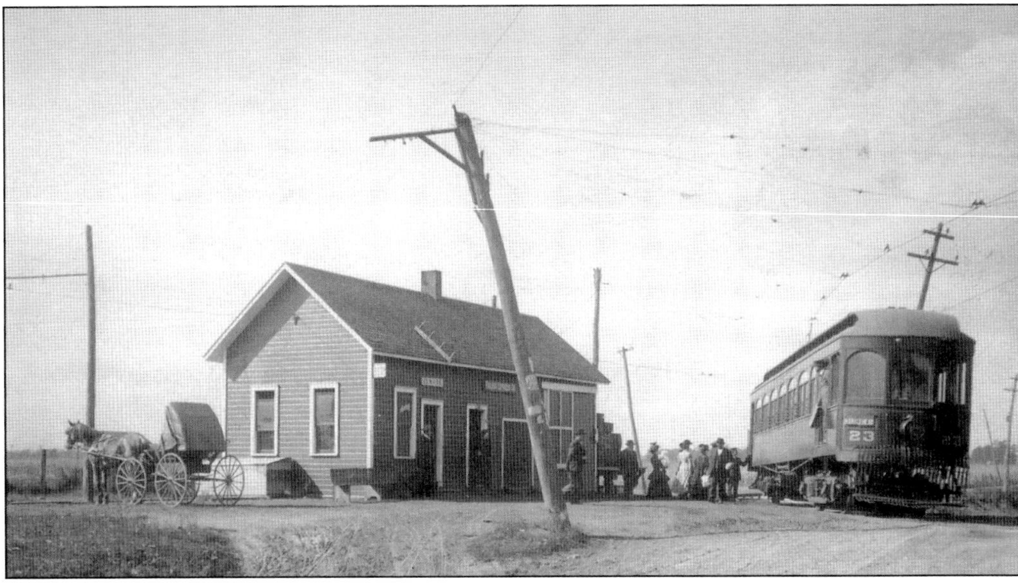

Passengers are getting ready to board the TPCL streetcar at the corner of Routes 51 and 105. The depot later became the Girl Scout Building. The trolley had just come from Genoa and was heading east toward Oak Harbor, Ohio. (Bob Eoff, HEPL.)

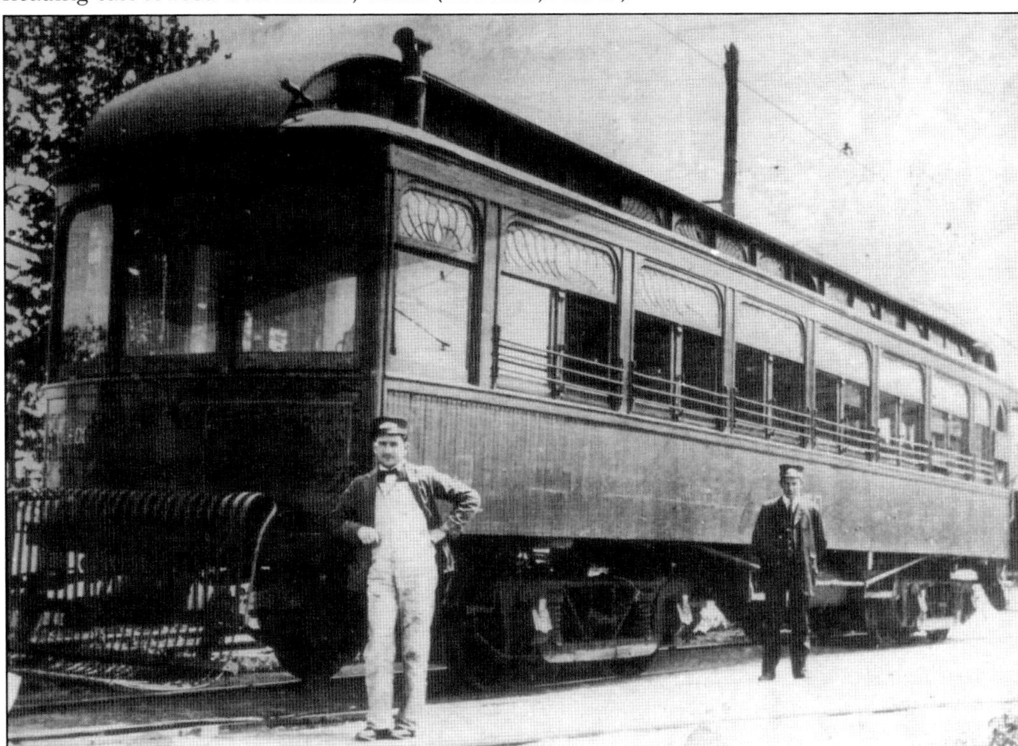

The conductor and brakeman stand with their trolley heading from Elmore to Toledo. The streetcars taking the longer trips to Toledo, Cleveland, or Detroit would advertise theater parties on the cars to gain more customers. Passengers could travel the route and pass the time by listening to bands onboard, playing cards, singing, and partaking in coffee and a light lunch. (HEPL.)

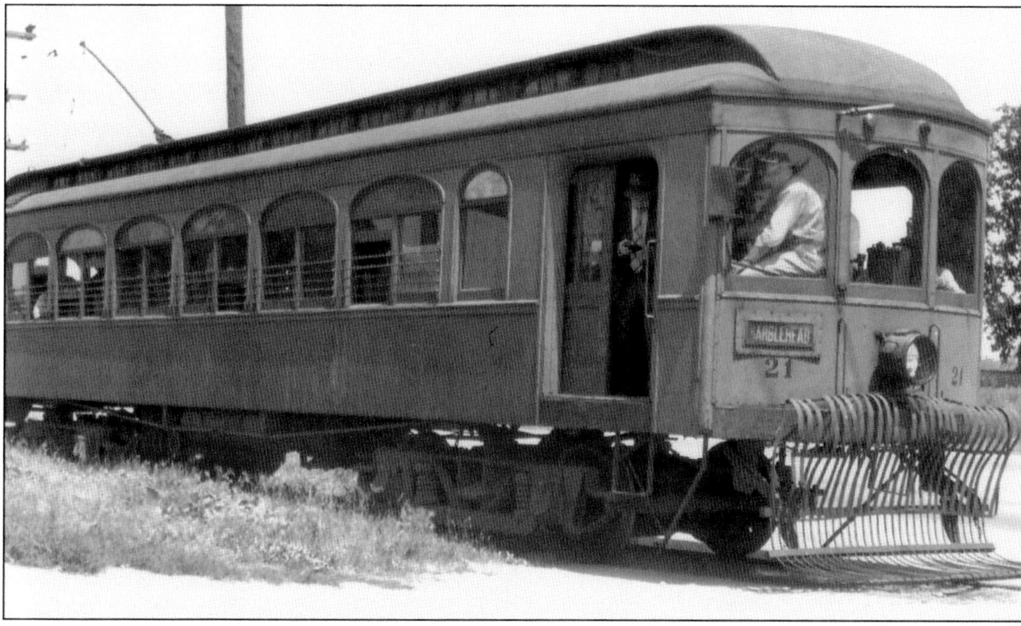

An unidentified man returning to Elmore takes advantage of the last passenger run for the Ohio Public Service interurban on July 11, 1939. The line continued to run until 1958, but it only hauled freight. This stop is the one on the corner of Route 105 and Route 51, and the trolley is no. 21. (HEPL.)

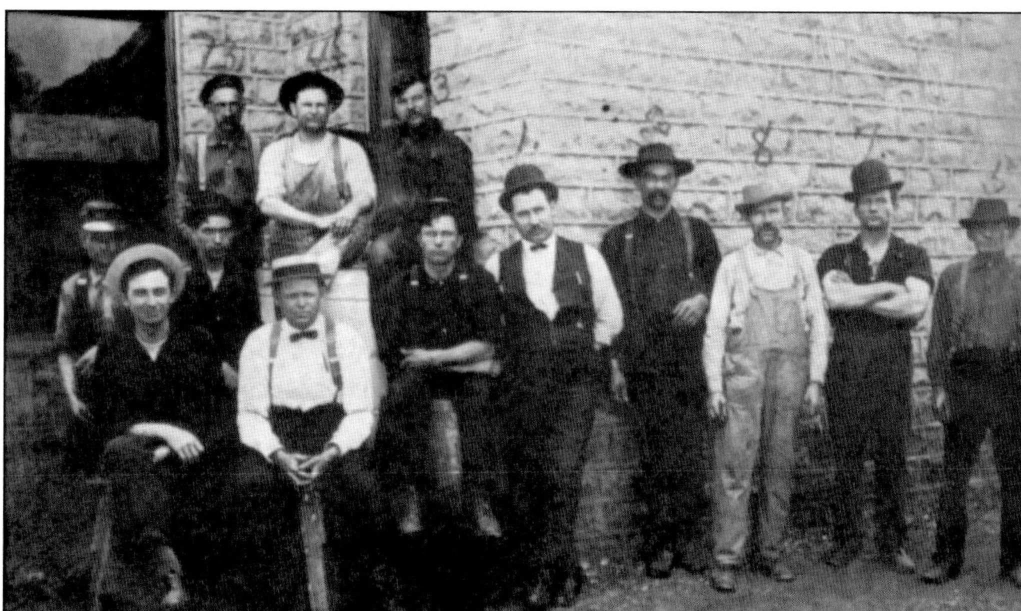

The Genoa car barn crew stands in front of the Toledo, Port Clinton and Lakeside station around 1915. It includes, from left to right, (first row) Richard Wager, William Hineman, Sherman Avery, Otto Sturtzinger, William Busse, John Berndt, Louis Avery, and Joseph Roofer; (second row) Hi Johnson and Fred Suess; (third row) Ernie Burge, Edward Snyder, and William Dreyer. (GPL.)

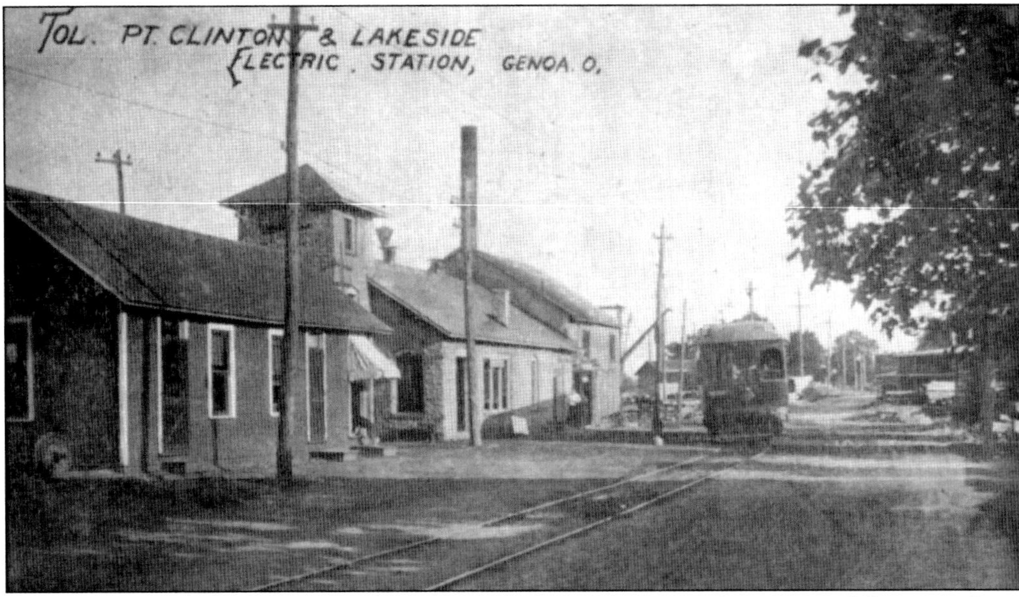

The Toledo, Port Clinton and Lakeside electric passenger station, substation, and shops are shown here in Genoa around 1910. In 1924, the TPCL became the Ohio Public Service. (Joe Badger.)

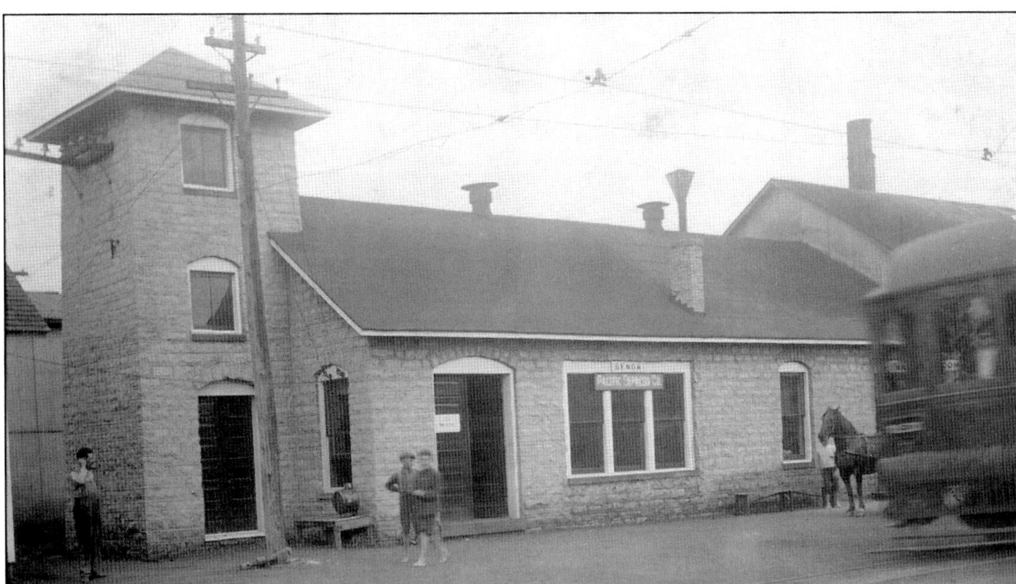

Pictured is the Ohio Public Service (OPS) interurban station on Washington Street in Genoa. During the 1930s, the OPS was referred to as "Mary Jane," most likely after the popular c. 1918 *Mary Jane* book series by Clara Ingram Judson. Mary Jane visited interurbans in the second book. In later years, it was known as "B and F E" (back and forth empty), when few passengers rode the streetcar. (Kirk Hise collection, via Eric Hise.)

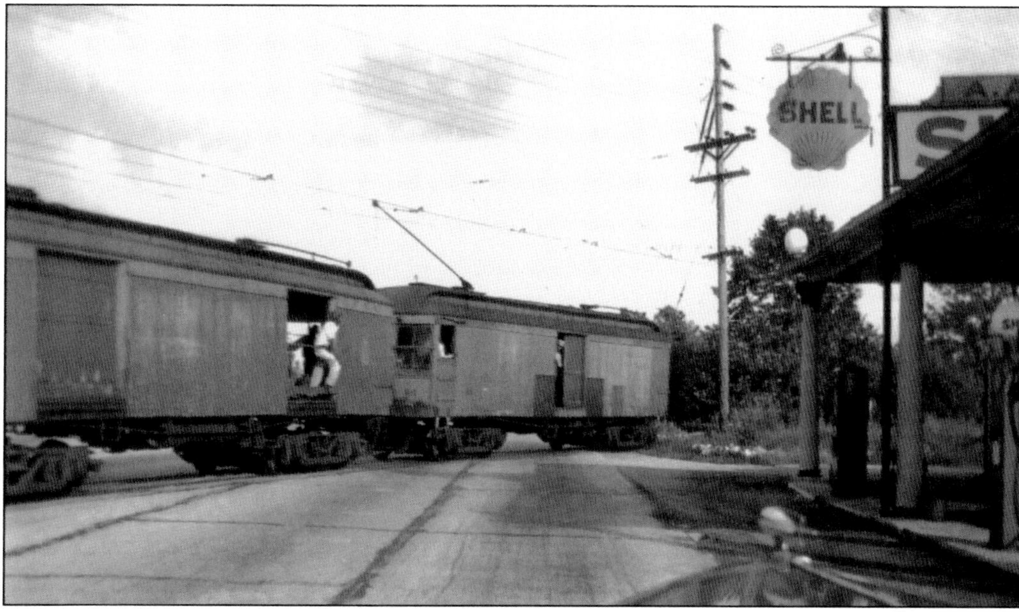

Ohio Public Service cars no. 40 and no. 41 are seen here at the Woodville Road (Route 51) crossing at Genoa in 1944. Both freight cars are turning down Washington Street to the station. Ambrose Rethy's gas station can be seen on the right. (Kirk Hise collection, via Eric Hise.)

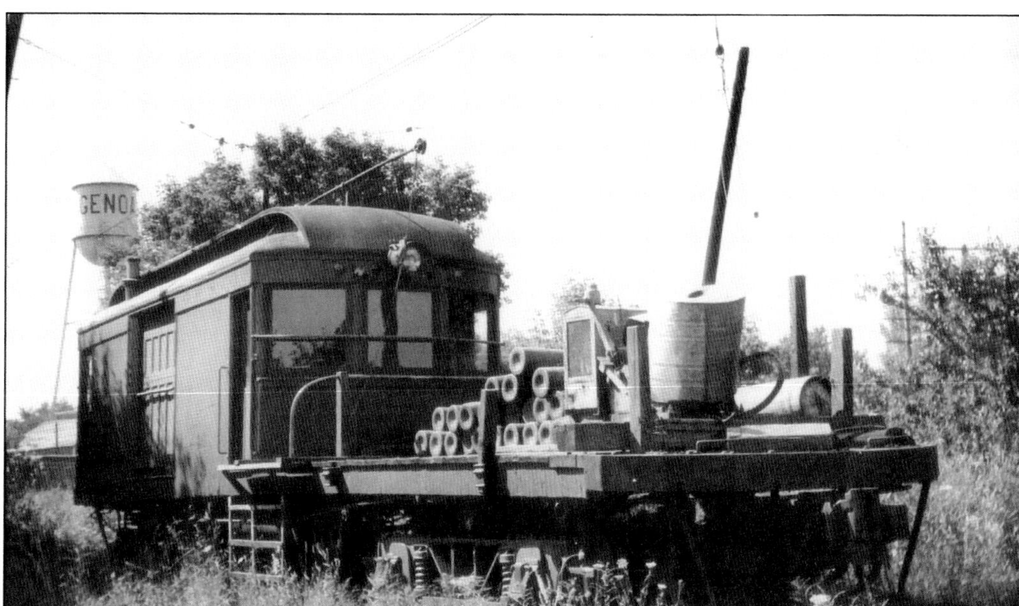

Ohio Public Service car no. 40 is removing rail to be discarded at Genoa in 1946. (Kirk Hise collection, via Eric Hise.)

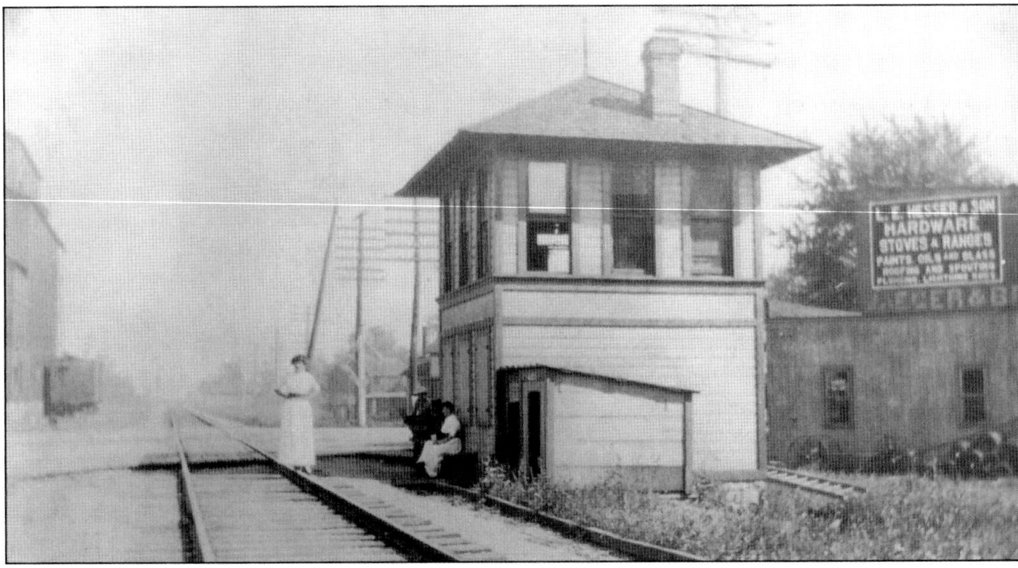

Passengers wait at the New York Central Railroad interlocking tower on Genoa's Main Street in 1915. The tower also protected the Lake Shore Electric Railway cars, as they crossed at this section of track. The structure was torn down in 1927. (Kirk Hise collection, via Eric Hise.)

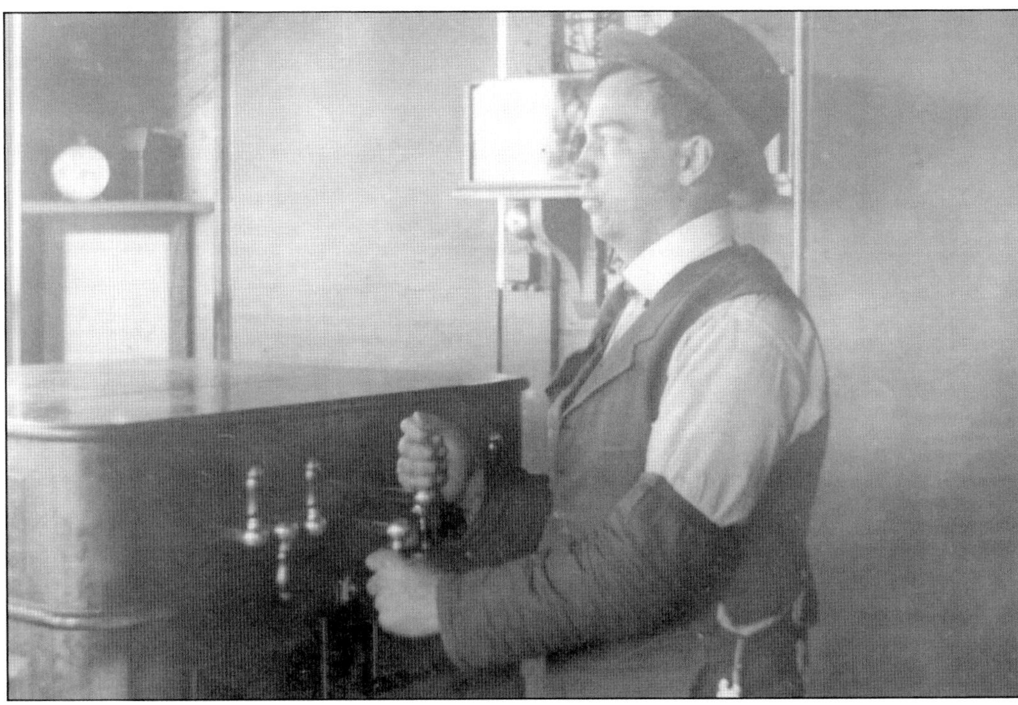

Wallace Gallup was the Genoa operator of the tower at the New York Central Railroad crossing and the Lake Shore station. The Lakeshore Electric Railway constructed a cutoff between Sandusky and Fremont, Ohio, taking off nearly five miles along the route between Cleveland and Toledo. (Kirk Hise collection, via Eric Hise.)

A Lake Shore Electric streetcar rolls down Main Street in front of the McIntyre Building in Genoa. (Edna Turner collection, GPL.)

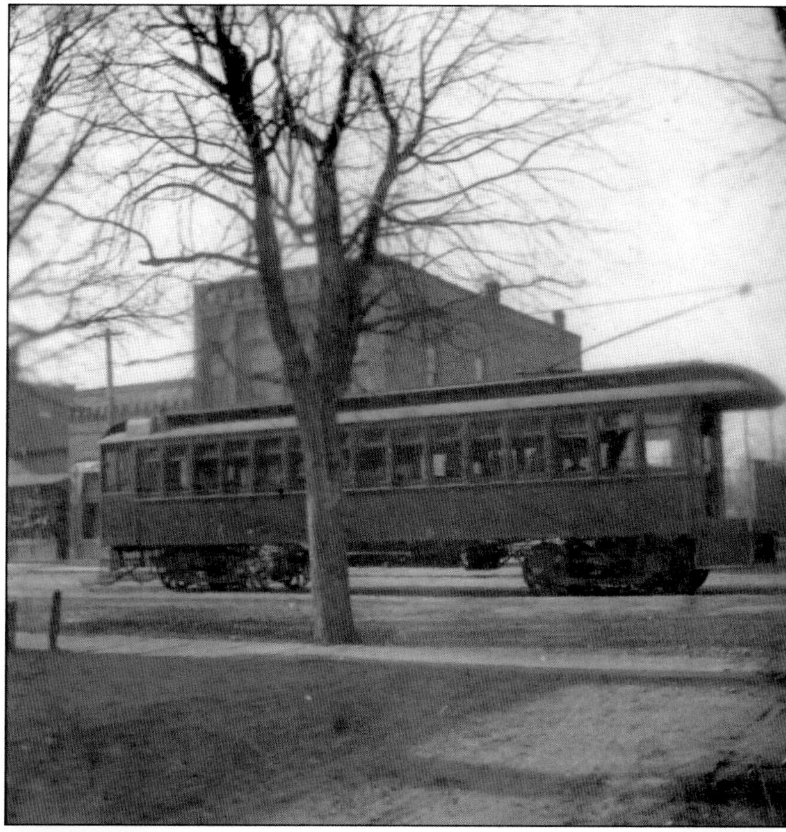

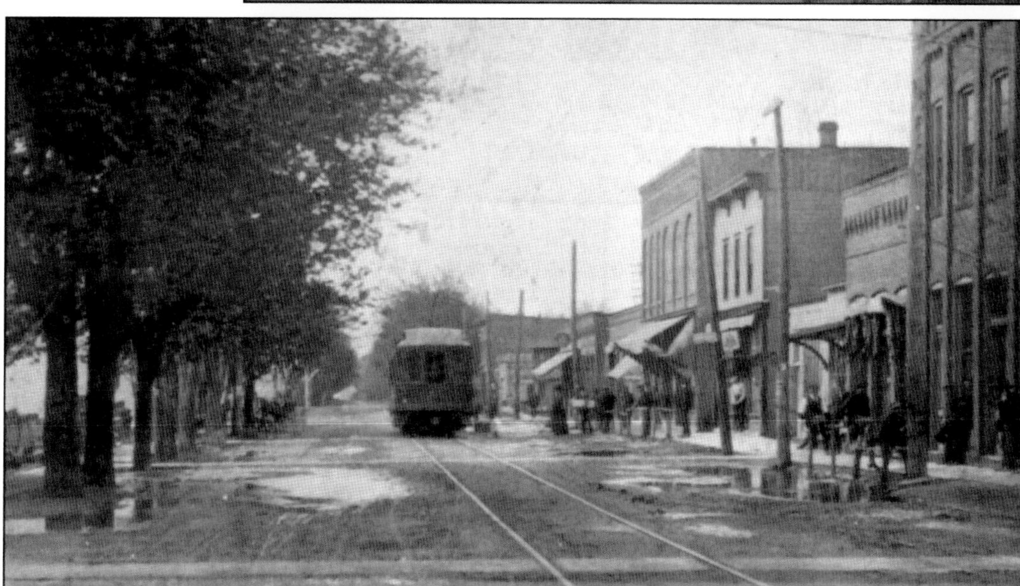

In 1907, a Lake Shore Electric interurban rides down Main Street in Genoa. The Lake Shore stations often promoted quicker service to Toledo than the Toledo, Port Clinton and Lakeside cars, but Genoa was fortunate to have these two lines running half-hourly service. (Courtesy of Joe Badger.)

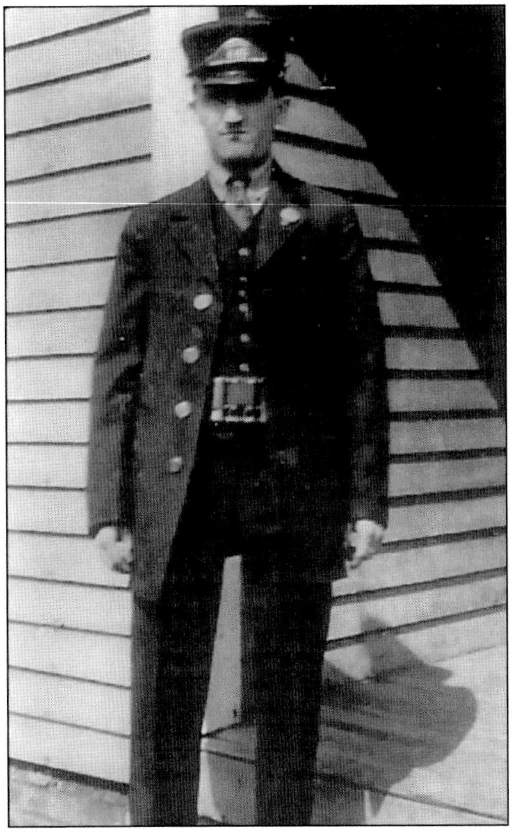

This is an unidentified Genoa brakeman from the Lake Shore electric station in the early 1900s. (Kirk Hise collection, via Eric Hise.)

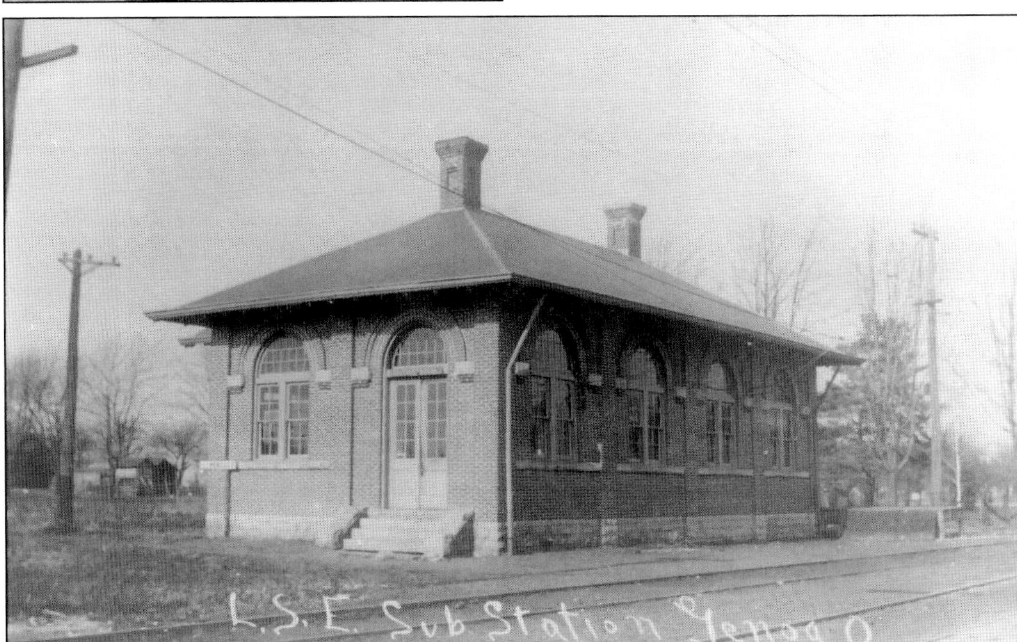

A 1907 shot shows the Lake Shore electric substation in Genoa. It provided the power for that particular section of the line. (Kirk Hise collection, via Eric Hise.)

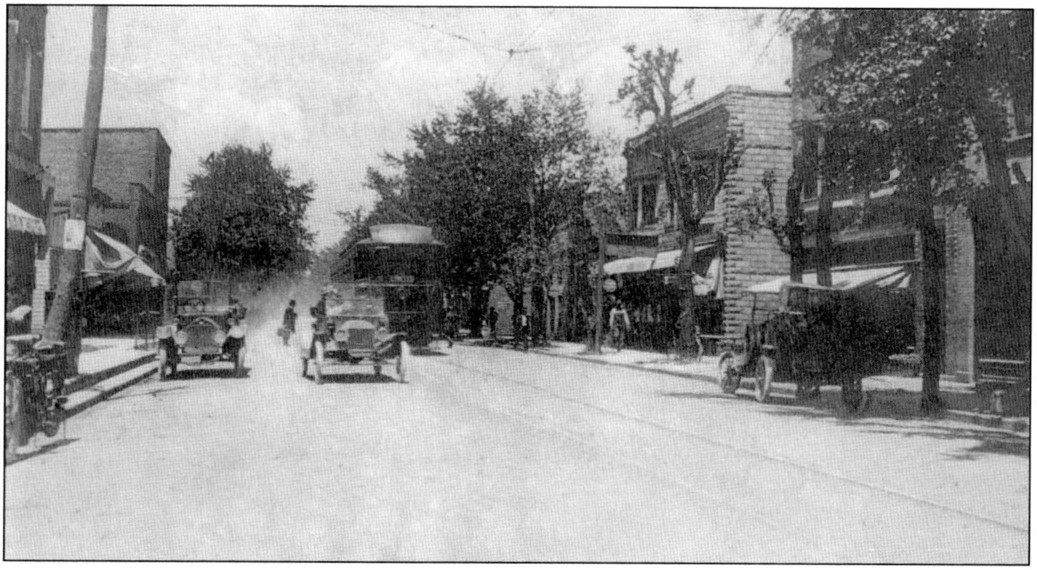

Another view of Genoa's Main Street shows a Lake Shore trolley narrowly missing pedestrians and automobiles near its tracks. There were numerous accidental deaths reported in the early years of streetcars, because there were few traffic laws to abide by when sharing the same street. (GPL.)

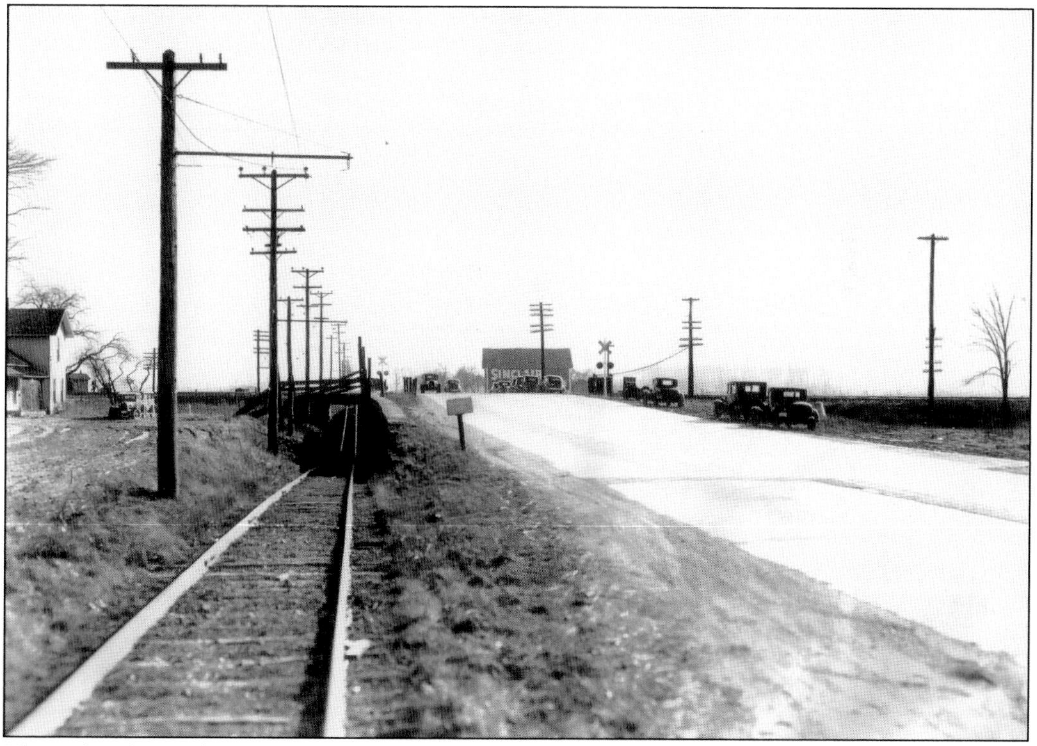

The Lake Shore Electric Railway tracks can be seen on the left running along Route 51 toward Genoa in this c. 1934 image. The New York Central Railroad tracks intersect the streetcar run at the crossing ahead. (Kirk Hise collection, via Eric Hise.)

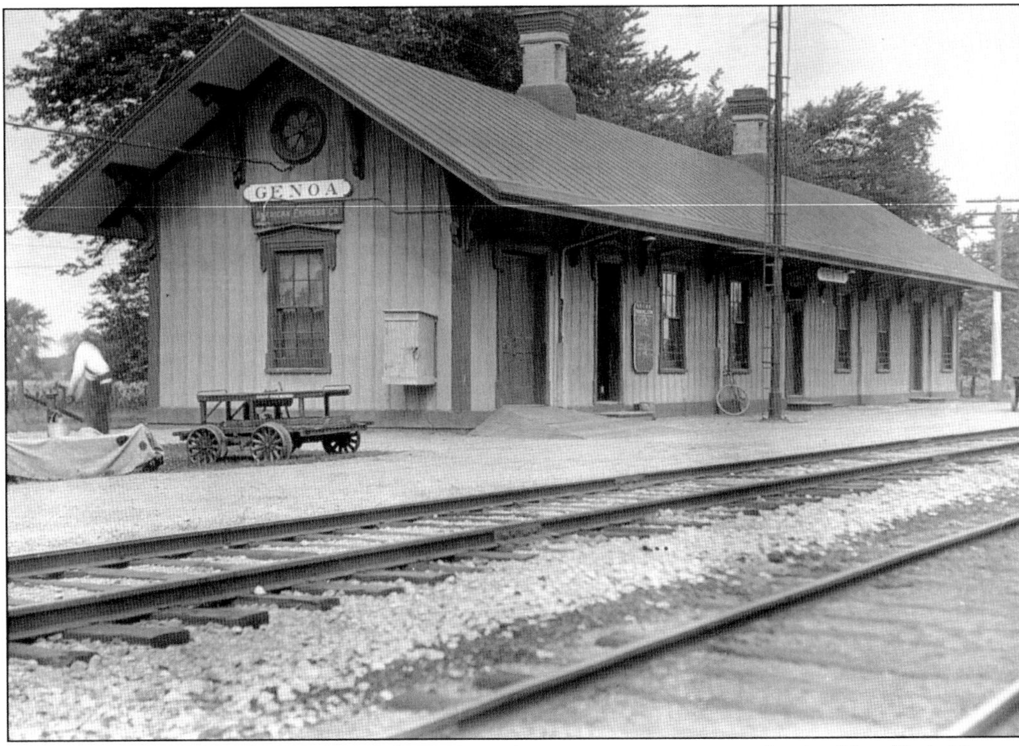

Built in the 1880s, the Genoa train depot served as a passenger station for the New York Central Railroad. It was located near Superior and South Railroad Streets. The depot is shown here in 1919, when it was starting to become less used due to electric streetcars. It was torn down in the early 1960s after years of disuse. (Kirk Hise collection, via Eric Hise.)

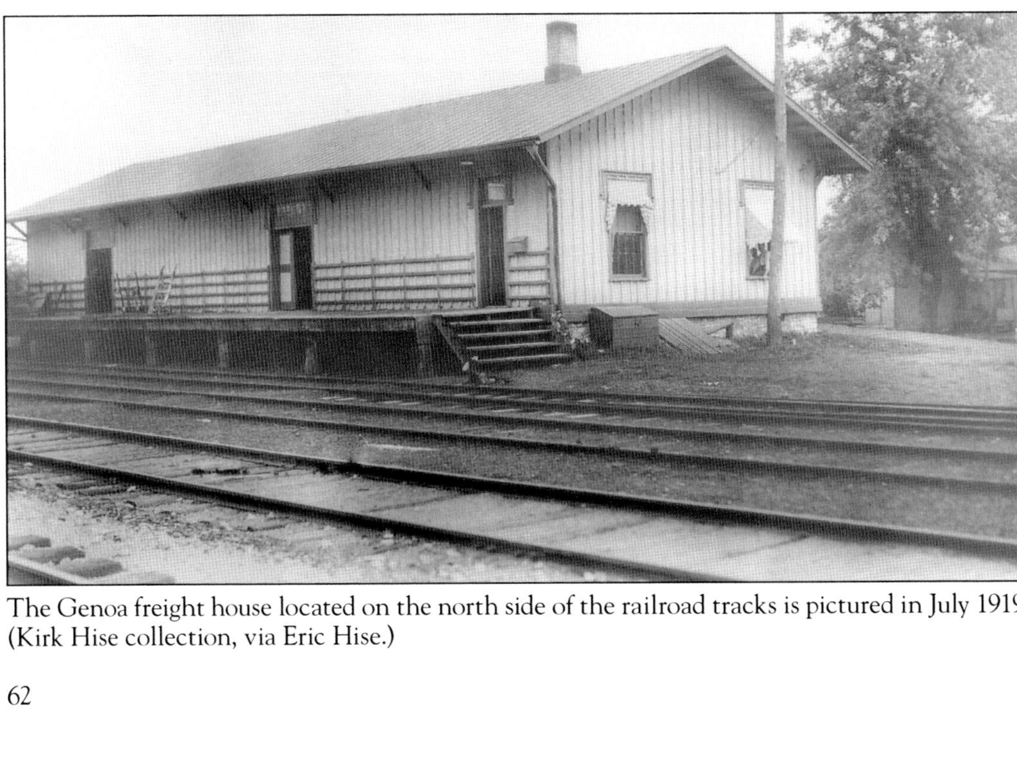

The Genoa freight house located on the north side of the railroad tracks is pictured in July 1919. (Kirk Hise collection, via Eric Hise.)

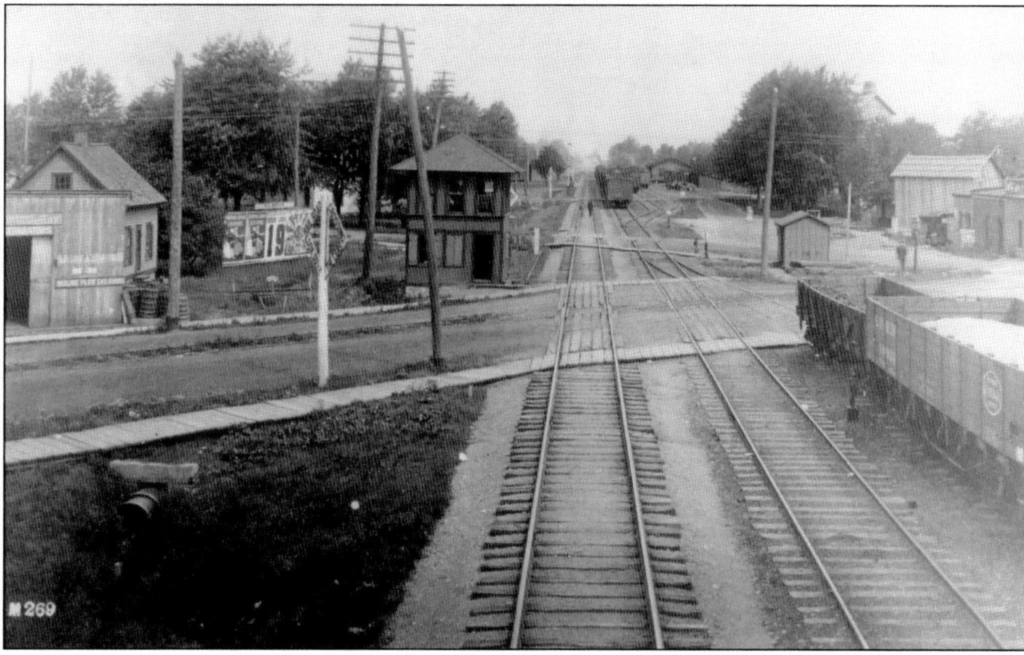

Looking west on the Genoa Lakeshore and Michigan Southern Railroad tracks in 1906, on the right are the stock-loading pens beyond the freight station. (Kirk Hise collection, via Eric Hise.)

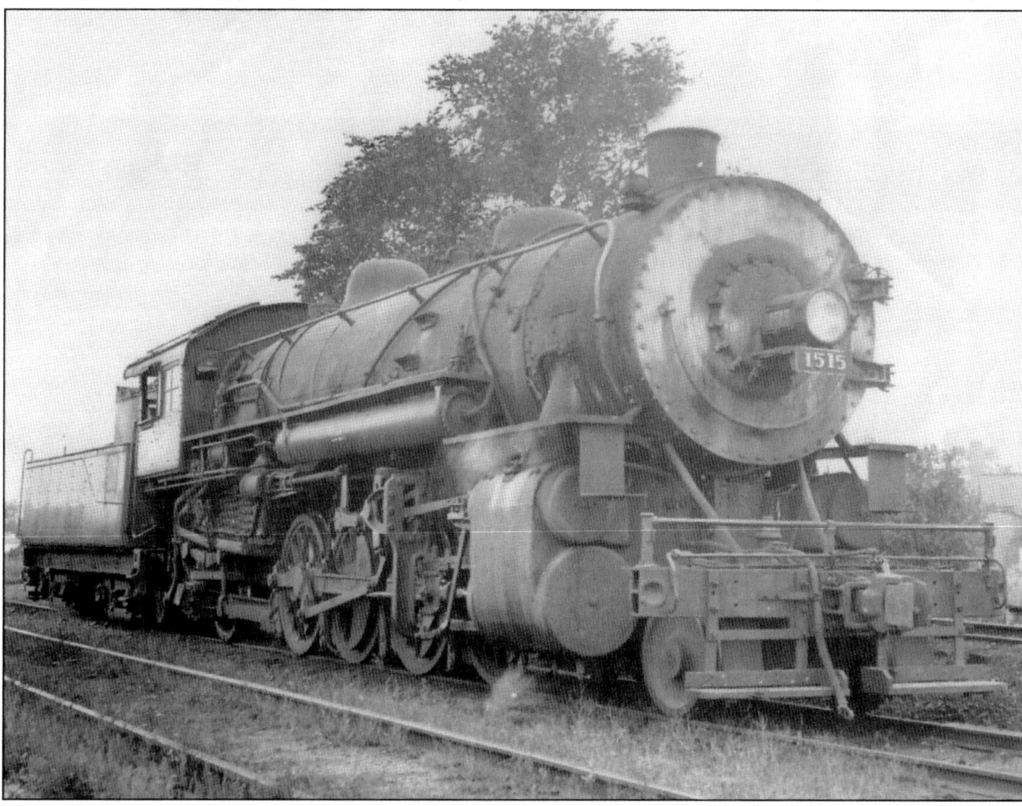

This is one of the engines used on the Genoa switch line that ran through Elmore. (HEPL.)

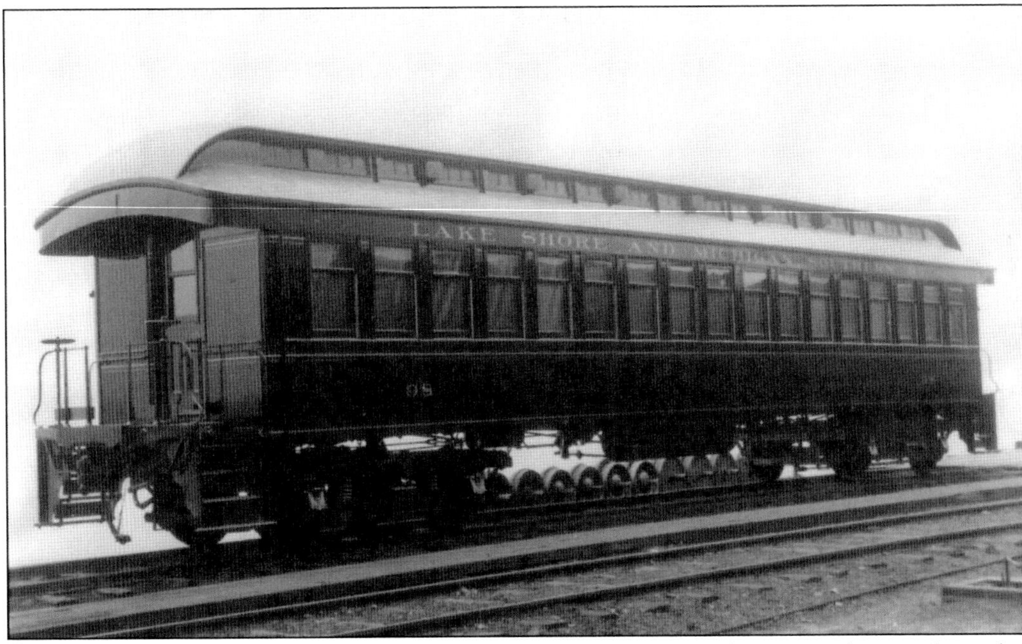

This image shows an example of the one of the Lake Shore and Michigan Southern railcars that operated in Elmore and Genoa from the 1870s until 1906. (HEPL.)

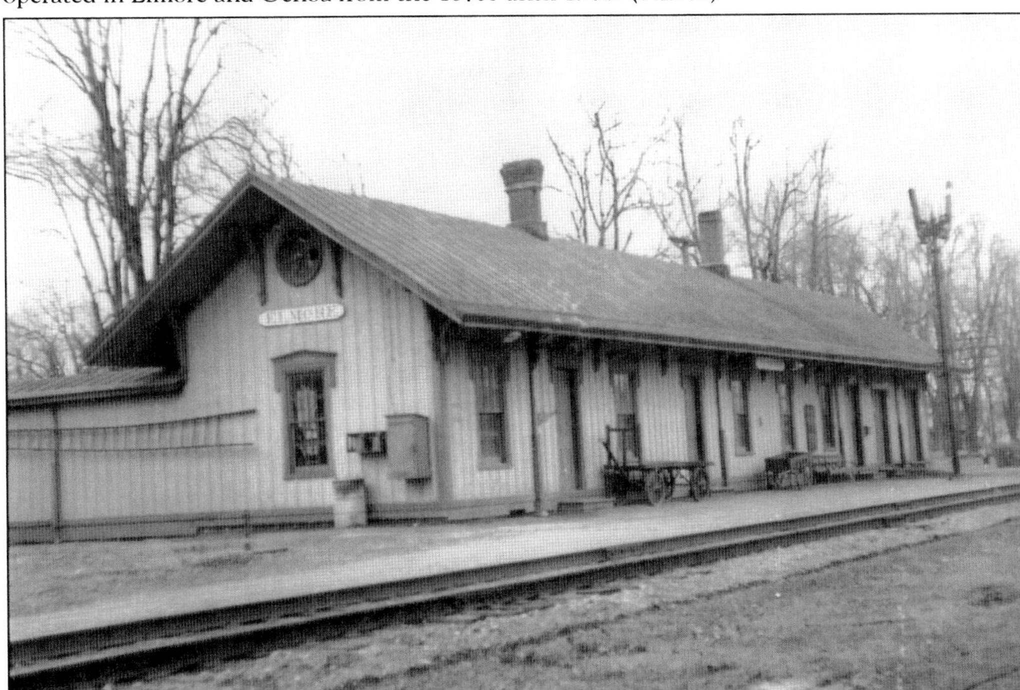

The Elmore Railroad Depot was completed in December 1869. Freight was shipped to Elmore from all over the country, and passenger service was bustling in the 1870s, helping the village to prosper. Passenger service ended in 1949, but freight continued until the 1970s. The Elmore Historical Society restored the depot in 2001, and it currently houses the Elmore Historical Museum and the Elmore Railroad Club in 2011. (HEPL.)

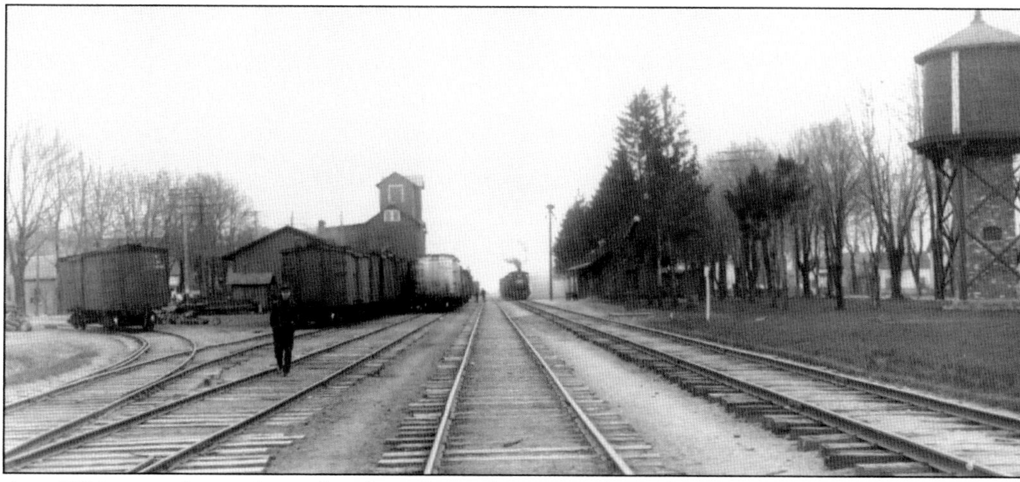

A c. 1906 view shows the railroad tracks and train yards at the site of the Lakeshore Depot in Elmore. Note the sidetrack curving off to the left heading toward what was once Metsch's Flour Mill on Clinton Street. (HEPL.)

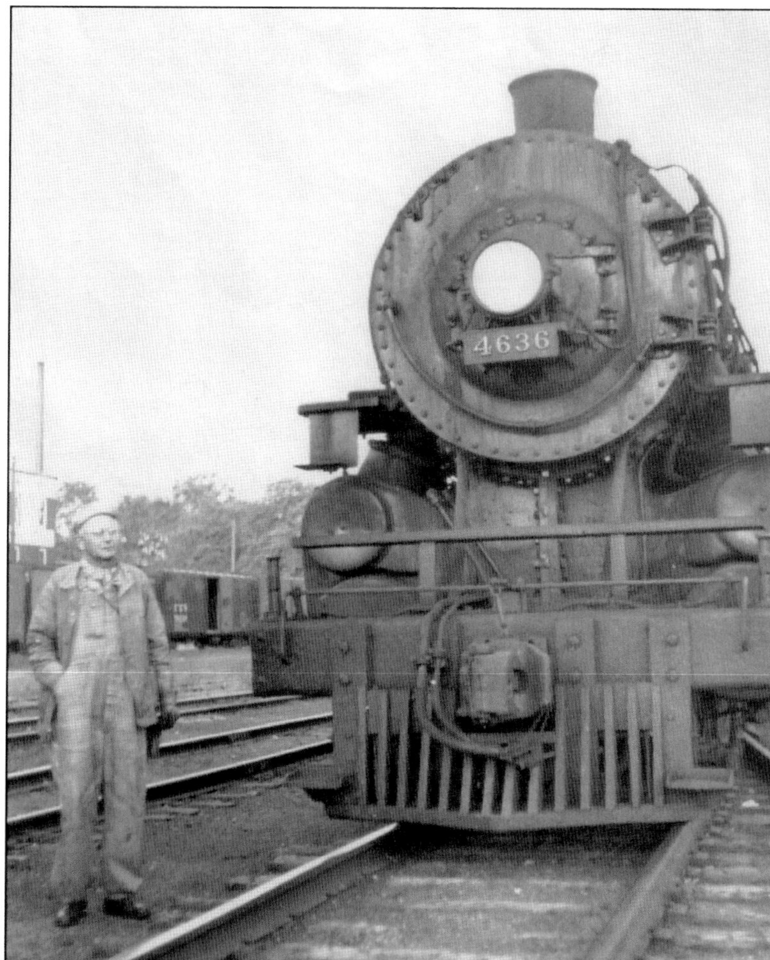

Engineer Herman Sabroske stands in front of train engine no. 4636 of the Lakeshore and Michigan Southern Railway in the Elmore train yards. (HEPL.)

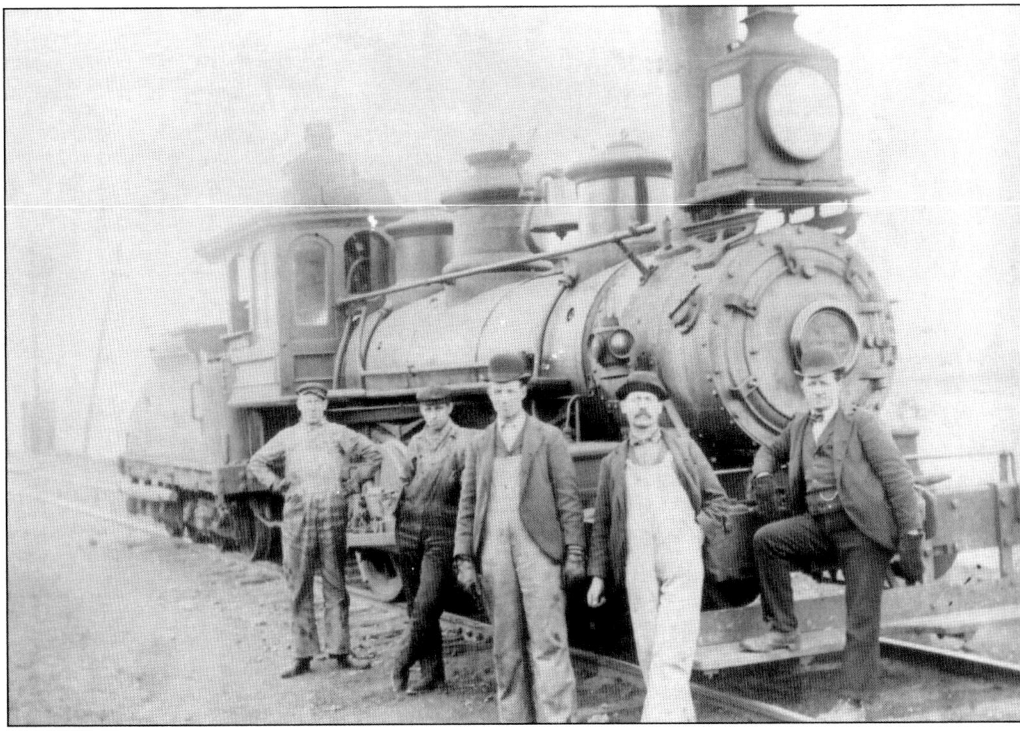

Stanton Oster (far right) stands in front of one of the Elmore train engines with a group of unidentified people during the later portion of the 19th century. Oster was the brother of Suel, Edward, David, Clara (Oster) Witty, and Stella (Oster) Ames. (HEPL.)

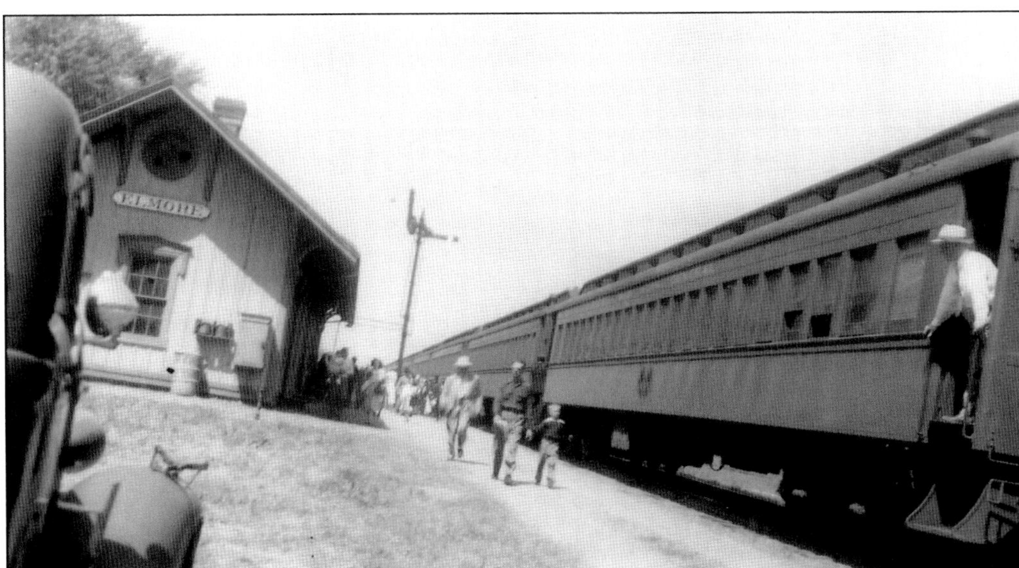

Harry Witty peeks out of the last passenger train to enter Elmore on August 24, 1951. Passenger service discontinued in 1949, but a special excursion train stopped in Elmore as part of the village's centennial celebration on August 25, 1951. More than 750 people boarded the train in front of the depot to travel to Toledo and back that day. (HEPL.)

Four

Elmorites and Genoans

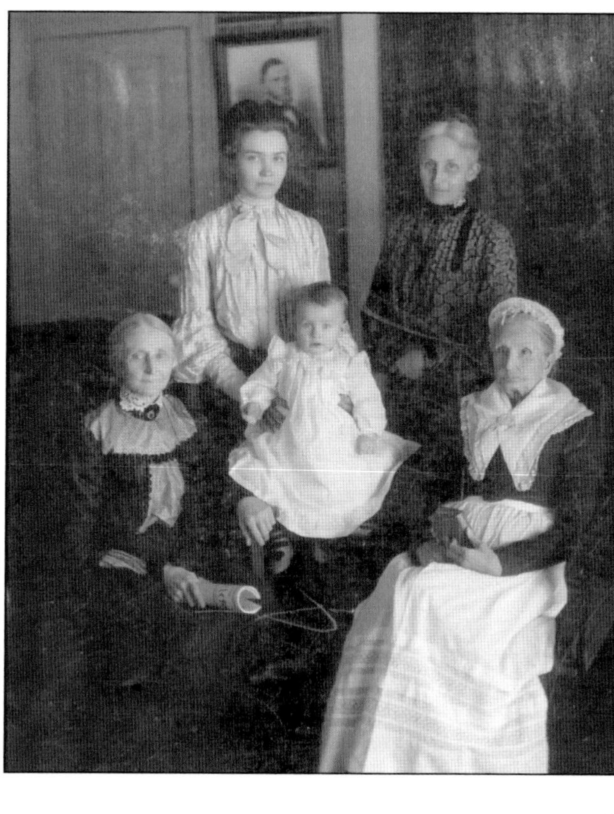

Five generations of a family that has its roots in Elmore and Genoa pose in this photograph taken in 1906. They are, from left to right, (first row) Lydia Banks Powers Deering, Richard Miller, and Pamelia Phillips Banks Warriner; (second row) Caroline Jaeger Miller and Helen Powers Jaeger. In 1867, Pamelia Warriner married Harvey Warriner, one of the original settlers of Genoa in the 1830s. The Jaegers were a prosperous Elmore family. (Elaine Jaeger, HEPL.)

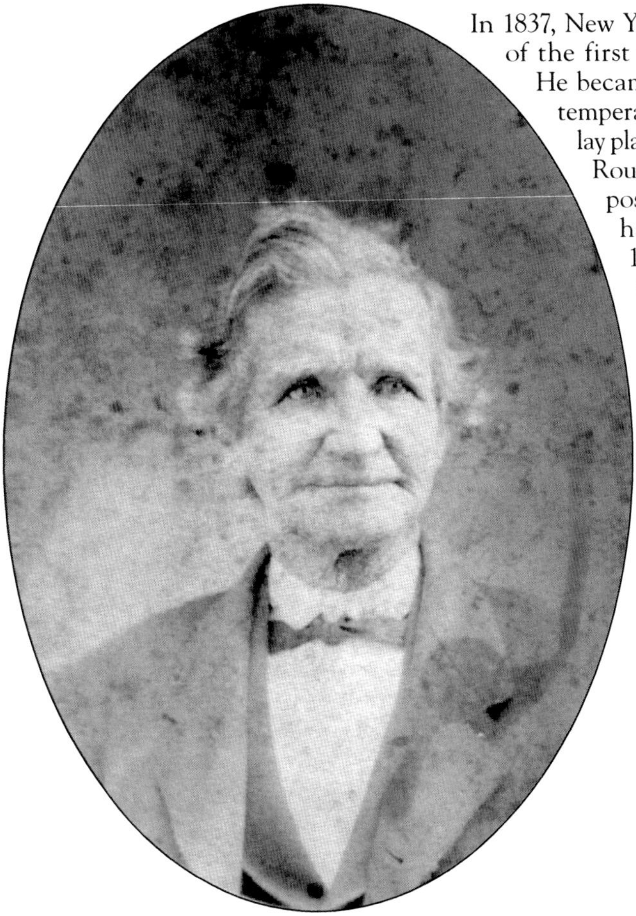

In 1837, New Yorker Harvey Warriner became one of the first white settlers in the Genoa area. He became the leader of the Carson League temperance organization and also helped to lay planks to form the Corduroy Road (State Route 51). Additionally, Warriner ran a post office, lodging rooms, and dance hall on his homestead from 1854 to 1868, when he sold out to Frank Holt. (John Jaeger.)

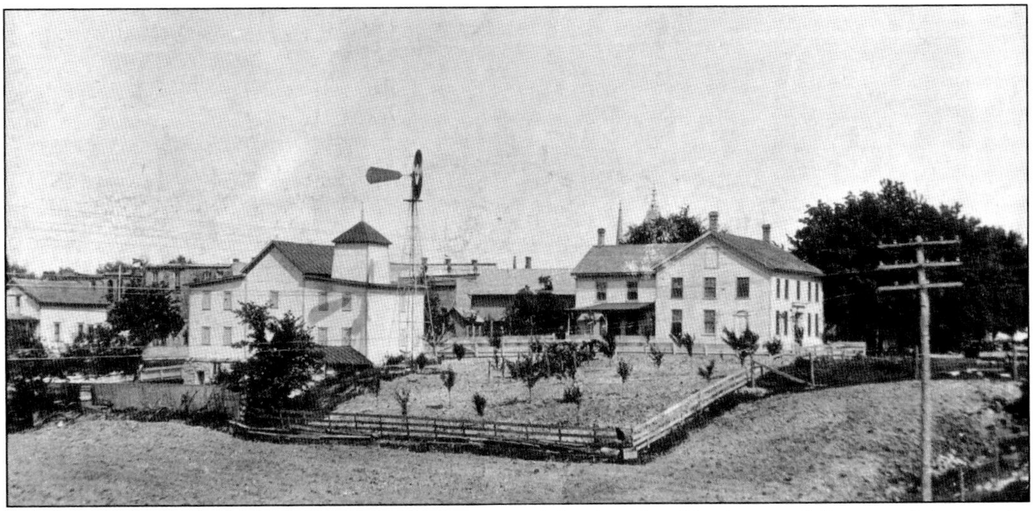

In 1824, Judge Ezekiel Rice settled near Elmore with his brother Rueben and Bennett Havens. In 1851, Rice built a house in town on the corner of Maple and Harris Streets (pictured) and used it as a tavern and inn. In later years, his daughter Jennie Hunt used it as a ballroom to host grand parties and wedding events. It became known as Riverside Manor. (HEPL.)

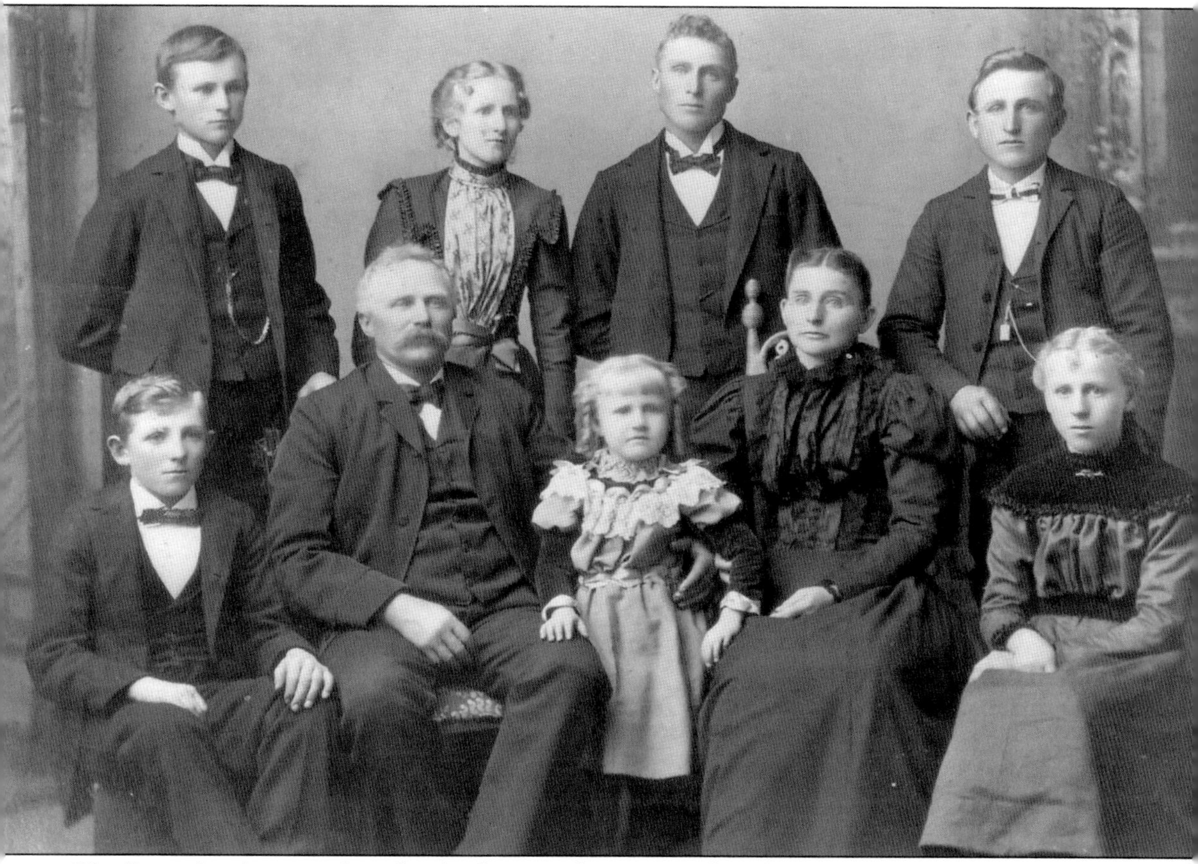

The Damschroders pose for a family photograph in 1900. This Elmore family ran a general store from 1864 until the 1960s. Each family member shown here was the proprietor at some point. Pictured from left to right are (first row) Artie, John W., Verna, Mary, and Nettie Damschroder; (second row) Rudy, Mamie, Bill, and Julius Damschroder. (Damschroder Collection, HEPL.)

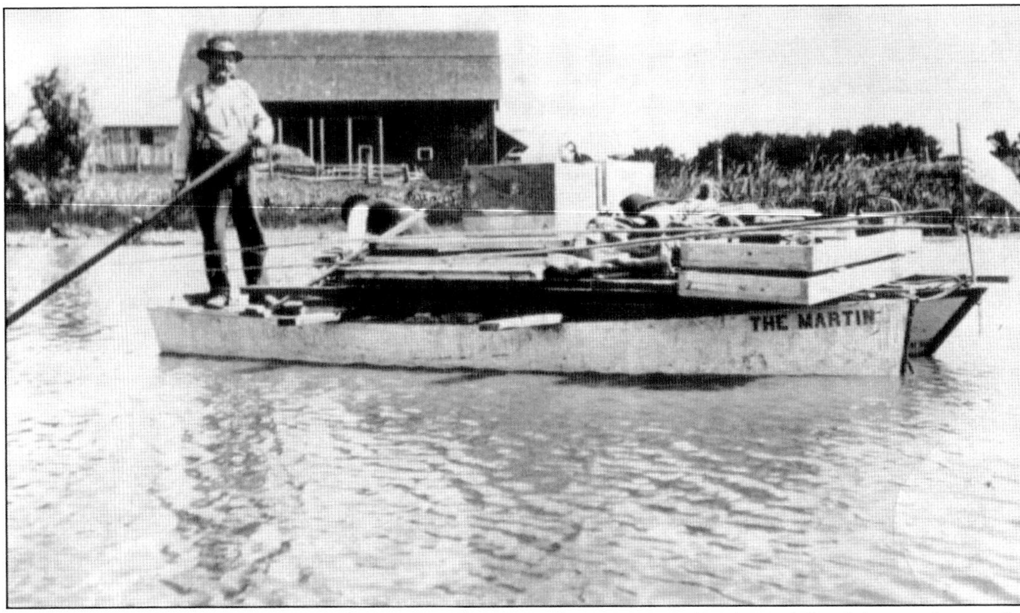

Augustus Buffington, one of Elmore's earliest residents, steers his boat *The Martin* down the Portage River toward Oak Harbor. Buffington was one of many who delivered lumber and other goods from the trains that entered Elmore to other towns via waterways. This was taken around 1900. (Betty Haar.)

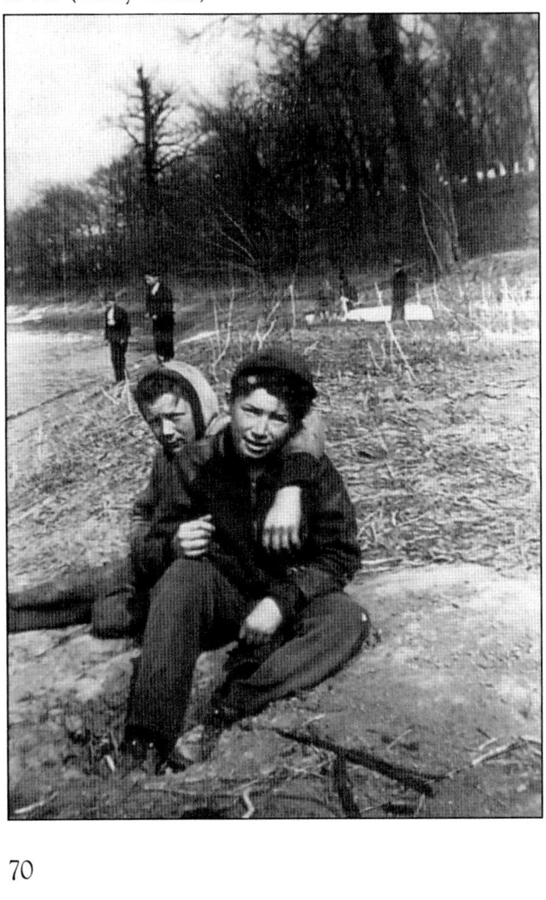

Buffington's grandsons are pictured here at the bottom of Reed's Hill in Elmore around 1939. They are William (left) and James "Corky" Murray. Corky was a longtime Elmore village councilman and played Santa Claus for various organizations for over 45 years. (Betty Haar.)

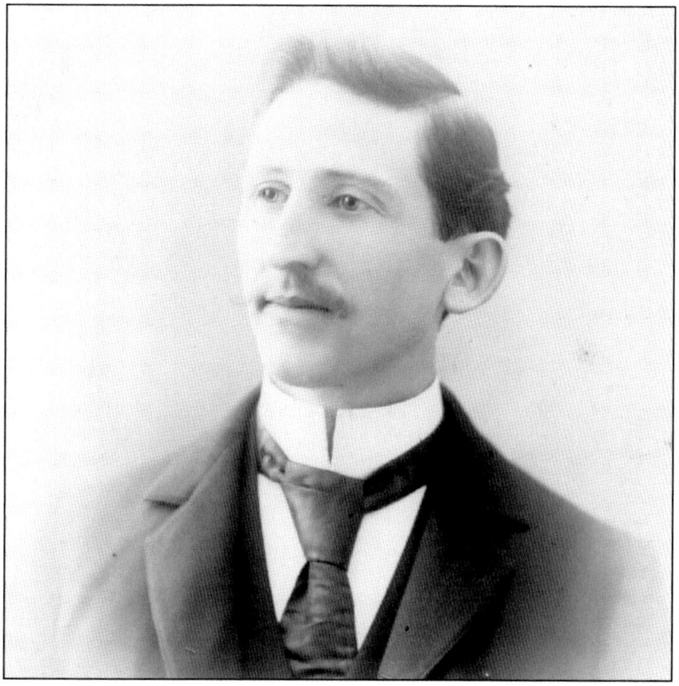

Burton A. Becker (pictured) went into business along with his brother James and father Harmon to form the Elmore Manufacturing Company. They were known for creating the Elmore bicycle and the Elmore car. The success of the Becker management attracted the attention of General Motors Company, which bought their interests in 1911 and continued to manufacture the Elmore car models for a few more years. (HEPL.)

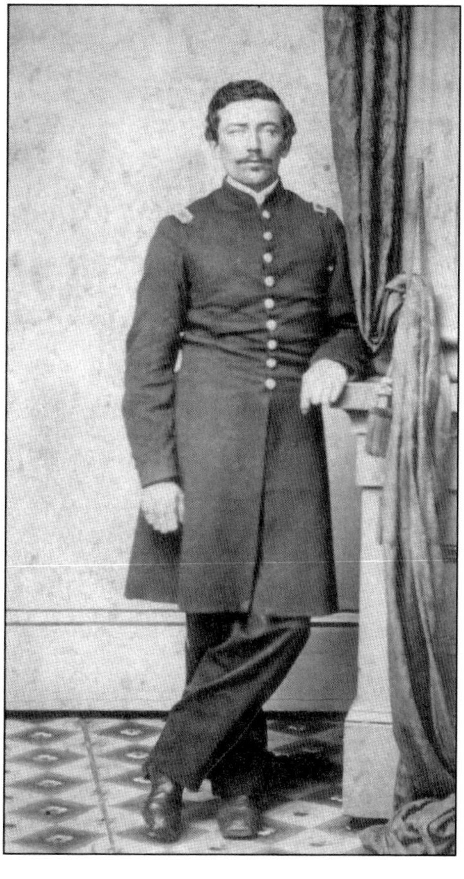

Gustavus Jaeger is pictured in his 21st Wisconsin Volunteer Infantry uniform. He moved to Elmore in 1870 and established the Jaeger Hardware Store. Fancying himself a preacher, Jaeger often closed early to preach sermons to a small group at his home on the Harris Street hill. It was called "Piety Hill" due to his meetings and the building of several churches near that area. (John Jaeger.)

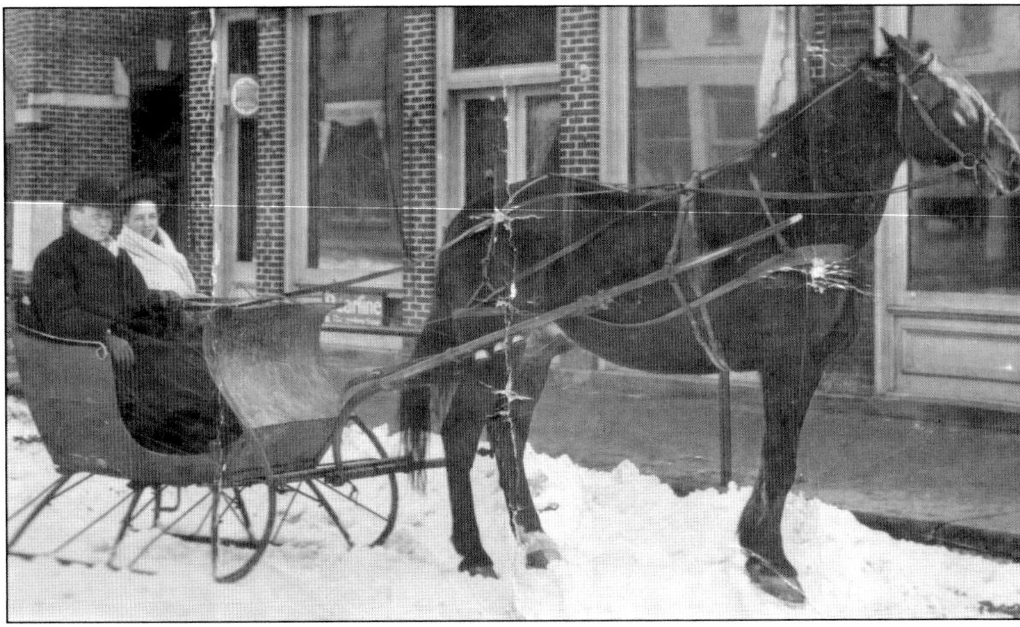

Fredrick von Vultee and his wife sit in a sleigh outside of their Elmore grocery store in the 1890s. Von Vultee opened the grocery and meat market in 1871 and retired in 1918, selling his interests to Brandes and Penfield. (HEPL.)

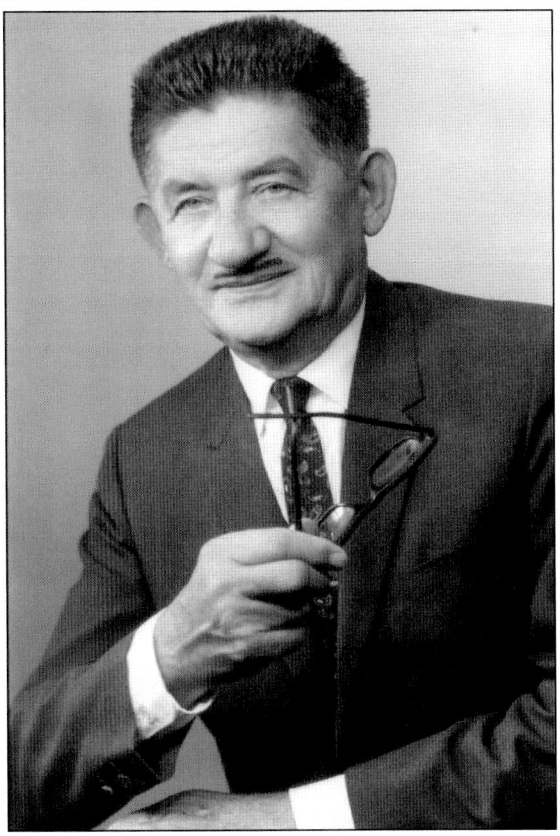

Joseph Schedel came to the United States in the 1920s. In addition to the Elmore arboretum he started in 1944, Schedel also founded the Dolite Company of Gibsonburg, Ohio. He later worked to raise rare and endangered waterfowl on his estate. In addition, his jade collection is said to be the largest private collection outside of China and is showcased in the 1974 book *The Splendor of Jade*. (John Foster, Schedel Foundation.)

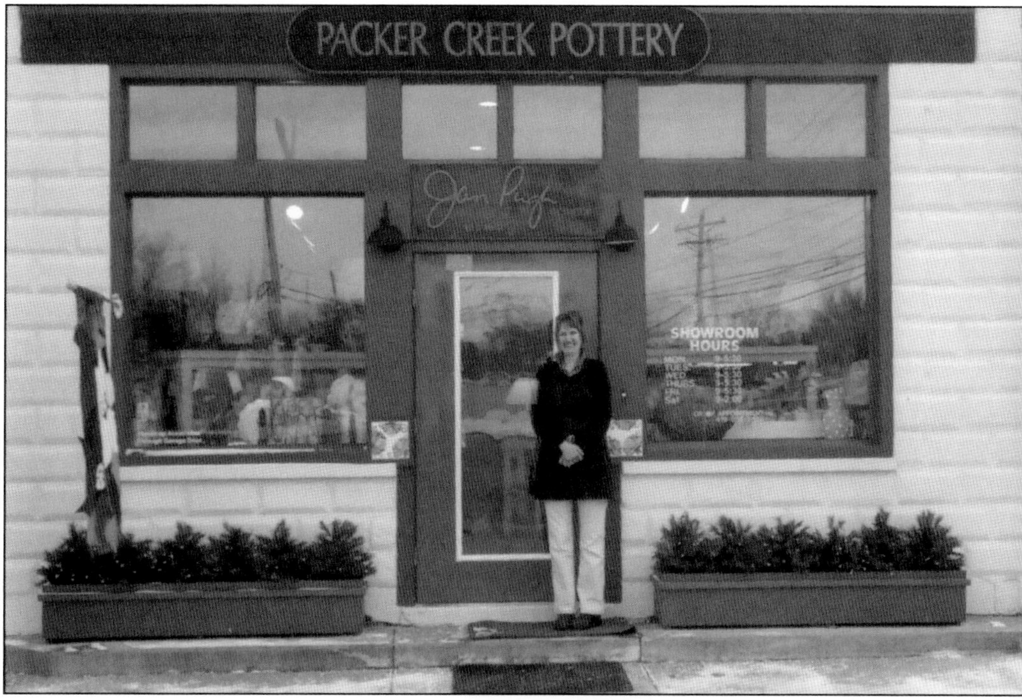

Jan Pugh began her pottery career at 14 and studied at the Toledo Museum of Art, the Rochester Institute of Technology, and the Kansas City Art Institute. She returned to her hometown of Genoa in 1980 to open Packer Creek Pottery, which features her majolica creations. Pugh's pieces can be found in the homes of celebrities such as Julie Andrews, Barbara Bush, Jerry Seinfeld, and Katie Holmes. (Don Wick.)

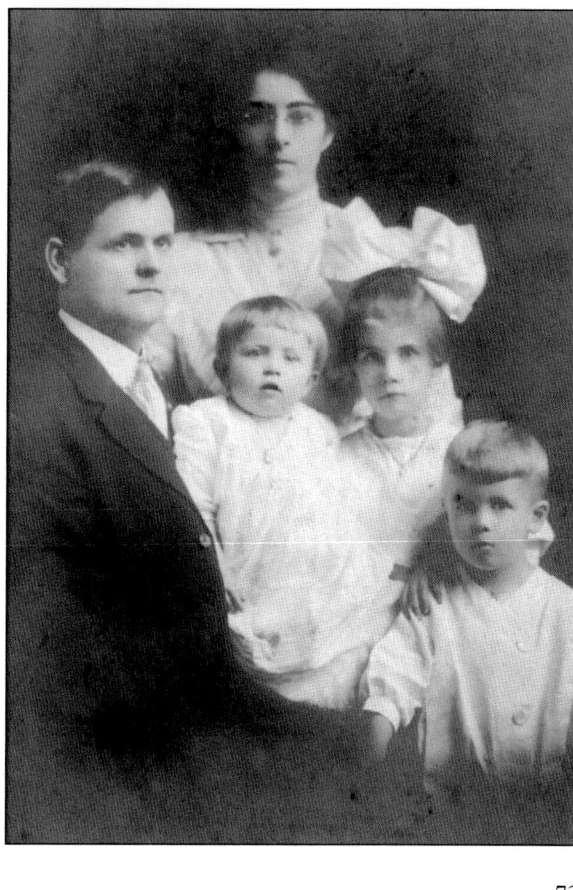

Genoan Albert F. Camper left home at 12 and earned money from odd jobs and bicycle races. He once rode six days on his bicycle from Toledo to Canada to New York, through Cleveland, and back to Genoa; it was a total of 1,117 miles. In 1904, Camper saved enough money to open a grocery business in town. He is pictured here with his family in 1914. (John Jaeger.)

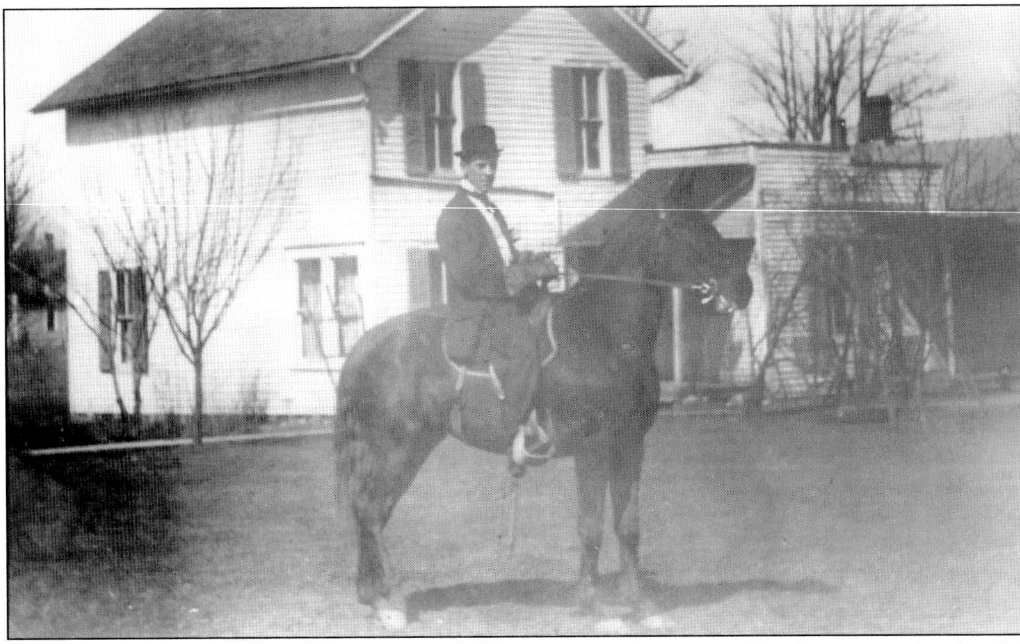

A member of the Edward Uthoff family, most likely Carl, sits astride a horse on the family's Buckeye Street property in Genoa. Carl is best known for opening Forest Park, an amusement park at Hickory Corners. The Uthoffs had a long history of business ventures in Genoa. (Kirk Hise collection, via Eric Hise.)

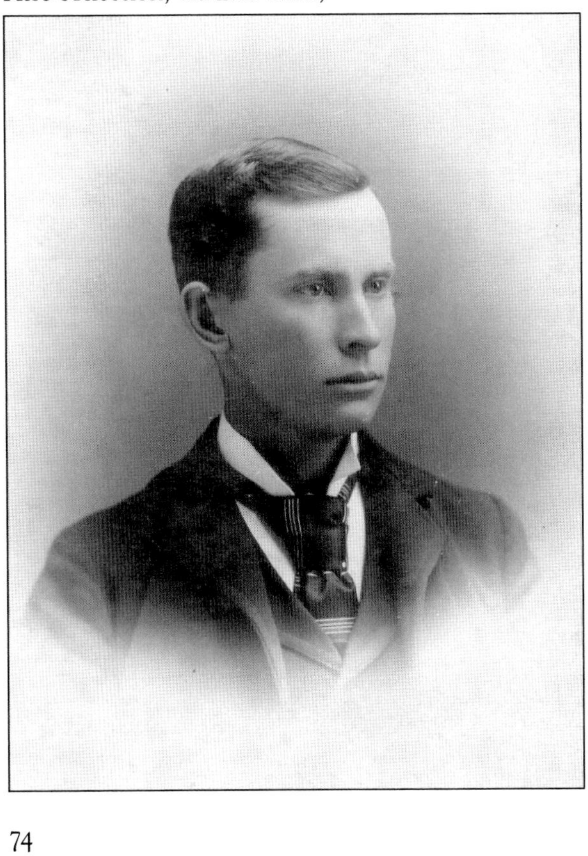

John Edgar Brunner was born in Macon County, Missouri, in 1872 and came to Genoa in 1915. He became the president of the Genoa Bank in 1923, was a member of the Ottawa County Board of Education for 25 years, and served on the Genoa School Board for eight years. An elementary school built in 1956 was named the Brunner School in his honor. (Brunner Collection, GPL.)

Clarence (left) and sister Mattie Heckman (far right) pose with an unidentified friend on their family farm on Nissen Road in Clay Township around 1919. Having also taught for 12 years in the rural areas of Ottawa and Sandusky Counties, Mattie was a popular elementary school teacher in Elmore for 39 years. The Heckman home was moved to Ory Park in Elmore as a historical attraction. (Heckman Collection, EHS.)

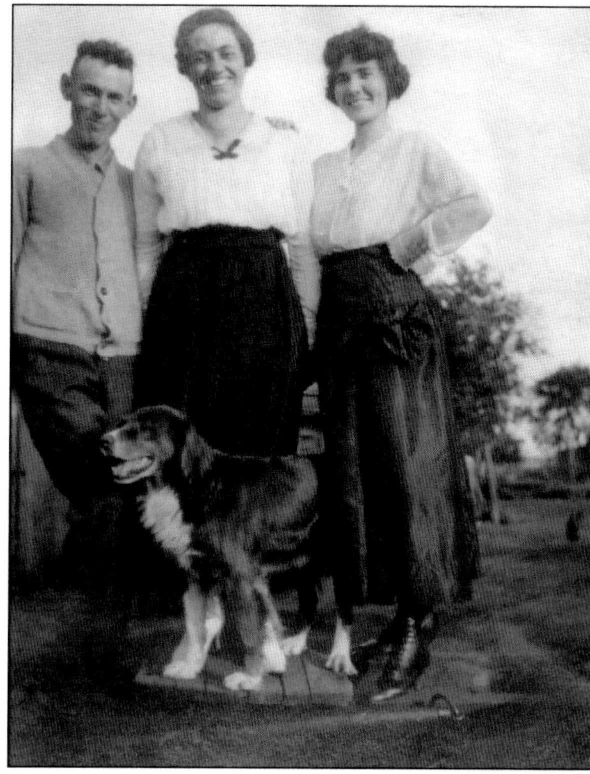

Elmore native Carl "Sox" Wainwright (first row, center) was well known as the pitcher of the Crimson Coaches and Paige Dairy. Both were professional fast-pitch softball teams in Toledo, Ohio. In his 25 years in softball, he led both teams to national championships and pitched 50 no-hit games. From the 1920s to the 1940s, he was considered one of the greatest softball pitchers in Ohio. (HEPL.)

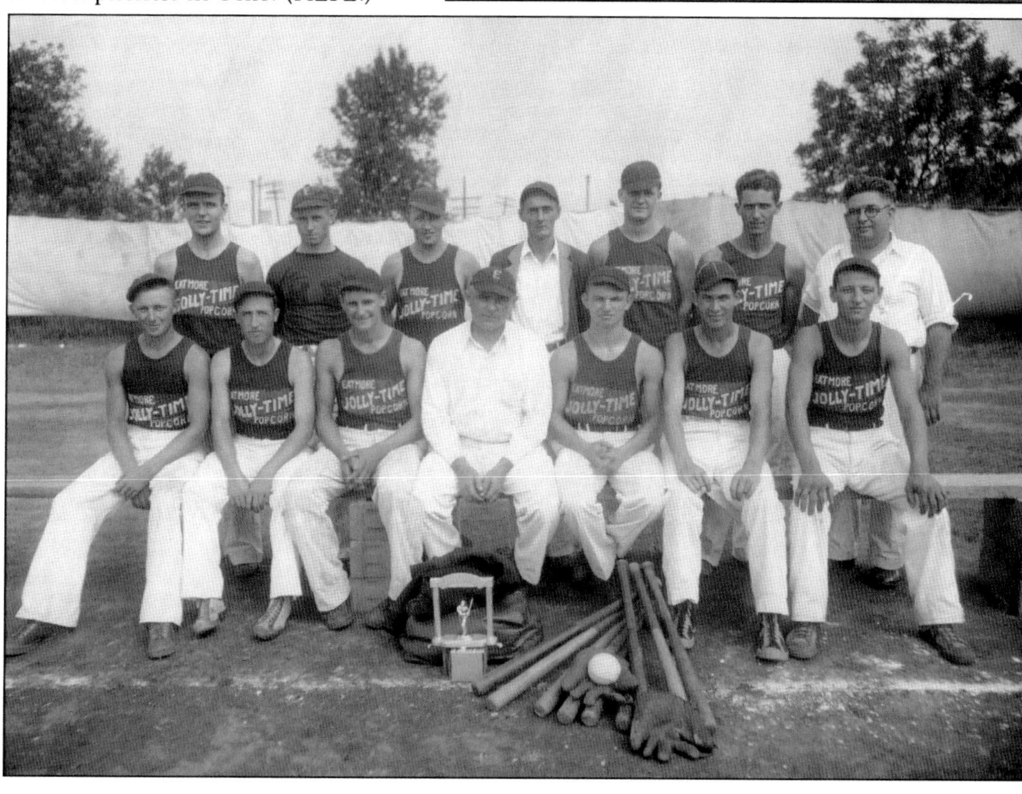

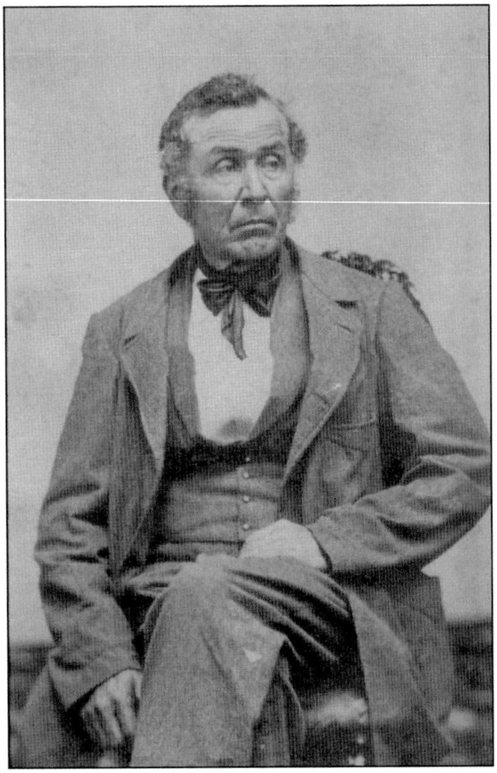

Leaving Germany in 1844, Dr. Frederick Jaeger came to Woodville, Ohio. He was fondly referred to as the "Black Swamp Doctor," and he made rounds to the settlements of Leatherport, Elmore, Hartford (Oak Harbor), Toussaint, Sugar Creek, and Perrysburg. Jaeger left medical journals that explain the harsh yet necessary treatments given. Medicines Jaeger used included aloes, castor oil, nitrate silver, unguent, and worm candy. (John Jaeger.)

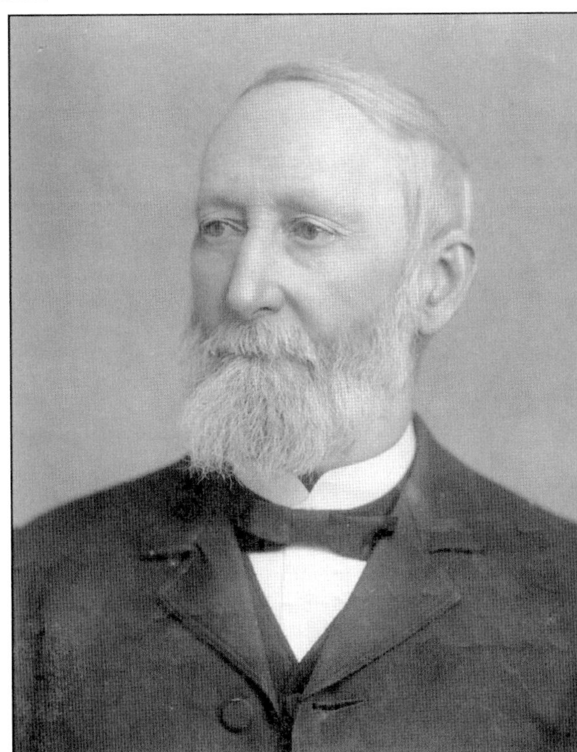

Dr. Joshua Permar was an Elmore dentist from 1873 until his death in 1897. His house and office was on the corner of Clinton and Toledo Streets. Permar spent the first week of each month at the Island House in Port Clinton, Ohio, and every Tuesday in Gibsonburg, Ohio, to pull teeth. He also performed stonecutting and ran a photography studio in his spare time. (HEPL.)

George Lafayette Nellis was born in 1840 in Pennsylvania and came to Elmore as a young man. An extremely bright individual, he suffered a nervous break at school and appeared to the Elmore public as an odd fellow with eccentric ways. He is well known for the detailed journal he kept about Elmore and its people, which spans the years 1895 to 1907. (HEPL.)

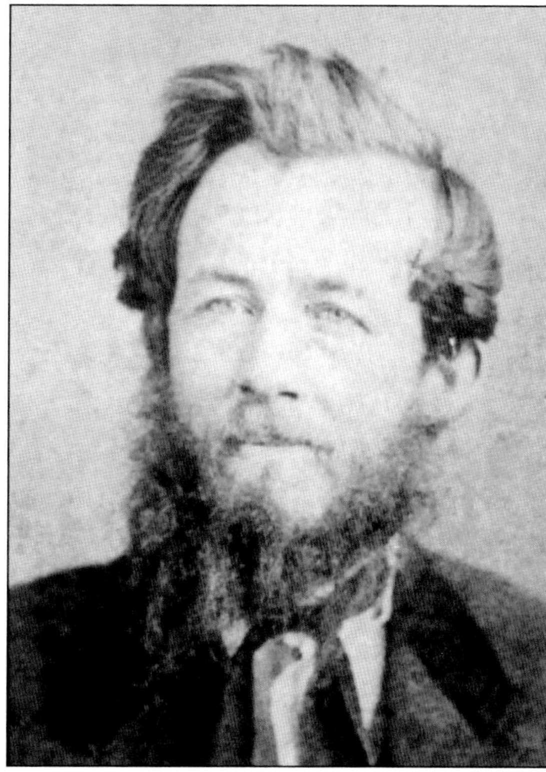

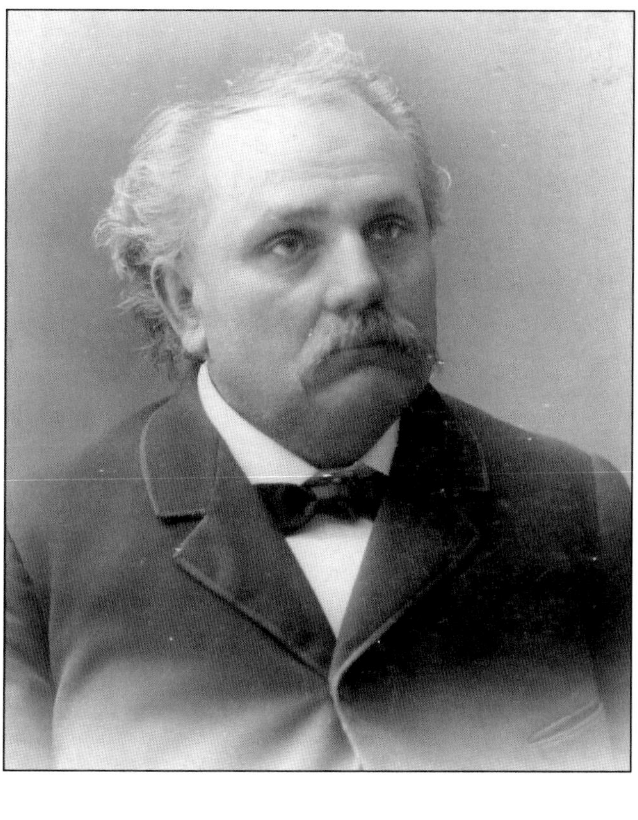

Henry F. Dischinger moved to Elmore in 1866 and quickly became the local artist. He painted backdrops at the Elmore Opera House, business signs, and intricate designs for carriages. He later delved into oil portraits and scenes and created over 300 canvases. His works can be found in many local homes and businesses, and several were sold at auction at the Bennett Art Gallery of Toledo in 1966. (Charles Dibert, HEPL.)

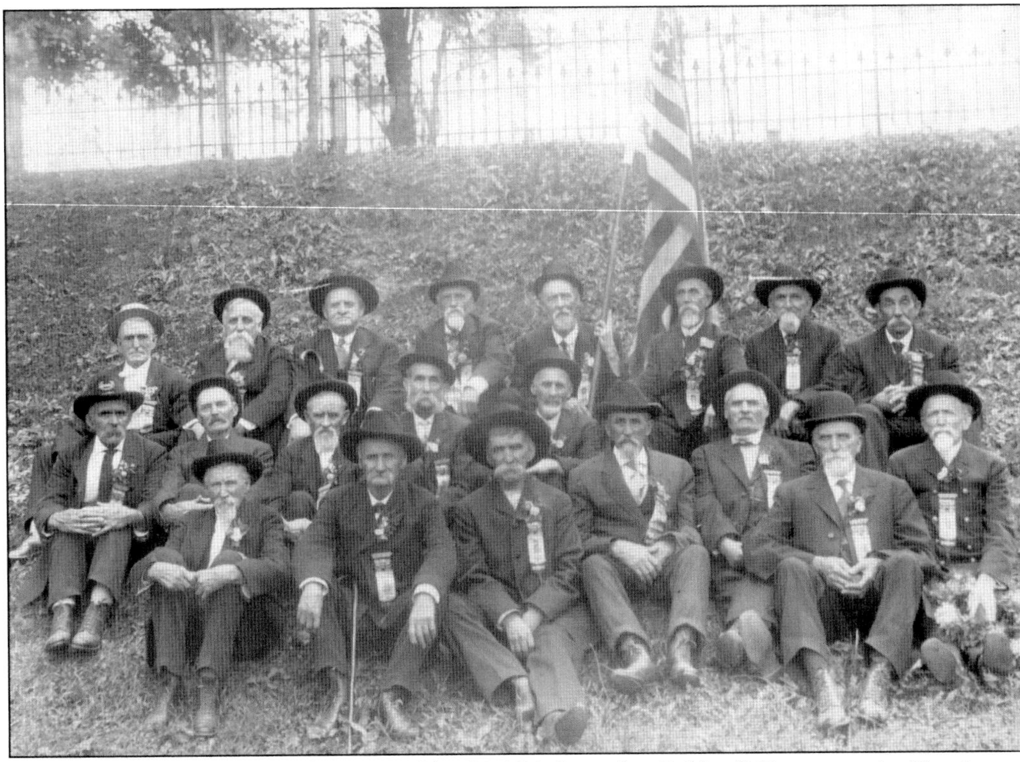

The Elmore Grand Army of the Republic (GAR) from the Caldwell Post poses in Harrington Cemetery in 1911. Members are, from left to right, (first row) Manoa Long, James Merrill, Isaac Logan, Lyman Ames, John Moore, Jacob Yeasting, and Gustavus Jaeger; (second row) William Luckey, Henry Rymers, Lysander Ames, Scott Stevens, and Gabriel Dubrie; (third row) Dewilton Wood, Hosea Fields, Harlow Aldrich, George W. Keightly, Benjamin P. Kimball, John D. Foster, Henry Bothe, and Samuel Groves. (HEPL.)

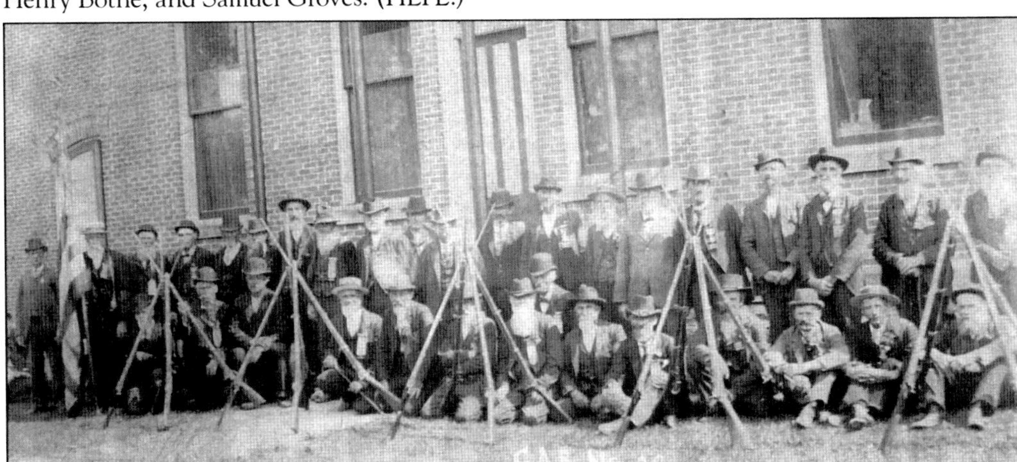

Members of the Genoa GAR gather at the town hall on Memorial Day 1895. The Elliot Wyman Post 39 held meetings in the old schoolhouse on Washington Street from 1867 to 1908; the group shared the building with the Women's Relief Corps. The post disbanded in 1956. The structure on Washington Street is one of seven remaining posts out of the original 725 used during and after the Civil War. (GPL.)

Fashionable, unidentified Elmore ladies have a portrait taken together in the late 1880s. (HEPL.)

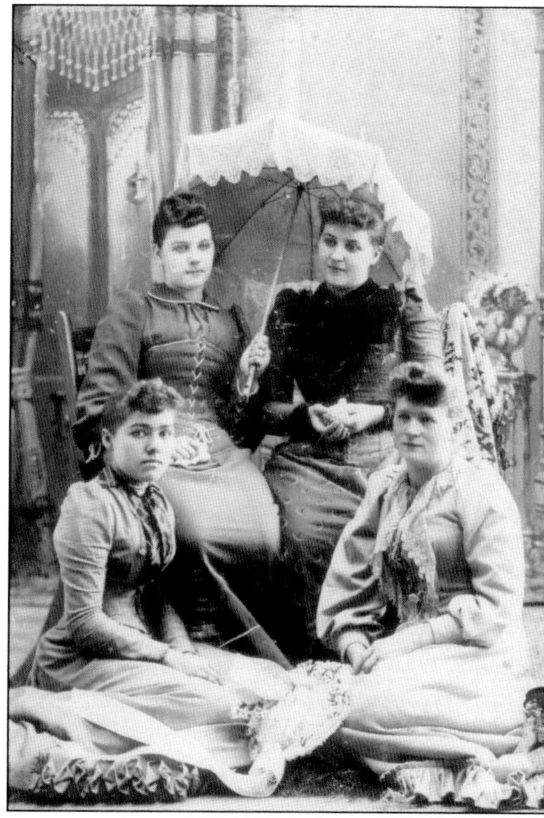

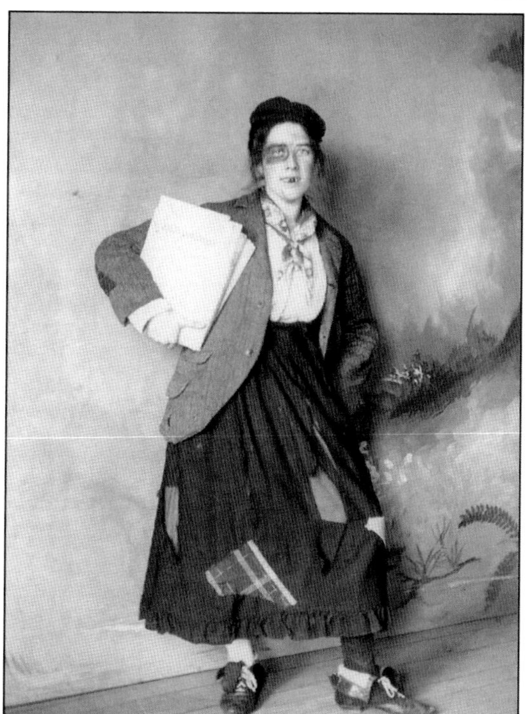

Young Elmorite Daisy Hall stands for her first-prize photograph after winning the August 1900 Industrial Carnival costume contest. Hall's winning costume is a local newsboy. (Loren Hall Collection, HEPL.)

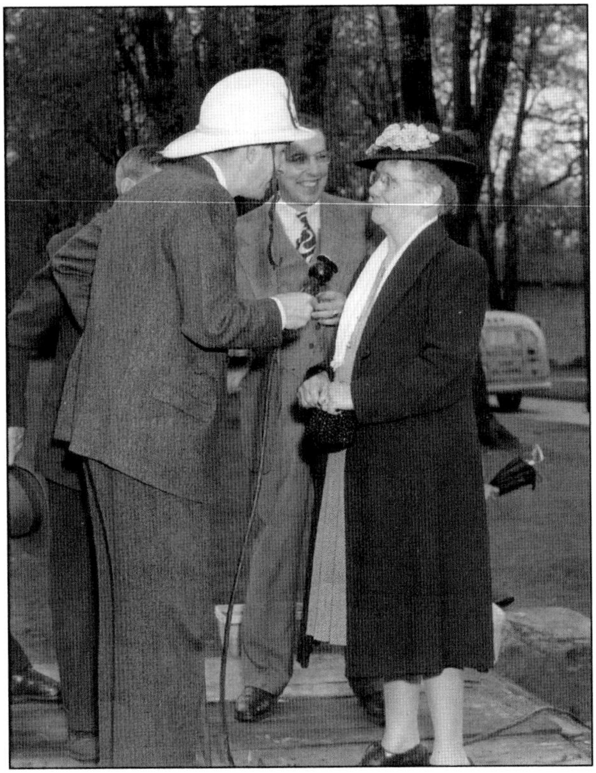

This photograph was taken at a radio broadcast in the Railroad Park in Elmore on April 27, 1948. Pictured are Art Barrie (left), George Brandow (center), and Nellie Linker. (HEPL.)

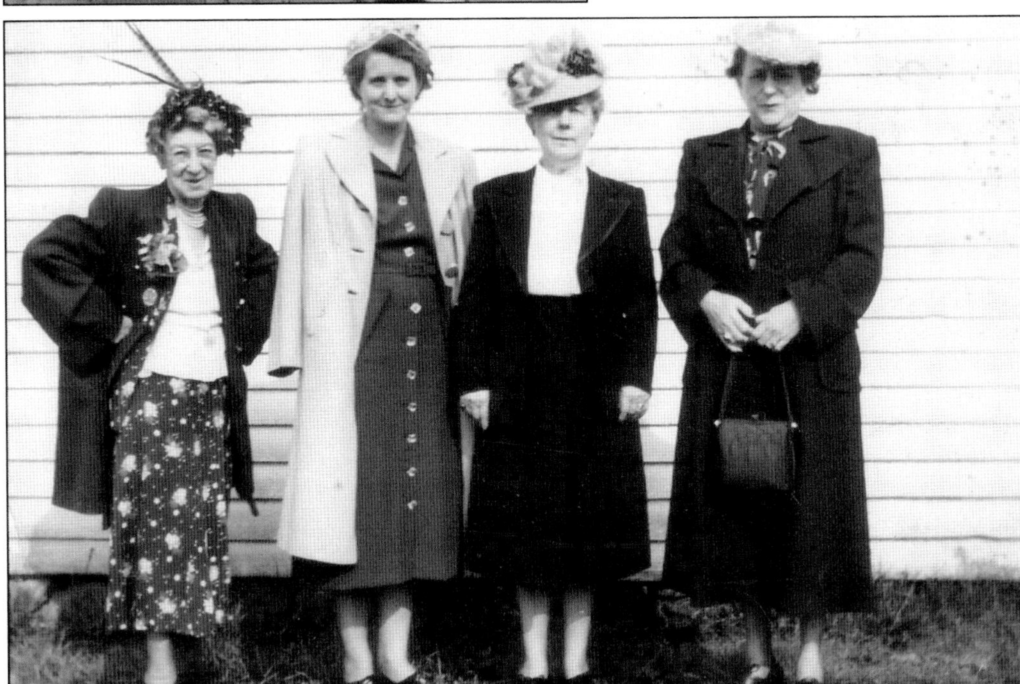

These Genoa ladies are most likely waiting for church in the 1940s. They are, from left to right, Nell Wood, Cora Digby, Ella White, and Henrietta Uthoff. (Tomme Bergman.)

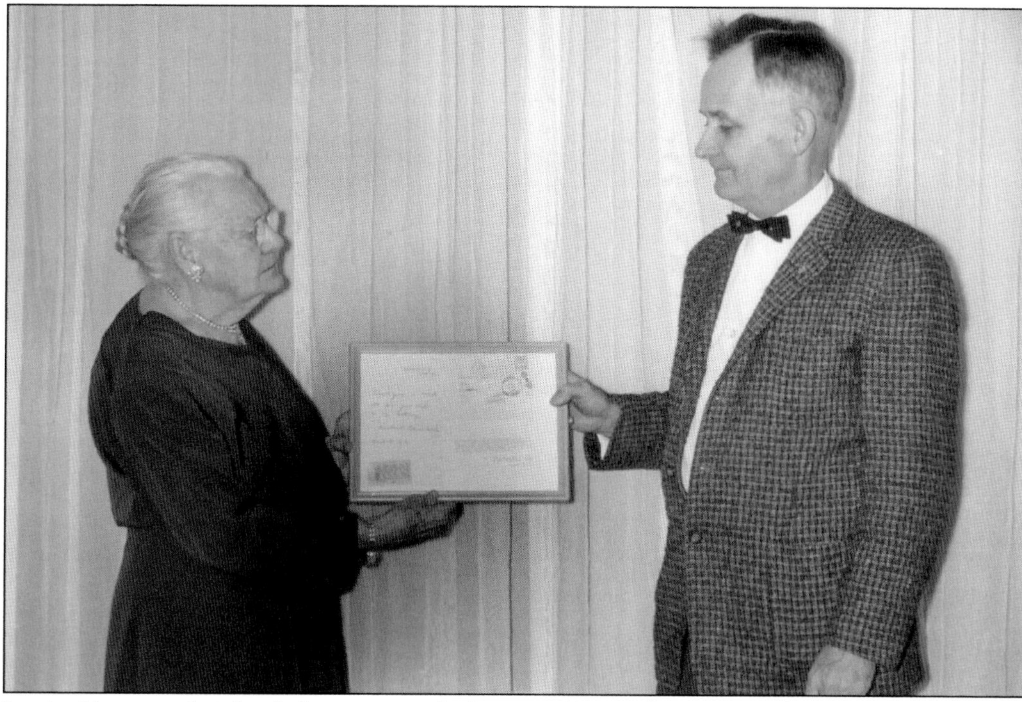

Inspired because their birth dates are nearly the same, Francis Dart wrote a letter of congratulations to Winston Churchill on the occasion of his 86th birthday on November 30, 1960. She received a reply from Churchill and is pictured here presenting the letter to the board president of the Genoa Public Library, David Platt. (GPL.)

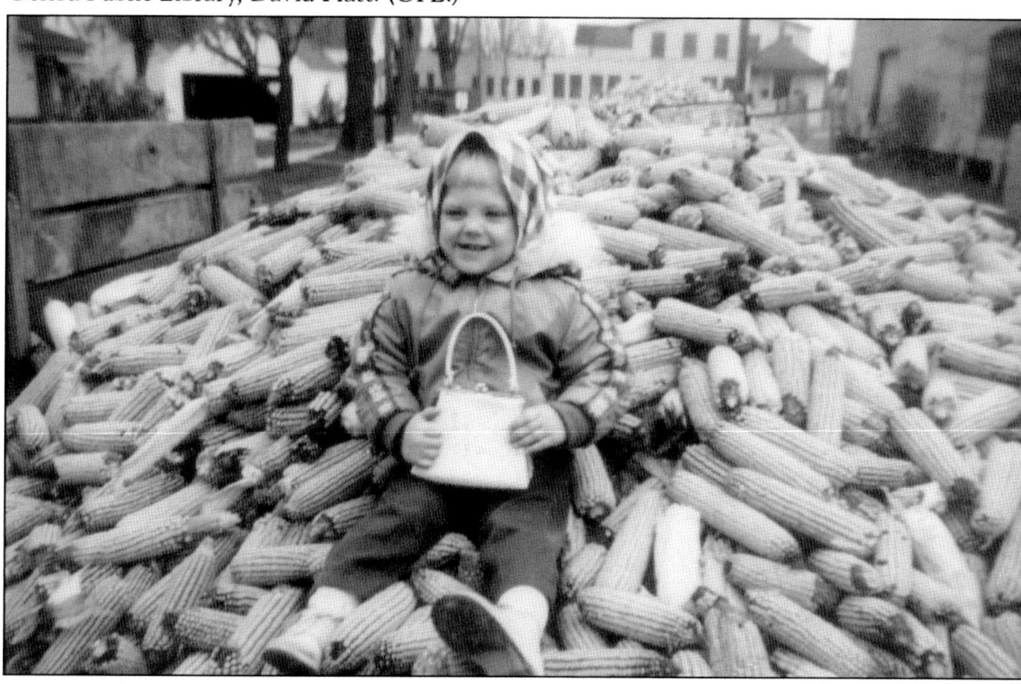

Young Becky Lieske rides a wagon full of corn. This was taken outside of the Elmore Farmer's Elevator in 1966. (Merlin Lieske.)

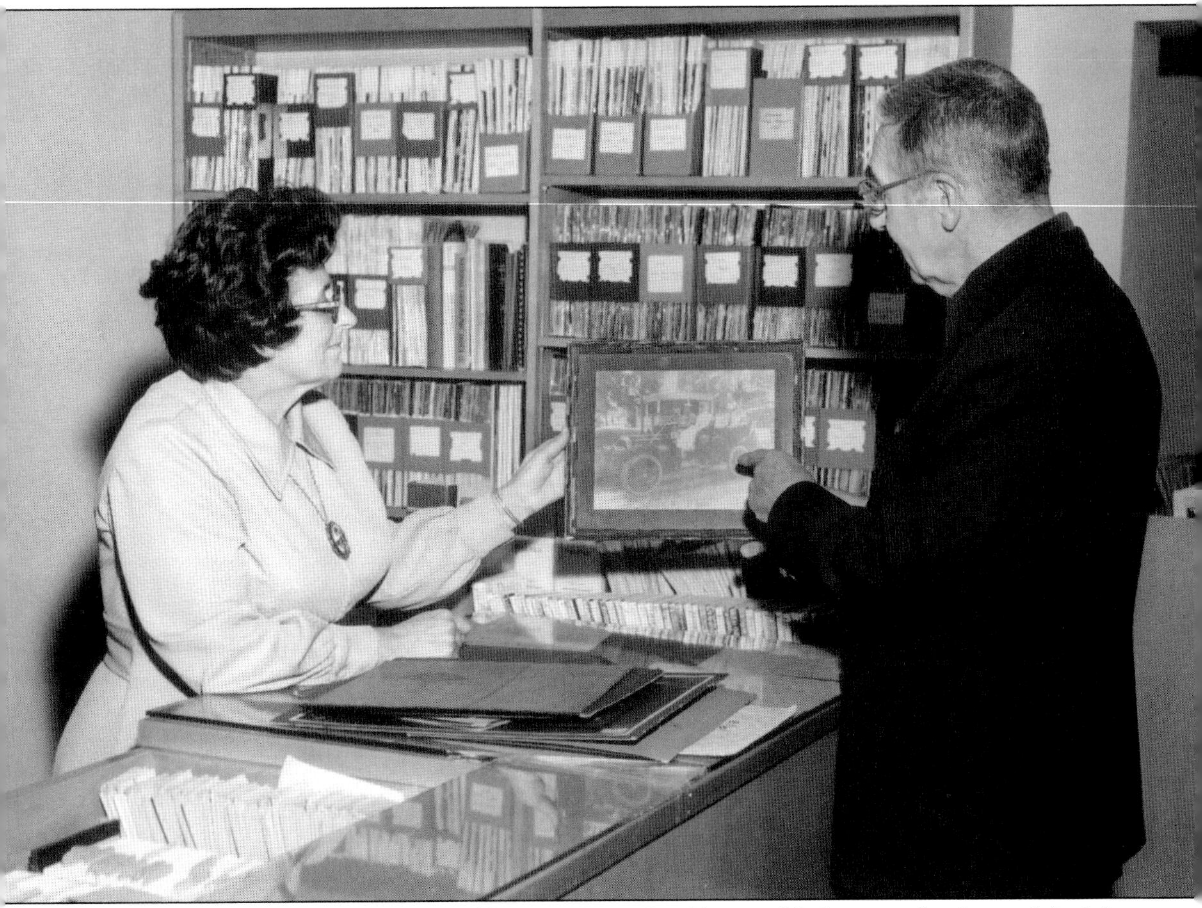

Laurie Dolph (right) is presenting librarian Grace Luebke an old photograph of a model of the Elmore car. It was manufactured in Clyde, Ohio, by Dolph's great-uncles, the Beckers of Elmore. Luebke also created the renowned, eponymous Grace Luebke Local History and Genealogy Room at the Harris-Elmore Public Library. (HEPL.)

Five

School Days

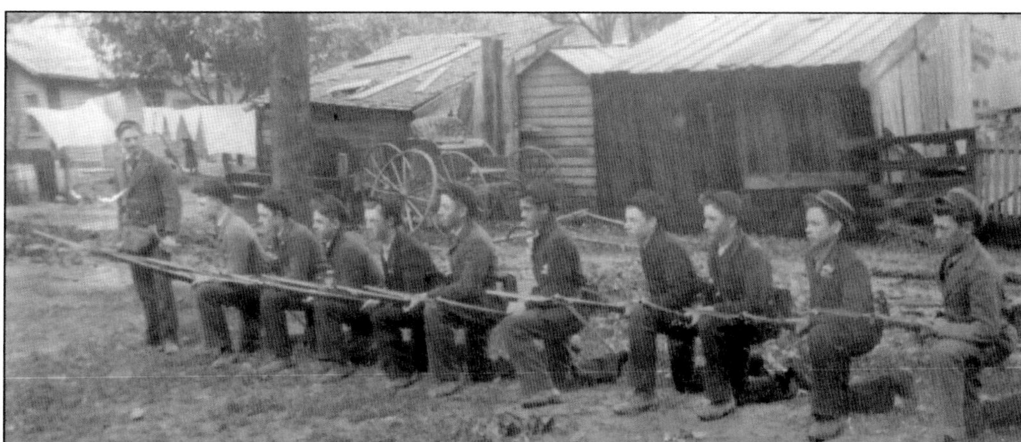

A group of Elmore High School students formed the Cadets in 1893–1894 to practice and drill as a sort of precursor to an Army ROTC. The Elmore GAR allowed them use of its Civil War muskets—but only for drill purposes. The students trained for a week, during which they camped at Shepard's Grove and participated in activities such as marching, swimming, drilling, and boating. Identified from left to right are Robert Rymers (captain), Charles Bliven, Guy Barnhart, Gene Sarnes, Wesley Crozier, Frank Rice, Donald Worst, Rudy Hasselkus, George Weis, Elmer Weis, and Bill Marwilsky. (Charles Bliven Collection, HEPL.)

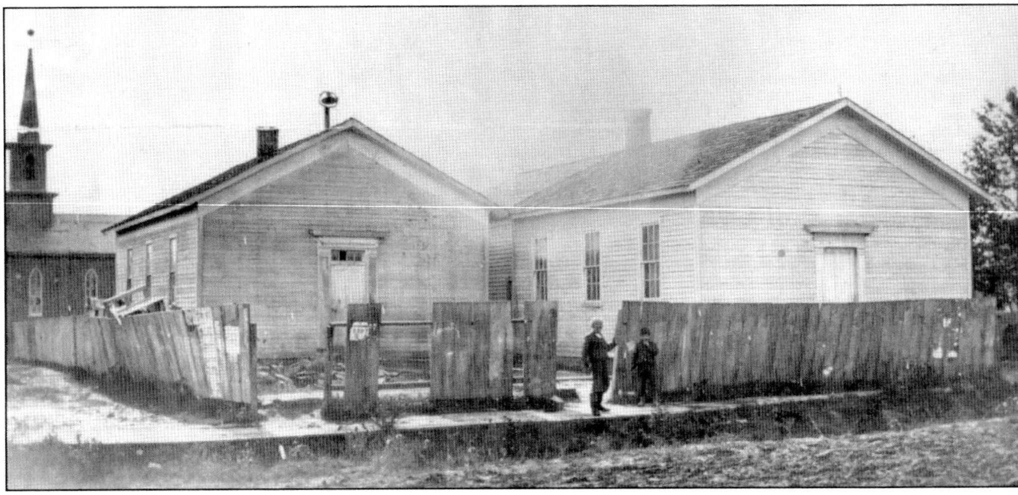

The first schoolhouse in Elmore was built about 1855 on the corner of Rice and Congress Streets. It was composed of two frame buildings for primary and high school students. The principal at that time was J.B. Gambel. (HEPL.)

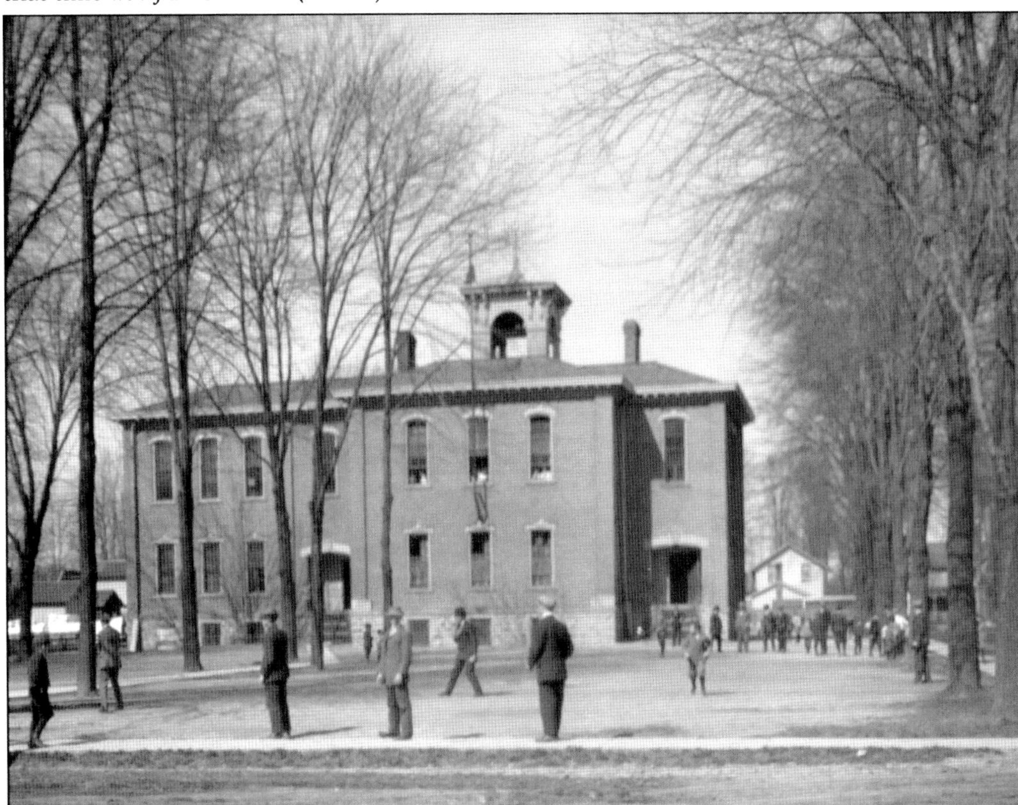

The Union School in Elmore was built in 1871 and was located on the corner of Maple and Fifth Streets. This was Elmore's second school. It was razed in 1931 after the opening of the Harris-Elmore High School. After the demolition, a metal box was found in the cornerstone that held a number of Elmore documents and memorabilia, including Civil War–era coins, voting lists, and church bulletins. (HEPL.)

This is the first graduating class of Elmore High School in 1879. The students are, from left to right, (first row) George Smith and Louis Eoff; (second row) Emma Stange, Mary Becker Dromgold, and Katie Buckey McCarty; (third row) Mame Quincke Willett and Emma Johnson Croomer. (HEPL.)

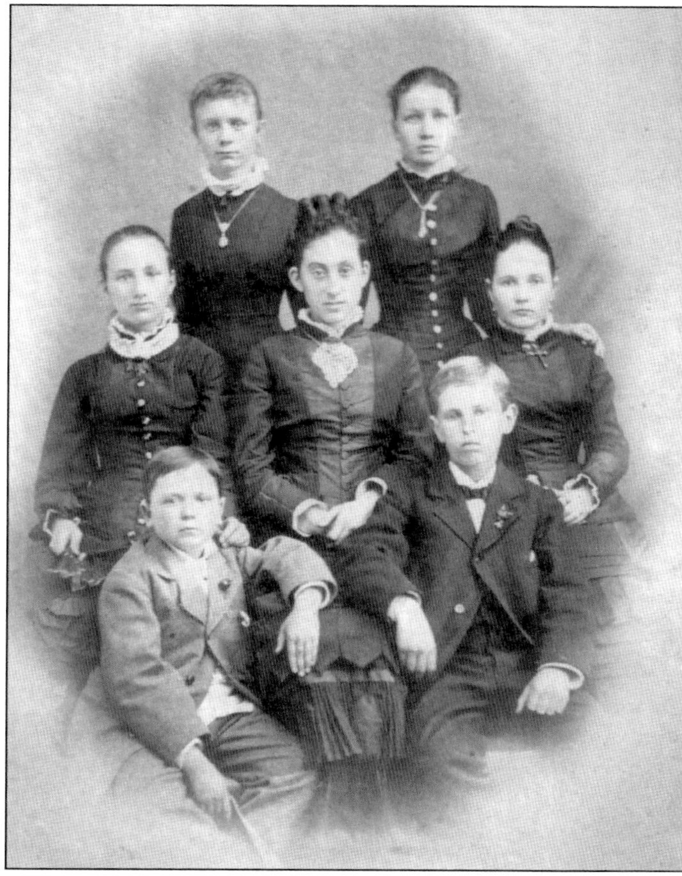

This is the second grade at Union School in Elmore during the 1907 school term. (HEPL.)

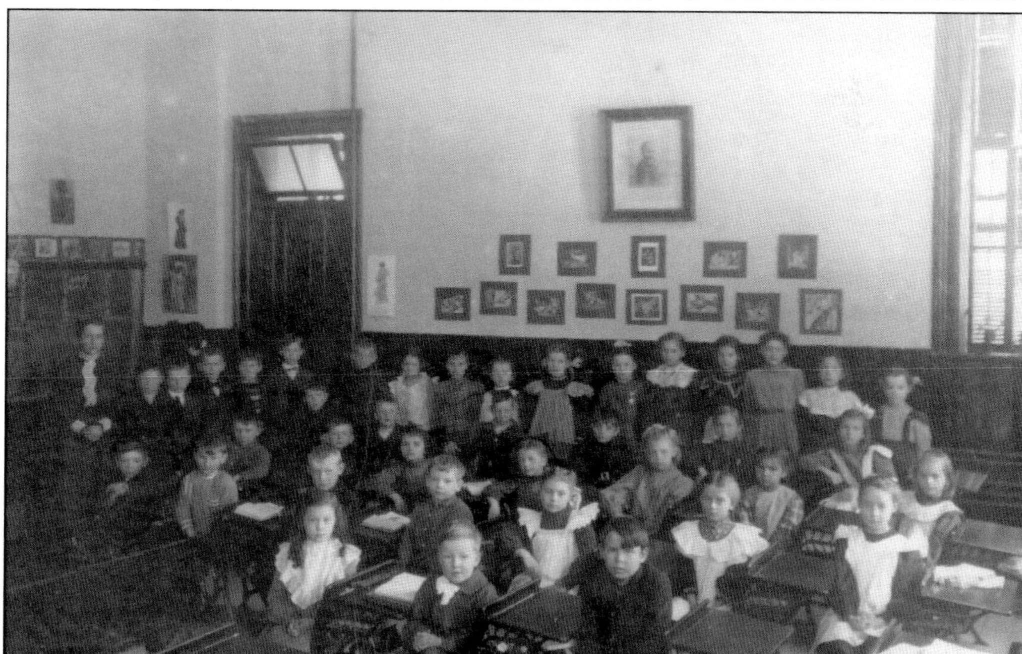

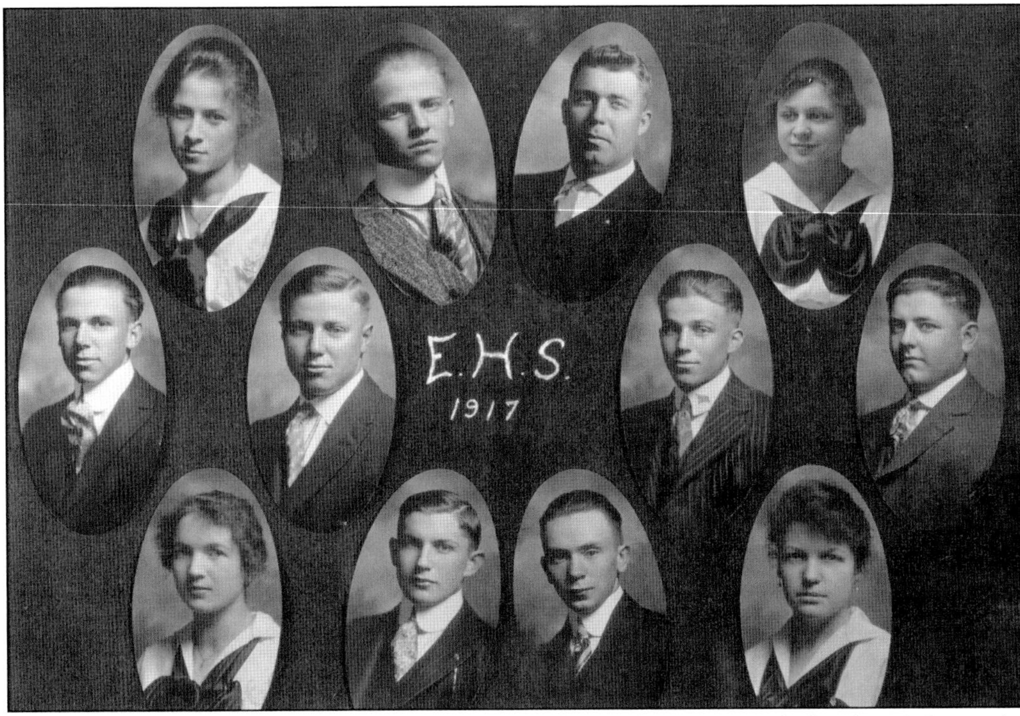

The Elmore High School senior class of 1917 is seen here. This image includes, from left to right, (first row) Doris Reynolds Dischinger, George Myers, Benjamin Dunham, and Bertha Avers Yeagle; (second row) Cyrus Gnepper, Charles Arnold, Martin Arnold, and Godfrey Witte; (third row) Lucille Helwig Smith, Emil Knieriem, Lyle Baldwin, and superintendent Hazel Kern. (HEPL.)

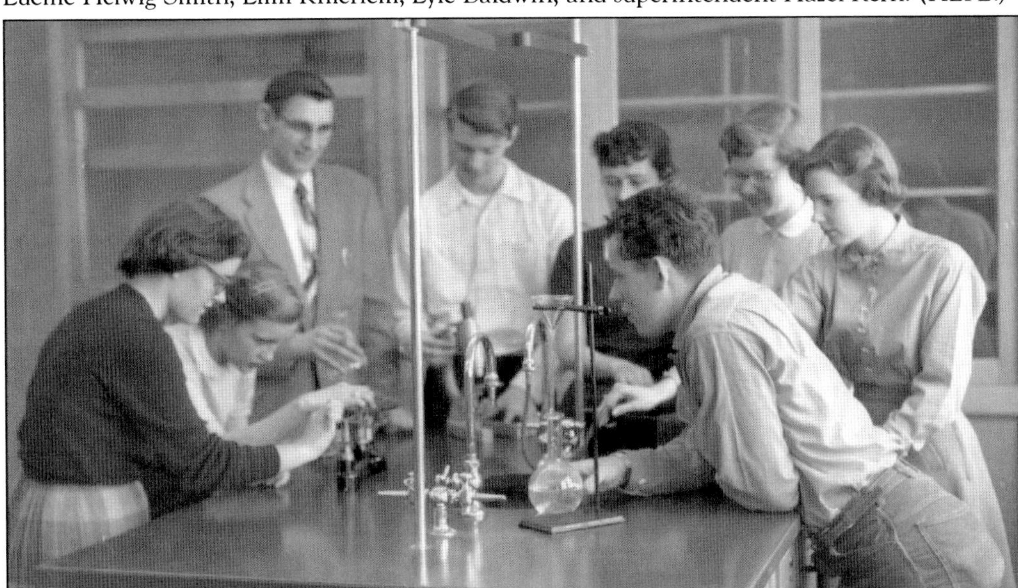

Students conduct a chemistry experiment at Harris-Elmore High School during the 1953–1954 school term. Pictured from left to right are Karen Jacobs, Barbara Moellman, Charles Rymers, John Votaw, Karen Hetrick, Marilyn Nissen, Lisa Sparks, and James Bolander. (Doug Pickard Collection, HEPL.)

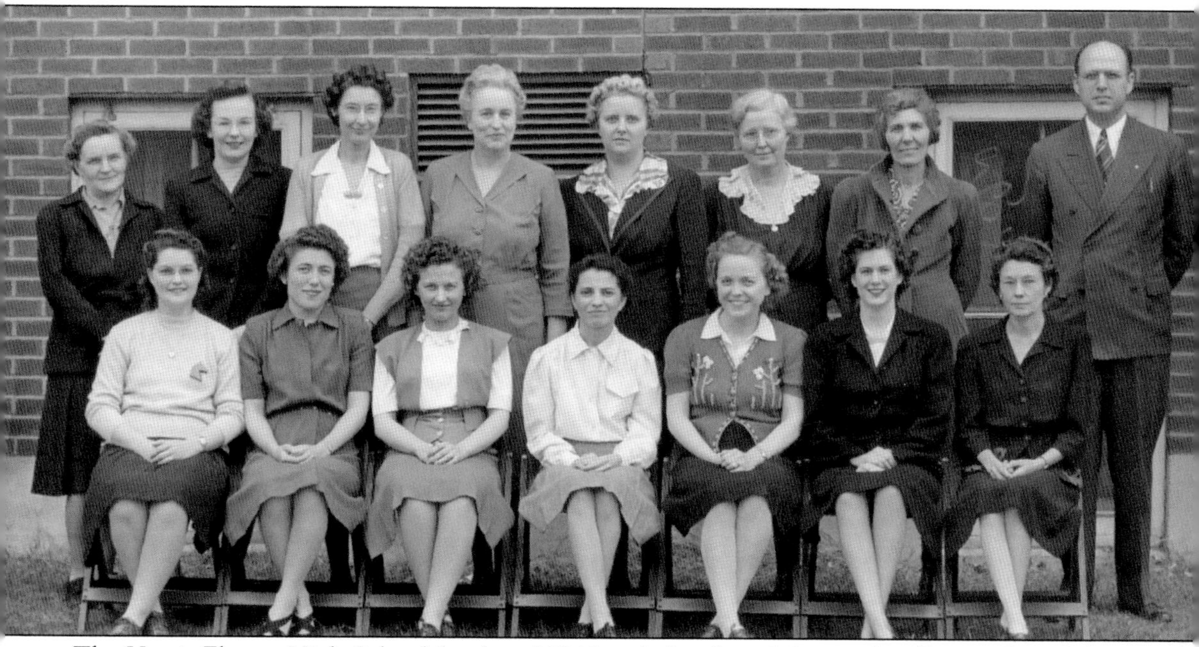

The Harris-Elmore High School faculty of 1944 includes, from left to right, (first row) Buelah Temple, Catharine Anstead, Wilma Pelton, Garnet Weber, Lois Eoff, Mary Monahan, and Grace Myers; (second row) Helen Mercer, Eleanor Ruffing, Alvina Kontak, Dora Coleman, Laurel Damschroder, Mabel Rozine, Mattie Heckman, and Lamar Hetrick. (HEPL.)

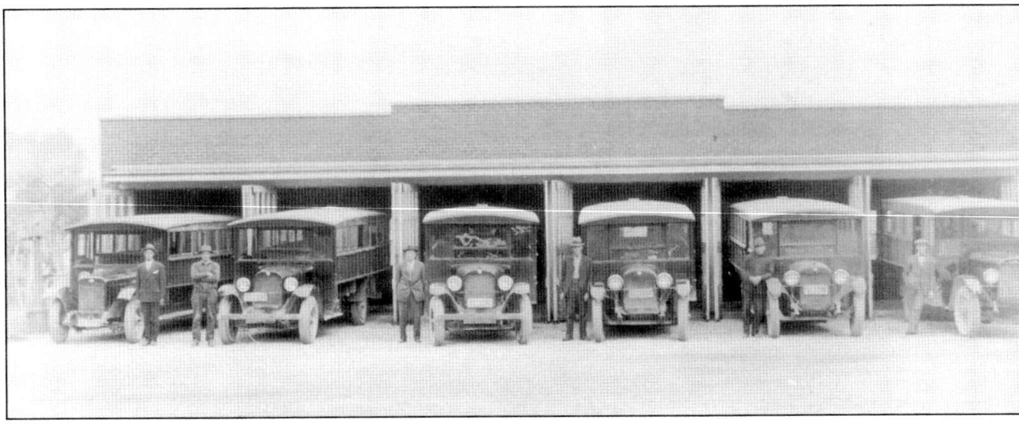

A slew of Elmore school buses and their drivers wait in the garage until school ends. Drivers in this image are, from left to right, Harold Holten, Christopher Arnold, William Tagg, Vincent Buck, Charles Kuhlman, and Rueben Rice. (HEPL.)

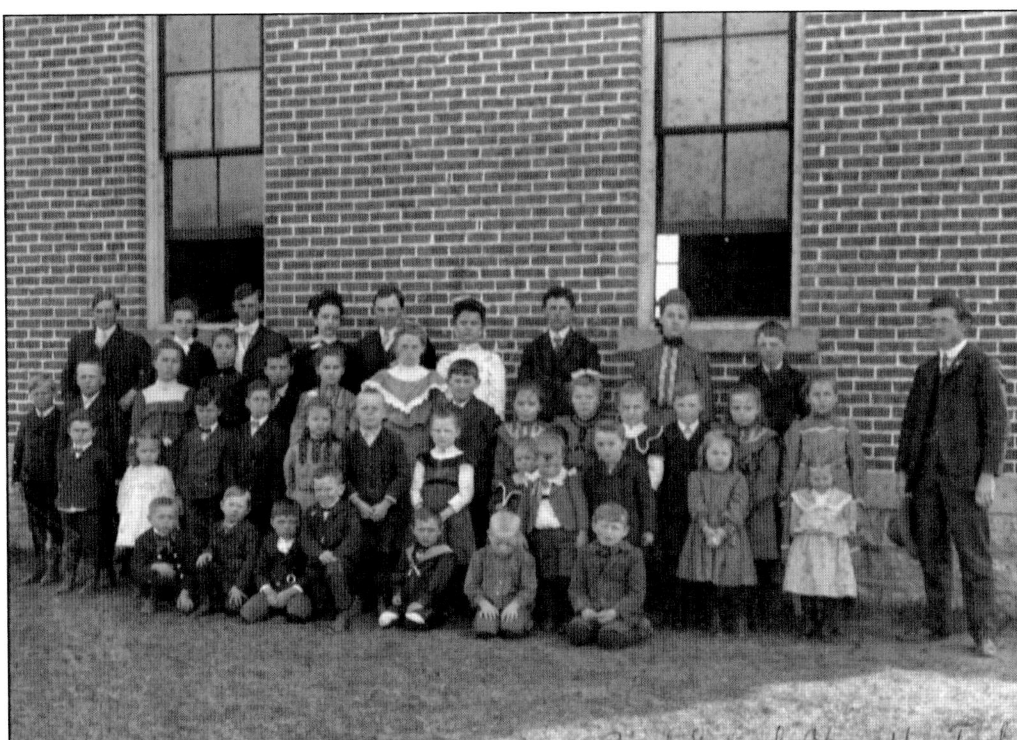

Students pose in front of the Hall Road School in Harris Township, near Elmore. This image was taken near the turn of the 20th century. Located on the far right is teacher Charles Hess. The school was situated on the corner of Elmore East Road and Route 590 and was converted to a butchering center soon after the rural schools were consolidated. (HEPL.)

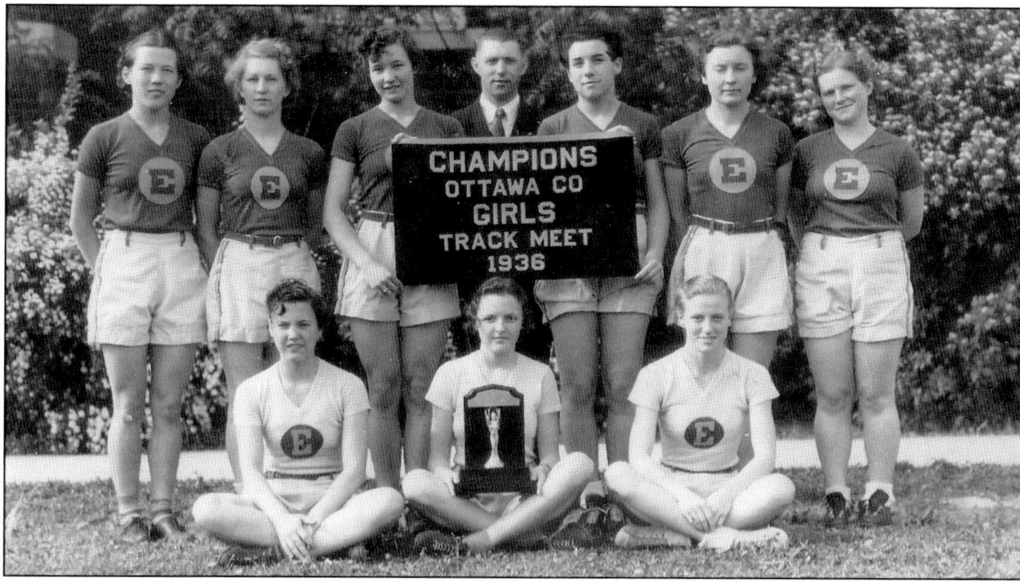

The Harris-Elmore High School girls' track team won the Ottawa County track and field championship in 1936. Four girls—Myrtle Lipstraw, Adelaide Hull, Mary Barnes, and Gladys Magsig—took part in the Olympic trials in Chicago that summer. In this photograph are, from left to right, (first row) Esther Magsig, Juanita Guthrie, and Mary Barnes; (second row) Adelaide Hull, Dorothy Rohloff, Gladys Magsig, coach B.W. Otto, Blanche Murray, Myrtle Lipstraw, and Mae Avers. (HEPL.)

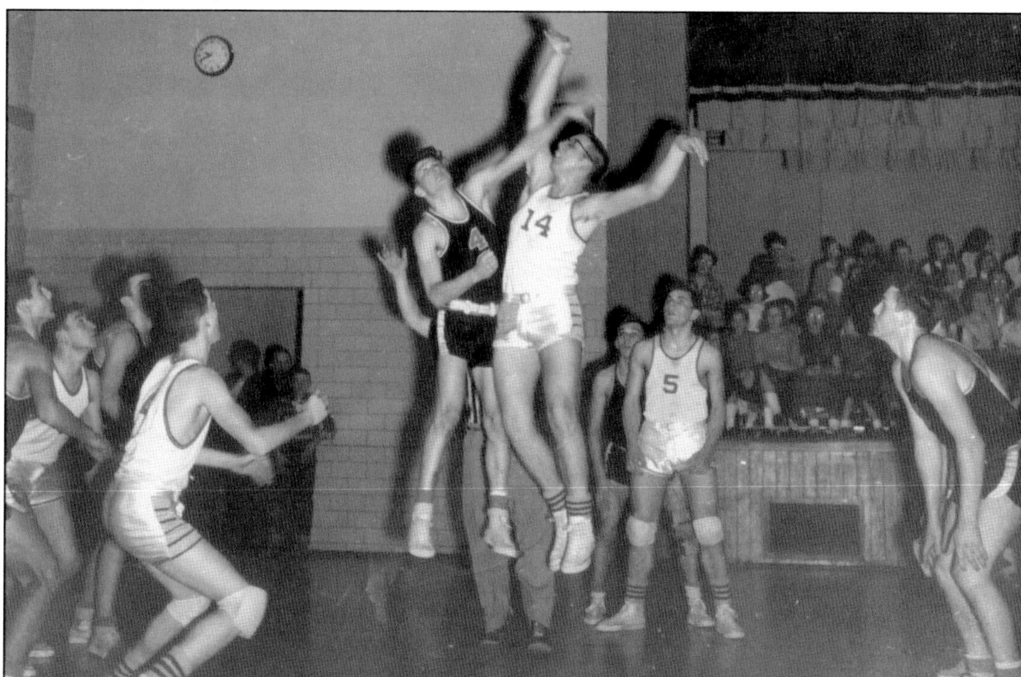

Players battle for the tip-off at a basketball game at Harris-Elmore High School during the 1950s. The Elmore team is pictured in white jerseys. From left to right are Don Laurer, Barrett Bates (no. 4), Bill Kuhlman (no. 14), Butch Lemke (no. 5), and unidentified. (Doug Pickard Collection, HEPL.)

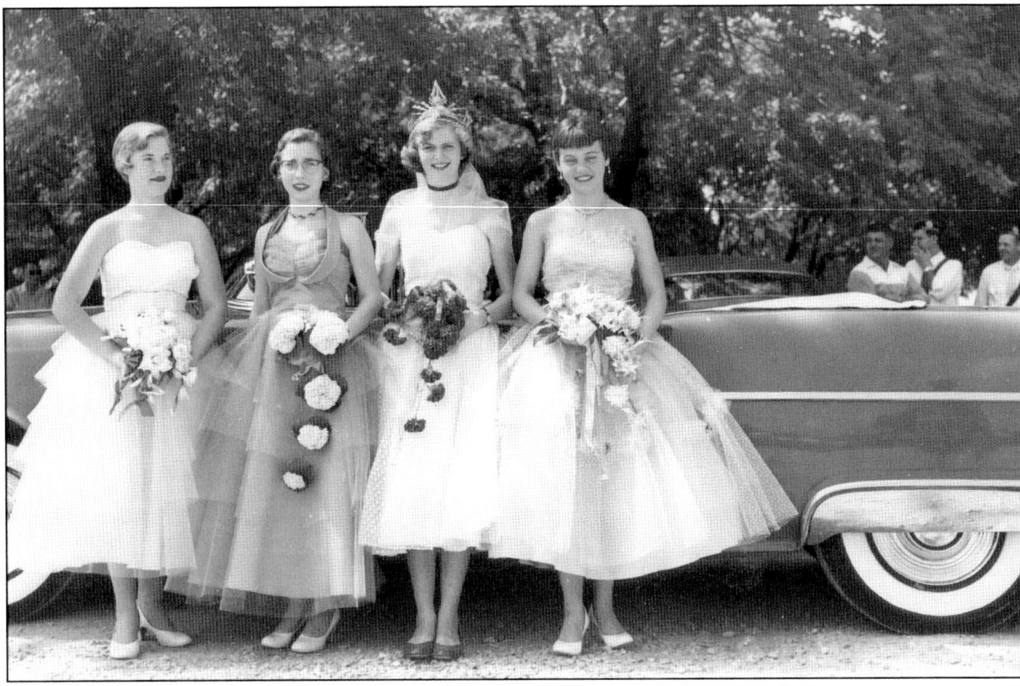

Elmore girls stand next to their ride while waiting to attend the school's homecoming parade sometime between 1953 and 1955. Pictured from left to right are Jean Vandersall, Judy Owen, Jane Damschroder, and Beverly Flick. (Courtesy of the Doug Pickard Collection, HEPL.)

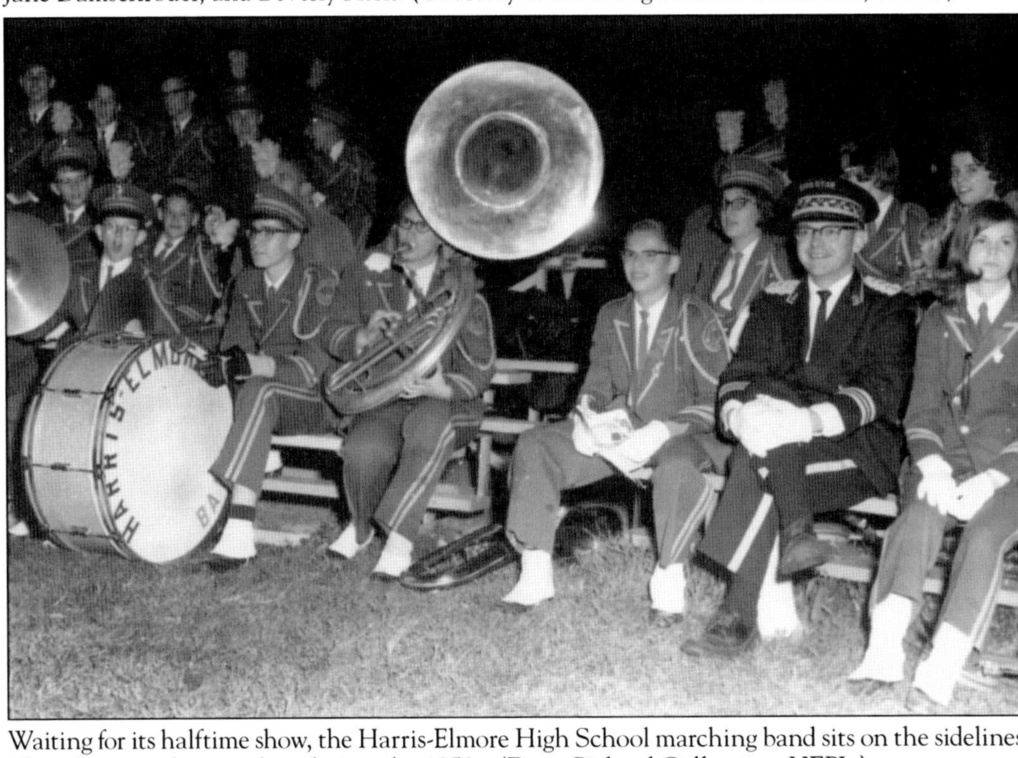

Waiting for its halftime show, the Harris-Elmore High School marching band sits on the sidelines. This photograph was taken during the 1950s. (Doug Pickard Collection, HEPL.)

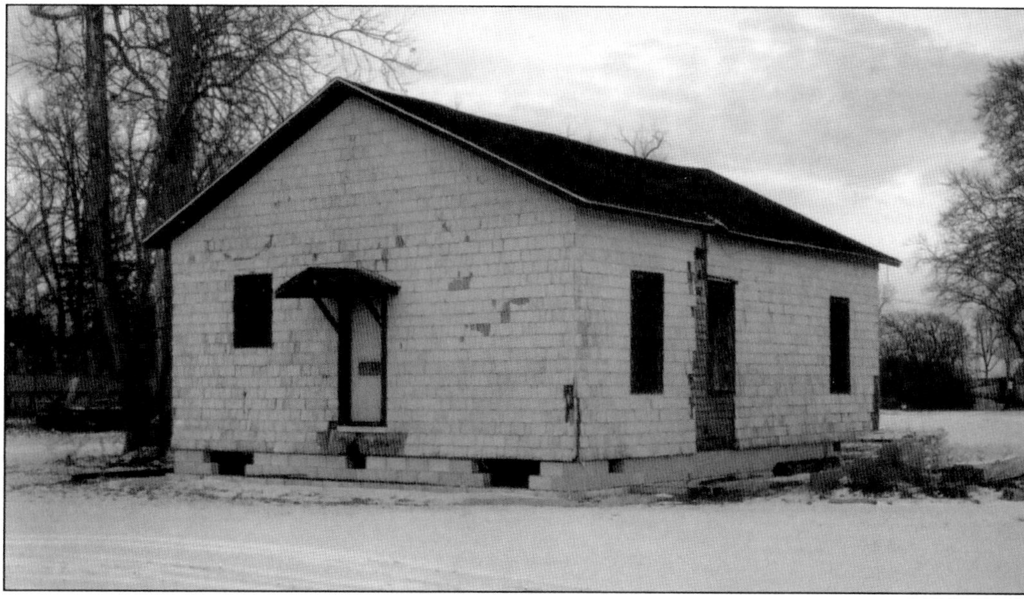

Known as the Genoa Women's Relief Corp (WRC) Hall, this building was first used in 1854 as a school. It was once located near Packer Creek but was soon moved to Washington Street. In 1858, nighttime foreign-language classes were taught here by a Mrs. Stotser. The village bought the structure in 1869, and it was used by the Genoa GAR for its headquarters. (GPL.)

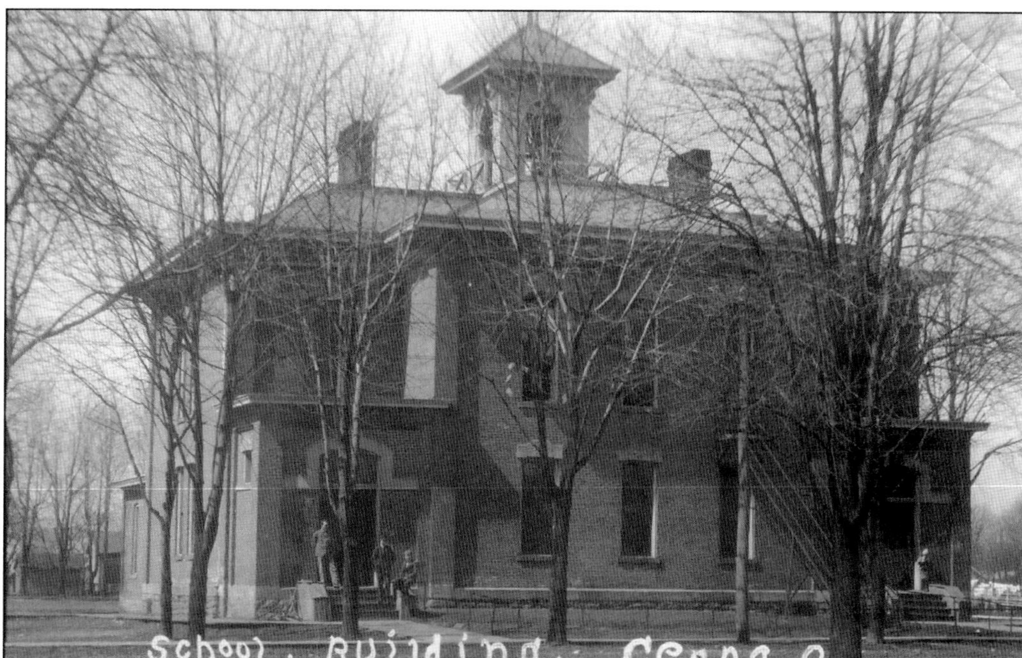

Built in 1870 and the first brick schoolhouse in Genoa, Union School housed students on the corner of Main and Fourth Streets. It was the first local school to place students in grades and to establish a separate high school. The structure was demolished in 1910 due to an increase in student population. The Camper School building was constructed in its place. (GPL.)

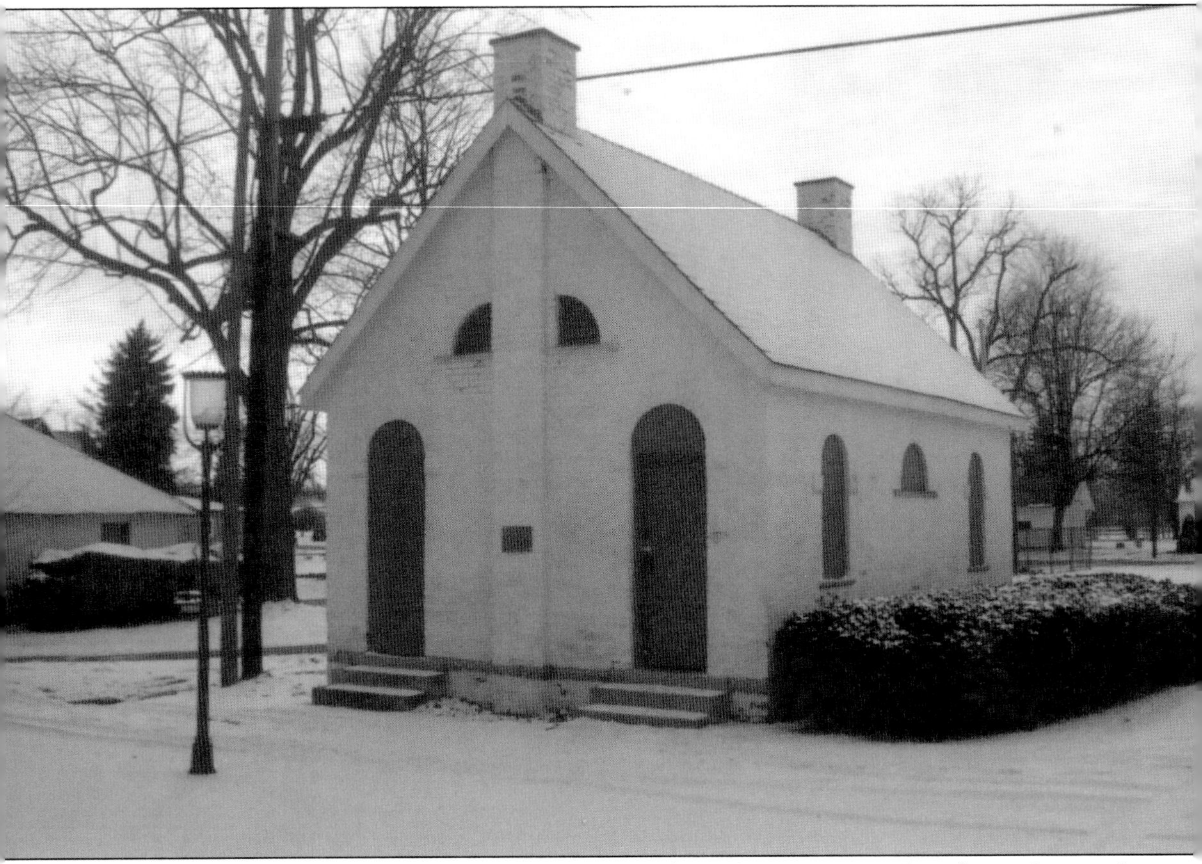

The old school privy (Little Building) was constructed in 1870 to accommodate the students and teachers of the Genoa School until 1929. This outhouse has four entrances: one each for male students, female students, male teachers, and female teachers. The 12-hole outhouse was made in the Romanesque Revival style, and its simple existence is astonishing as most schools prided themselves on indoor plumbing. The Village of Genoa restored the privy, and it was placed in the National Register of Historic Places in 1975. (Don Wick.)

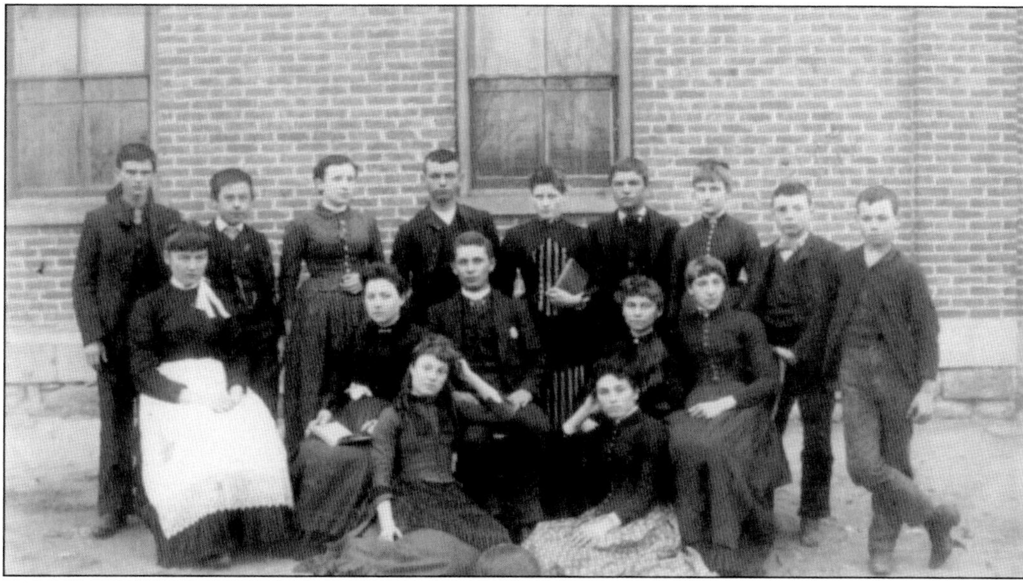

The Genoa High School sophomore class poses in a photograph taken on November 10, 1886. The students could not be identified, but the graduating class of 1888 included James F. Angus, Bertha Dryer, C. Will Null, Effie Bennett, Sarah Eyre, Clare Siglar, George Cross, Benny Kiewitter, and Gertrude Gregg. It is most likely that those listed are seen in this photograph. (HEPL.)

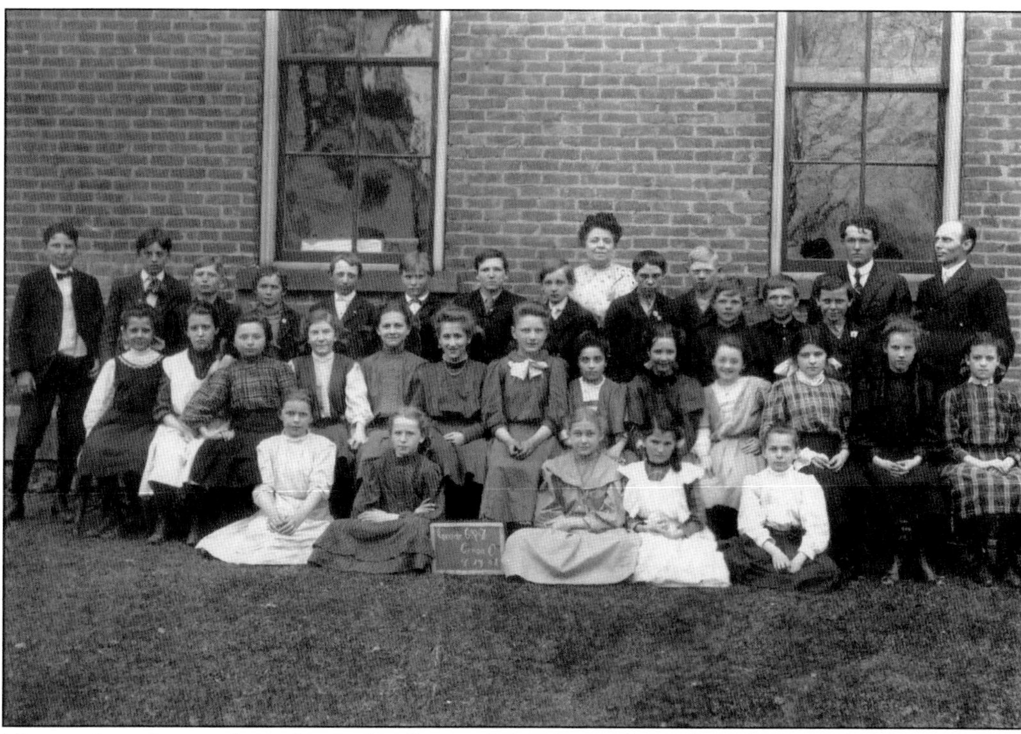

The sixth and seventh grades at the Genoa School pose for a class photograph taken on April 14, 1908. (GPL.)

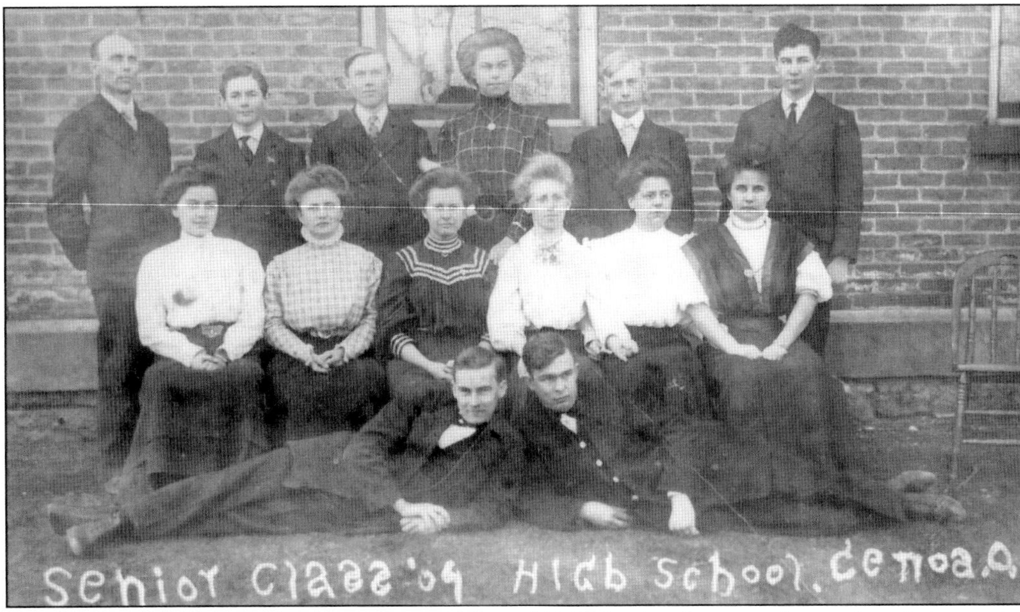

Pictured is the Genoa High School Senior Class of 1909. In the photograph are, from left to right, (first row) Jim Hennen and Merrill B. Rudes Sr.; (second row) Esther Bryant, Goldie Opher, Maggie Thone, Bertha Calkins, Bertha Bruggemeyer, and Lucy Ptak; (third row) principal S.S. Beard, Leroy Lindsey, Charles Truax, Bernice Skilliter, Albert Gosman, and Frank Shessler. (GPL.)

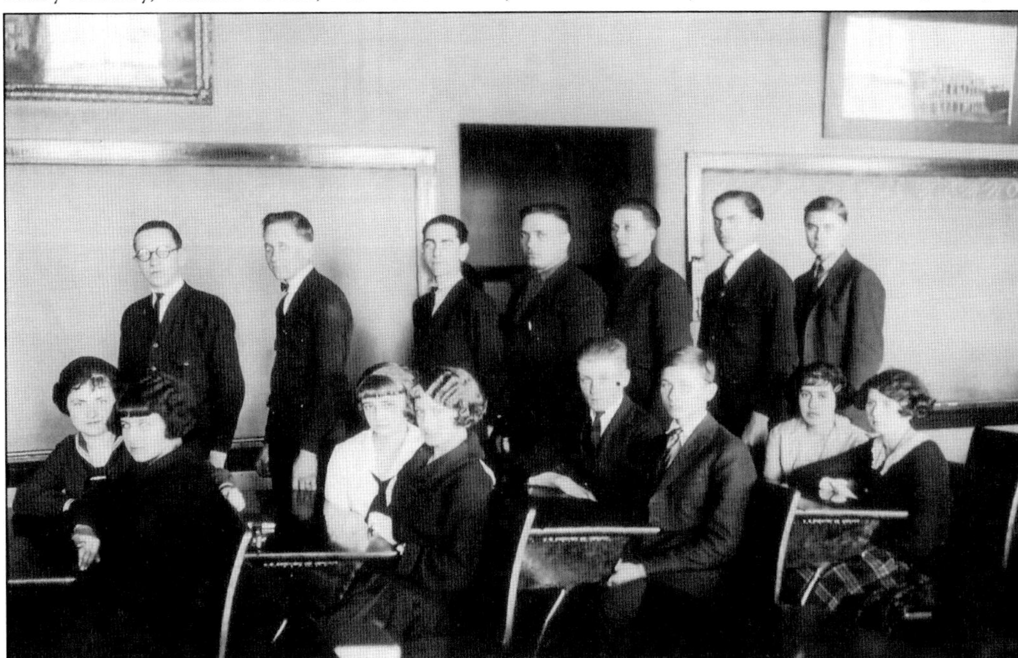

Members of the Genoa High School junior class sit in their classroom. In this April 20, 1923, photograph are, from left to right, (first row) Gertrude (Clark) Hansen, Hazel Lantz, Sadie (Clements) Hellwig, Clara Camper, Alvin Nickelson, Henry Krukemeyer, Esther Koehler, and Bessie Kroetz; (second row) Robert Gallup, Minor Buehler, Herbert Wood, John Dunn, Amherst Clough, Herman Turnow, and Ralph Riedman. (Tomme Bergman.)

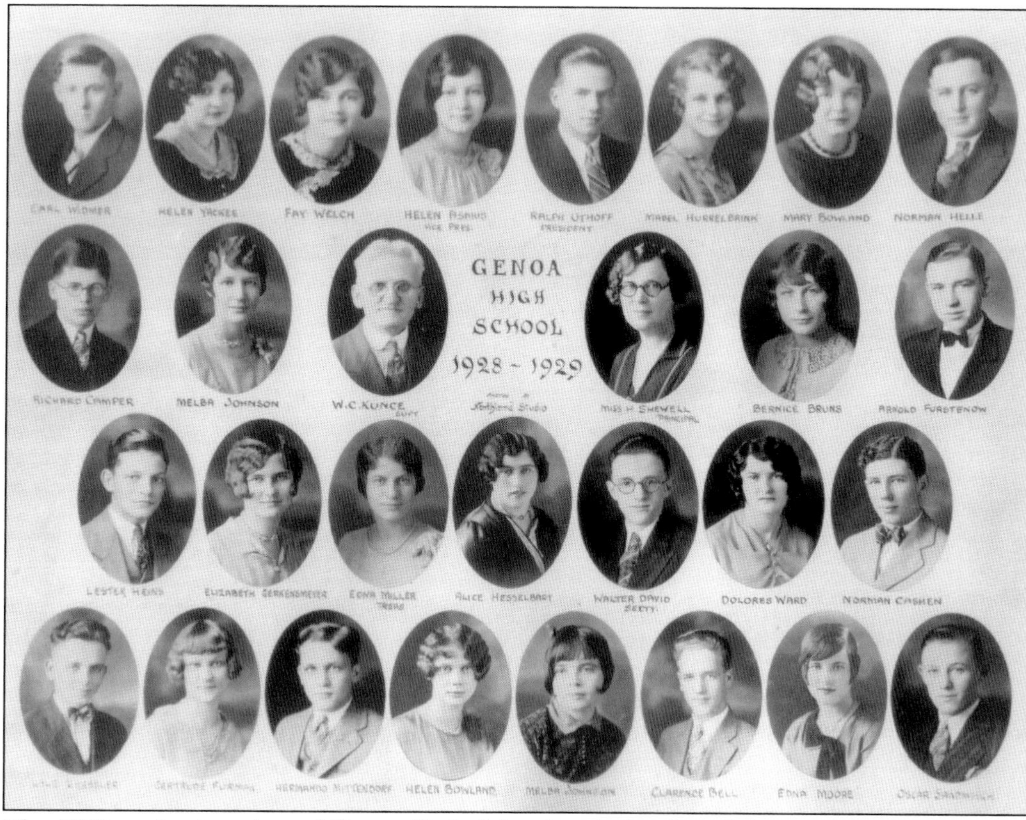

The 1929 graduating class of Genoa High School includes, from left to right, (first row) Lyle Shessler, Gertrude Furman, Hermando Mittendorf, Helen Bowland, Melba Johnson, Clarence Bell, Edna Moore, and Oscar Sandwich; (second row) Lester Heind, Elizabeth Gerkensmeyer, Edna Miller, Alice Hesselbart, Walter David, Dolores Ward, and Norman Cashen; (third row) Richard Camper, Melba Johnson, W.C. Kunce, Miss H. Shewell, Bernice Bruns, and Arnold Furstenow; (fourth row) Earl Widmer, Helen Yackee, Fay Welch, Helen Asmus, Ralph Uthoff, Mabel Hurrelbrink, Mary Bowland, and Norman Helle. (GPL.)

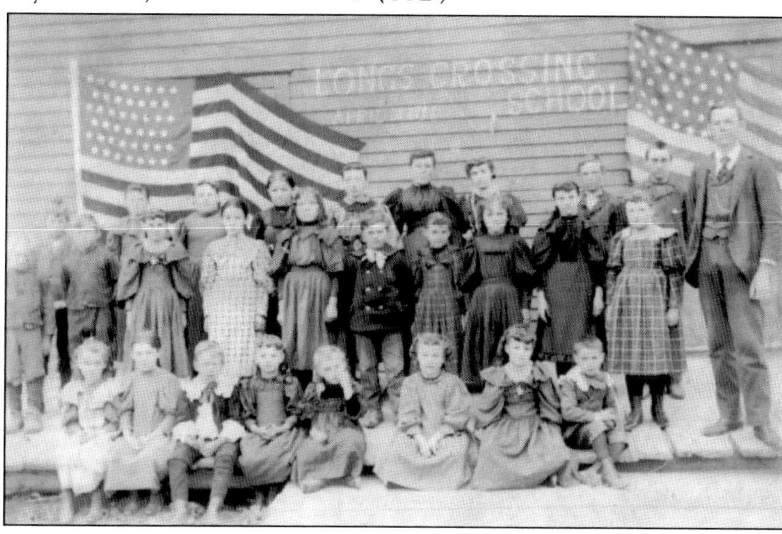

The school at Long's Crossing (District 4) was located at the junction of Hellwig Road and the New York Central Railroad crossing near Genoa. These unidentified students stand in front of the school on April 30, 1897, for their yearly photograph. (GPL.)

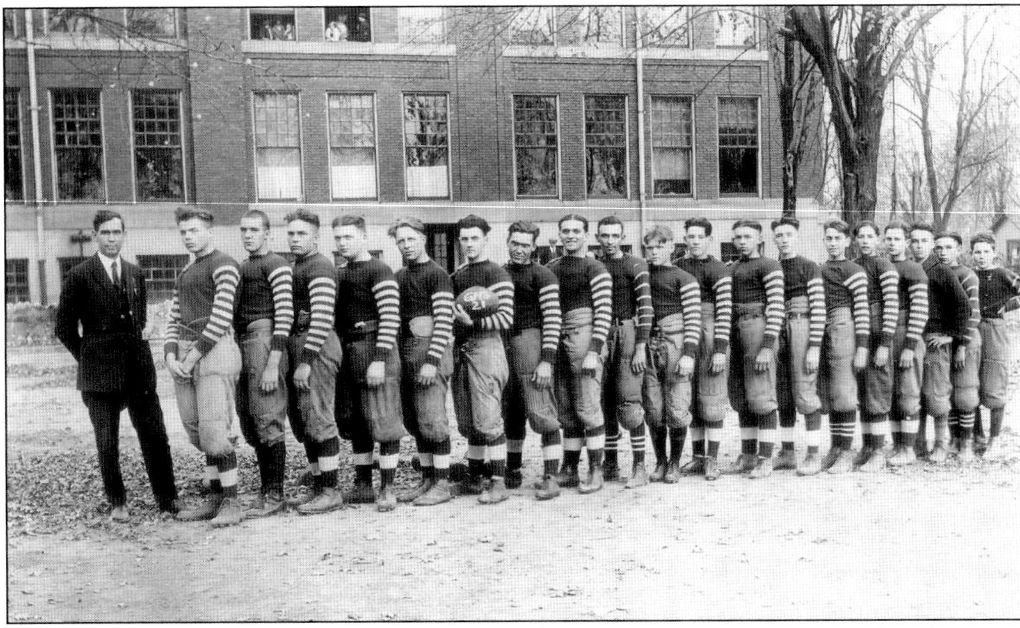

The 1921 varsity football team for Genoa High School lines up for a photograph. This image show, from left to right, superintendent Ray Carter, Herman Turnow, Polly Tillotson, John Dunn, Nelson Johnson, Lee Stewart, Marion LaPlantz, Afton Kelly, B.B. Huss, Walter Cashen, Ersam Kelly, Ed Kroetz, Sam Kroetz, Frank Rollins, Herb Wood, Dave Wood, Emerson Marsh, Howard Sorby, Leo Cashen, and Henry Krukenmyer. (Tomme Bergman.)

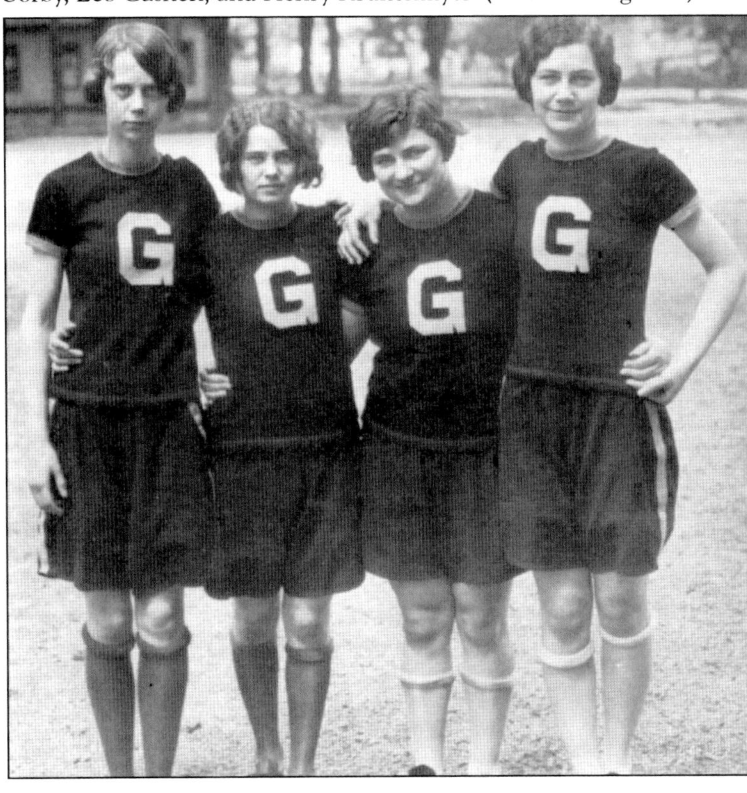

Genoa girls' track teammates, who won the county relay race in 1927, lock arms while posing for the camera. They include, from left to right, Helen Bowland, ? Apel, Anita Muslof, and Dorcas Tillotson. (GPL.)

Six

Put on Your Sunday Best

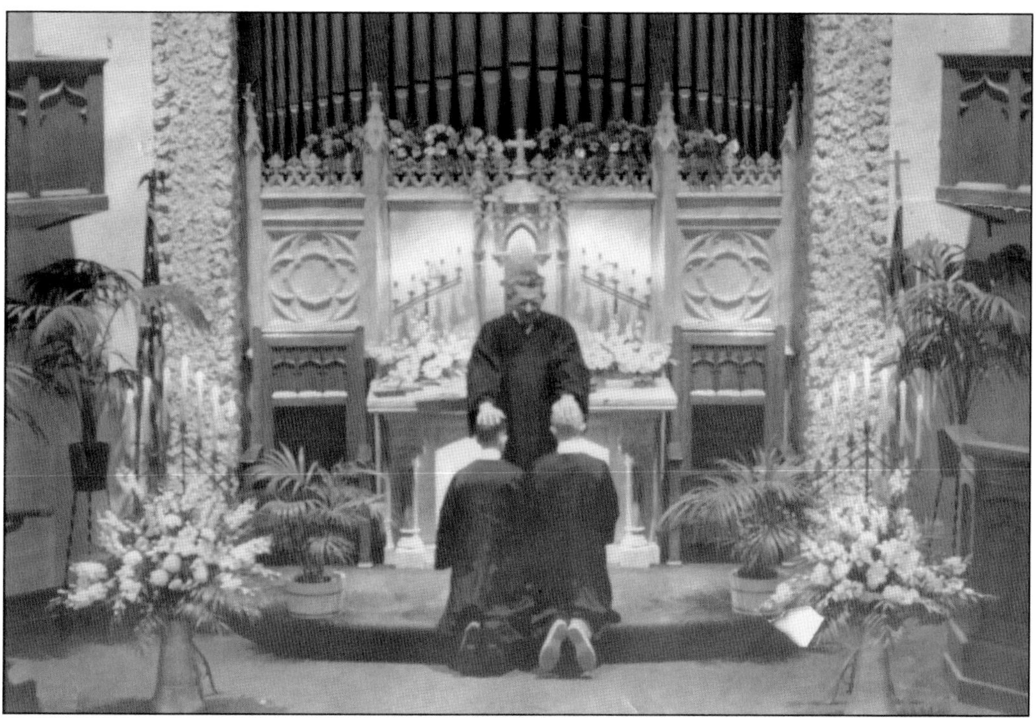

Rev. C. Ralph Schmidt of the St. John's Evangelical and Reformed Church of Elmore performs confirmation rites on David (left) and Dennis Haar in 1954. (Doug Pickard Collection, HEPL.)

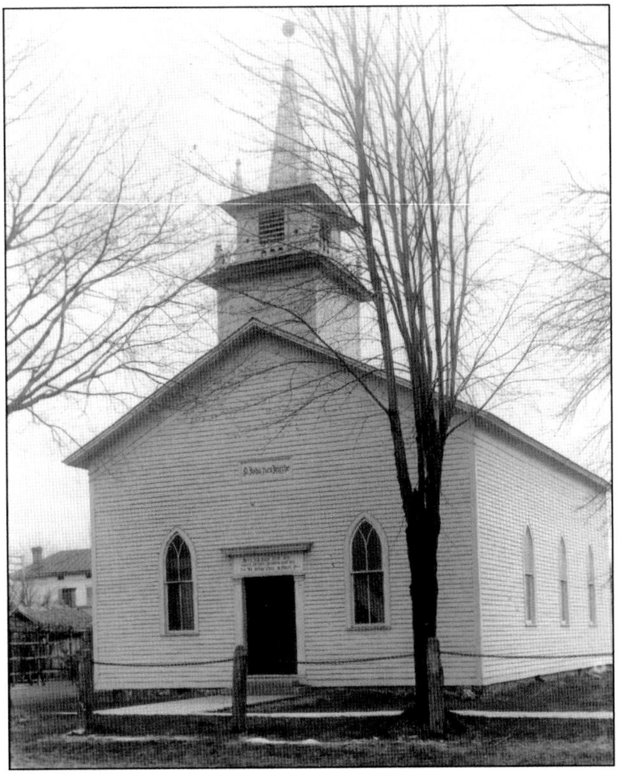

A c. 1900 view shows St. John's Evangelical Church in Elmore. It was built on Harris Street in 1860, when it was the St. John's Apostolistic Church. St. John's served the German people until 1921, when a new church was built on Rice Street. It was known as St. John's Evangelical and Reformed Church in the 1930s and became the St. John's Evangelical United Church of Christ in 1957. (HEPL.)

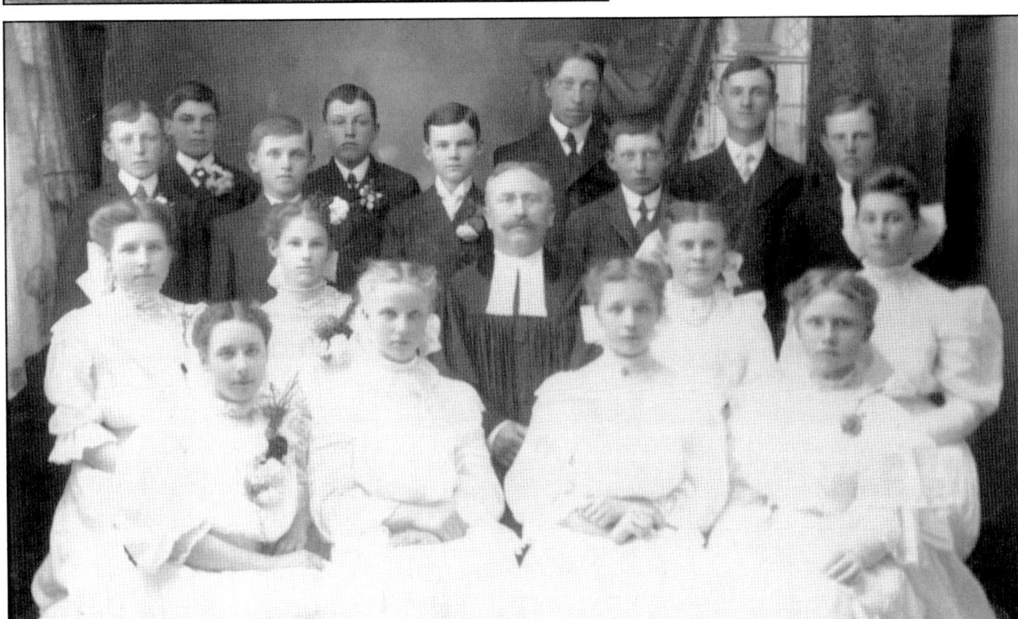

The 1906 confirmation class of St. John's Evangelical Church in Elmore includes, from left to right, (first row) Mary Kinker Muenzer, Mary Horner Magsig, Marie Villhauer Henry, Nettie Held Camper, Nina Lehman Melms, Clara Dierker Barnes, Emma Stange Wainwright, and Mabel Barkhau Ory; (second row) Jacob Geisler, Herman Waggoner, Otto Rozine, Fred Geisler, Leonard Horner, Rev. K. Buff, George Pafenbach, Alvin Geisler, William Hess, and Henry Behring. (HEPL.)

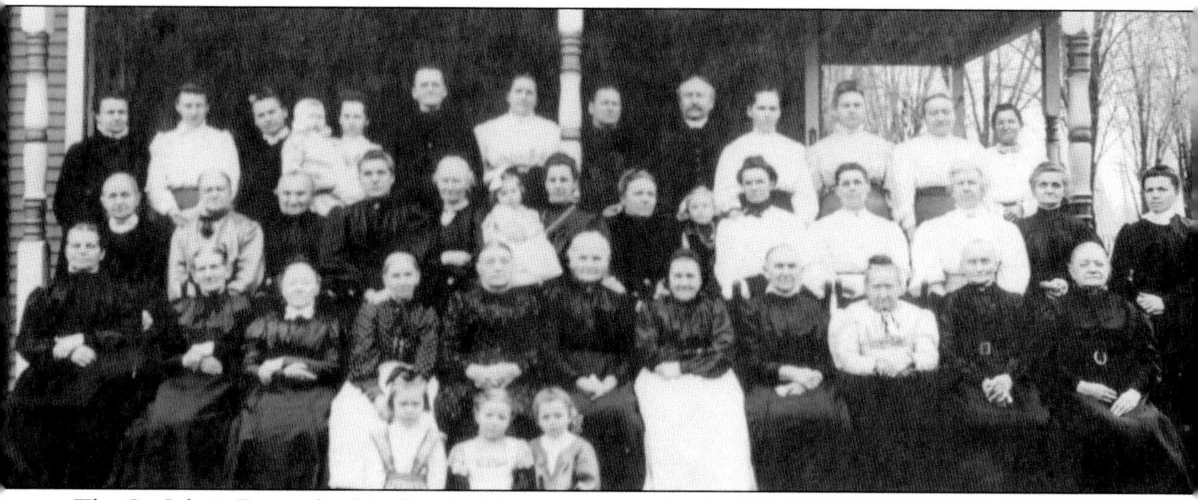

The St. John's Evangelical Ladies Aid Society met at the home of Andrew Feilbach on Toledo Street in Elmore. This January 28, 1909, photograph shows, from left to right, (first row) Kathryn Foster, Anna Voletta Vultee, and Lucille Klaustermeyer; (second row) Mrs. Joseph Widmer, Mrs. Fred Weis, Maria Quincke, Elizabeth Clay, Mrs. Kopp, Mrs. Whiteman, Mrs. Joseph Beck, unidentified, Mrs. Vultee, Mrs. Stange, and unidentified; (third row) Mrs. Henry Bothe, Mrs. Siefelt, Mrs. Kerbel, Mrs. Christ Loslie, Mrs. Fred Gerber, Mrs. Will Lohr, Eunice Lohr, Mrs. Henry Dierker, Mrs. Charles Langerman, Louise Langerman, Mrs. Andrew Feilbach, Martha Whiteman, Mrs. John Fulkert, and Mrs. Theodore Klaustermeyer; (fourth row) Janie Otto, ? Buck, Mrs. Clarence Truman, Mrs. Pat Lehman, Lillian Lehman, Mrs. Meyerholz, Mrs. Henry Kinker, Mrs. Matt Bader, Rev. Karl Buff, Mrs. August Rozine, Mrs. Henry Langerman, Mrs. Henry Geisler, and Kate Gerlach. (Richard Foster, HEPL.)

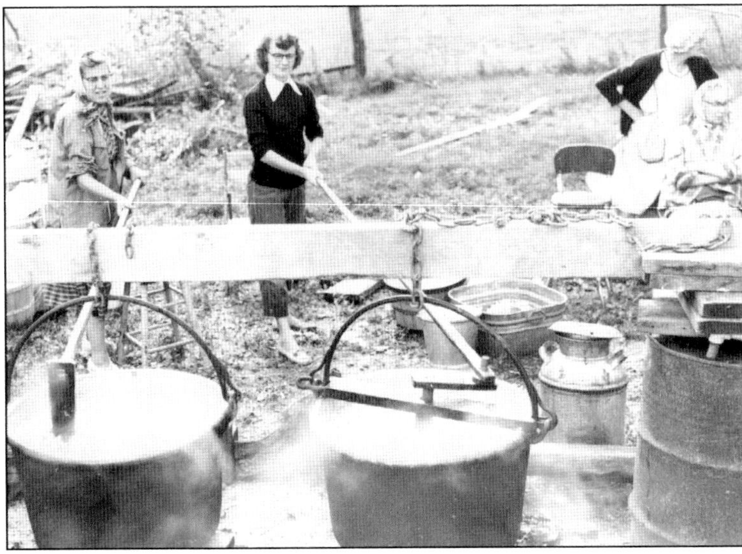

Members of the Elmore Bethel United Brethren Church are making apple butter as a fundraising activity in the early 1950s. The butter making took place on church grounds, located on the corner of Elmore Eastern Road and Route 590. Cooking the apple butter are Mrs. Cornell Overmyer (left) and Mrs. Royce Magsig. (Doug Pickard Collection, HEPL.)

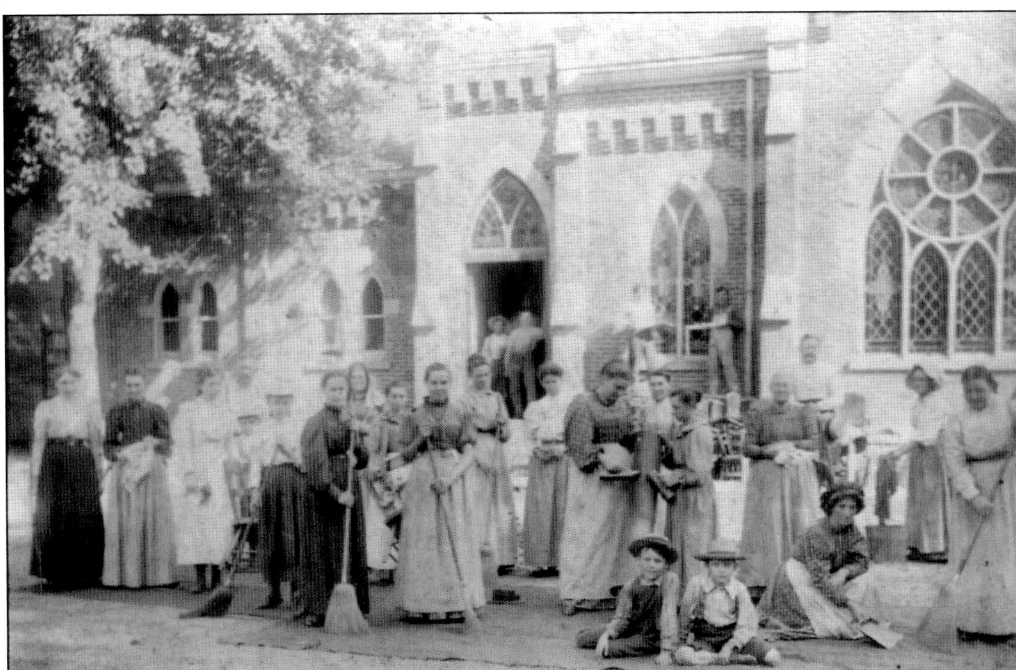

United Brethren Church members in Elmore are sweeping rugs outside the church in 1905. This congregation was likely the first organized in Harris Township and predated the city of Elmore. Its church was built on the corner of Toledo and Clinton Streets in the 1840s. The building pictured was raised in 1895. The church discontinued services sometime between 1916 and 1923, when the building was purchased by the Free and Accepted Masons. (HEPL.)

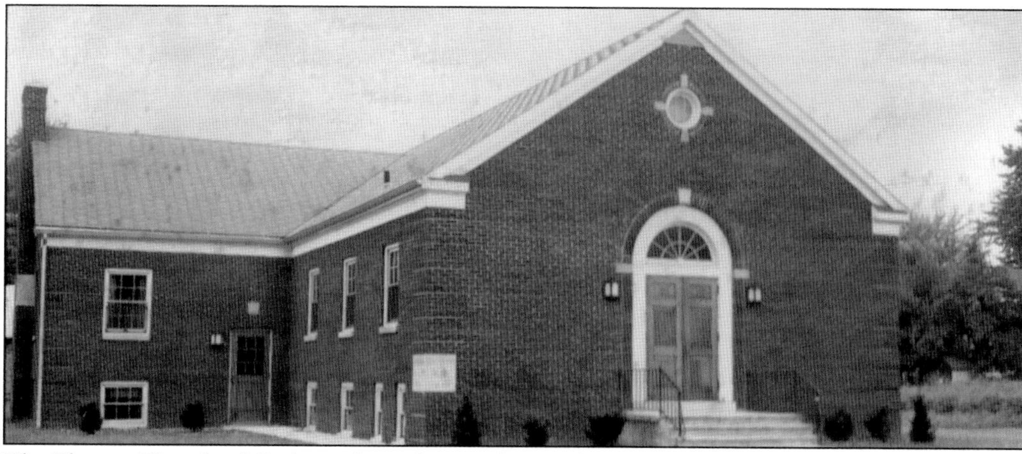

The Elmore Church of God was formed around 1913 through worship meetings at private homes, the Gleckler schoolhouse, and the town hall. In 1925, the church purchased the St. John's schoolhouse on Harris Street. In 1949, the building pictured here was erected on Congress Street during the pastoral residence of Rev. J.R. Richardson. The Church of God also conducted the first community Bible school in 1946. (HEPL.)

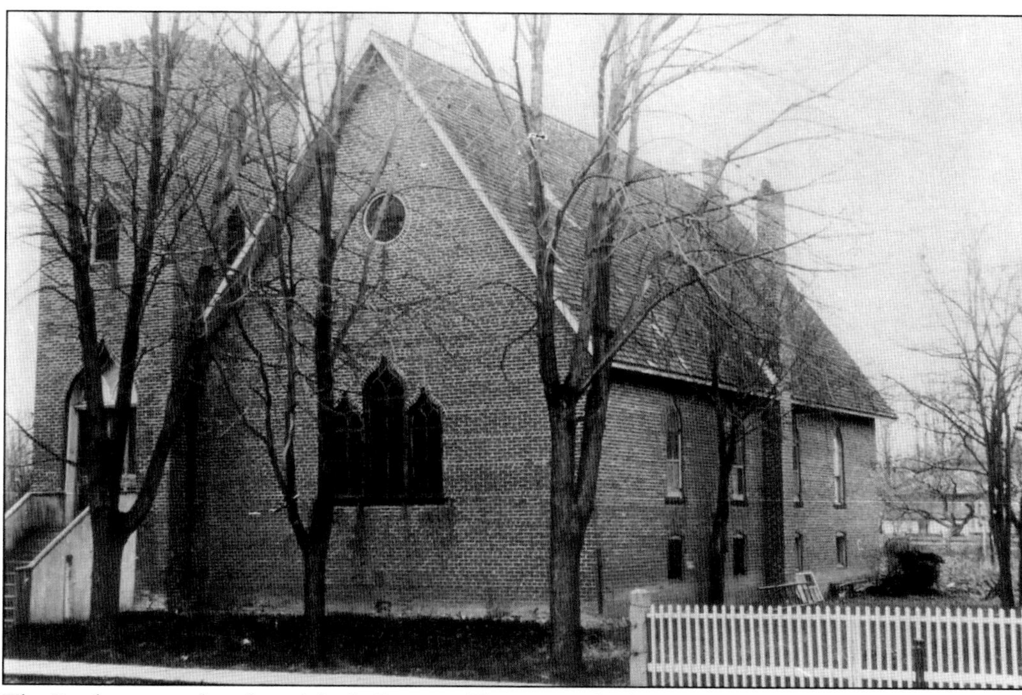

The Presbyterian church on Maple Street in Elmore was built in 1873. Around 1904, there were no regular ministers, so the church itself ceased to exist, though the church organizations continued for a time. In 1911, the structure was purchased by the Grace Lutheran congregation and used by them until they built a new church outside of town. (HEPL.)

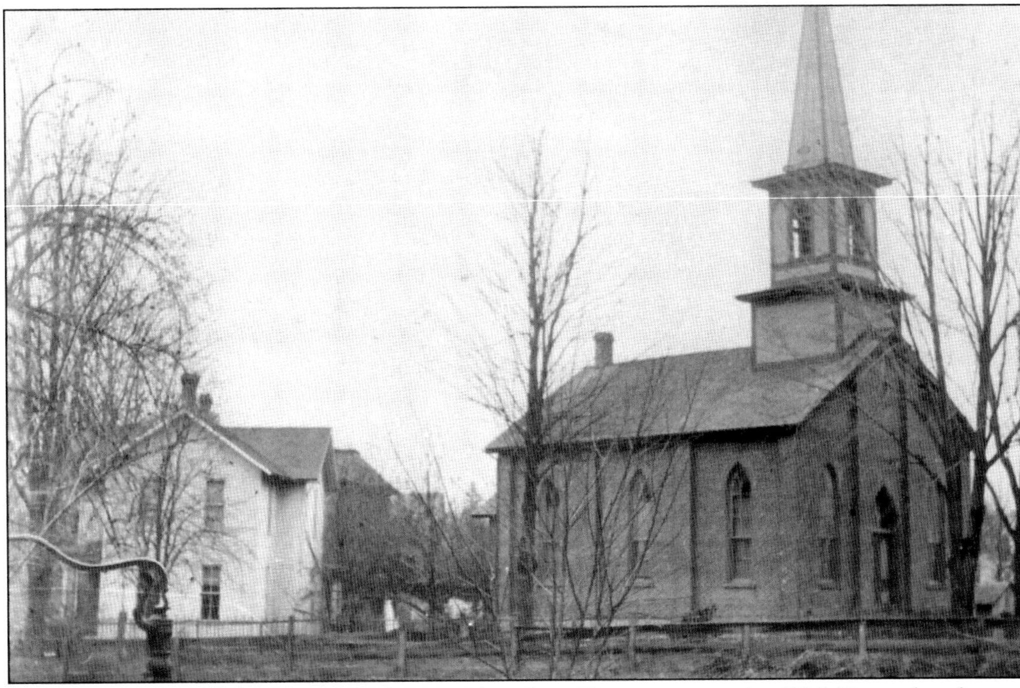

In 1865, members of the Trinity Lutheran Church at Elmore met at the C.H. Damschroder and Louis Frese store to form a congregation. The building pictured was constructed in 1866 on Congress Street, and Rev. George Cronenwett was the first pastor. (HEPL.)

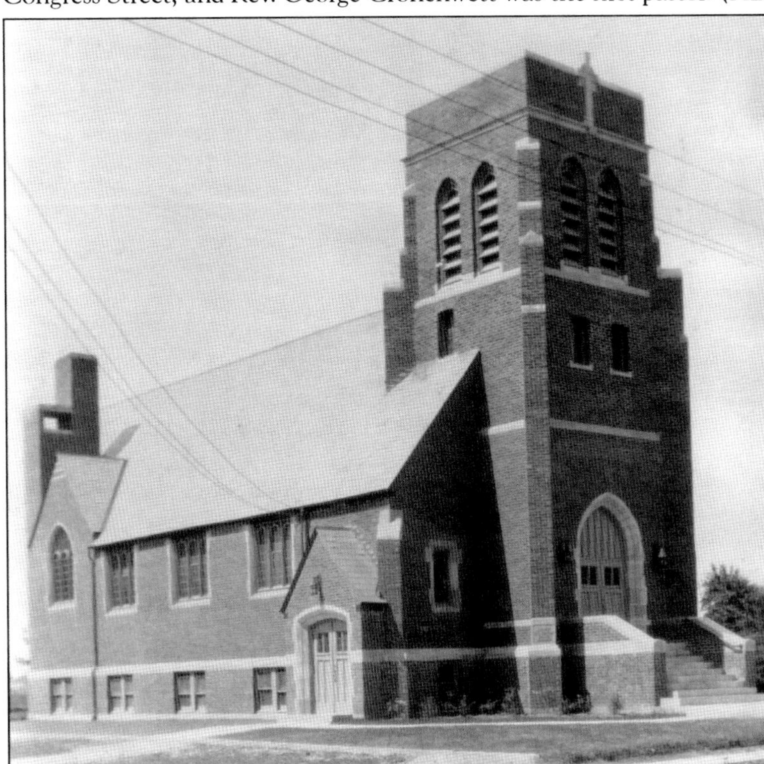

Elmore's Trinity Lutheran Church built a new church in 1925 under the direction of Rev. A.C. Thober. The church is located on Fremont Street. (Merlin Lieske.)

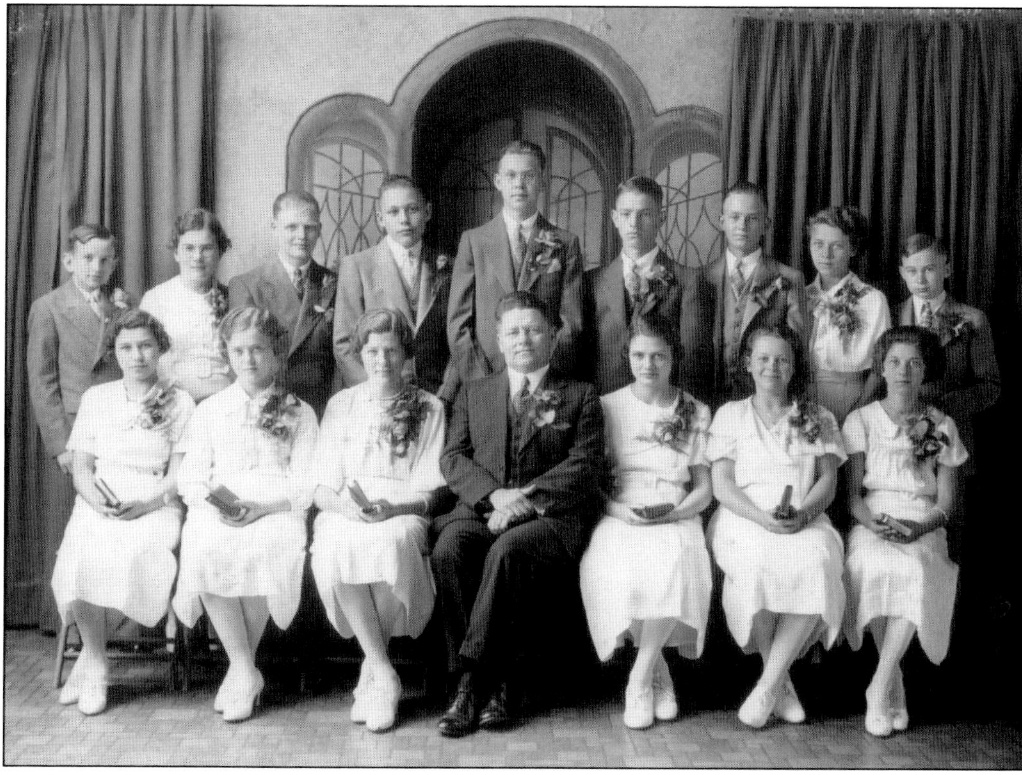

Trinity Lutheran Church of Elmore held confirmation ceremonies on June 1, 1935. In the photograph are, from left to right, (first row) Florence Deitemyer, Helen Dalling, unidentified, Rev. A.C. Thober, Wilma Deetz, Ruth Steinke, and Irene Wagner; (second row) Paul Wendt, Myrtle Juergens, Clarence Ninke, Edward Truman, Clovis Wortman, Gaillard Bach, Luther Avers, Arlene Deno, and John Musolf. (HEPL.)

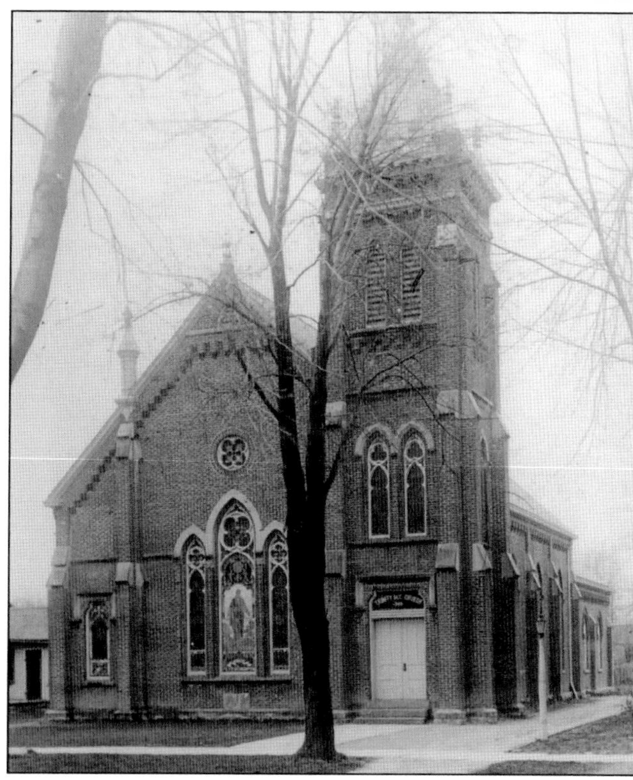

Pictured is Elmore's Trinity Methodist Episcopal Church in 1901 after it had been rebuilt due to fire damage the previous year. The congregation began in 1874 under Rev. C.J. Ferns. In 1954, the church joined together with St. Paul's Methodist to become the St. Paul's Trinity Methodist Church. (HEPL.)

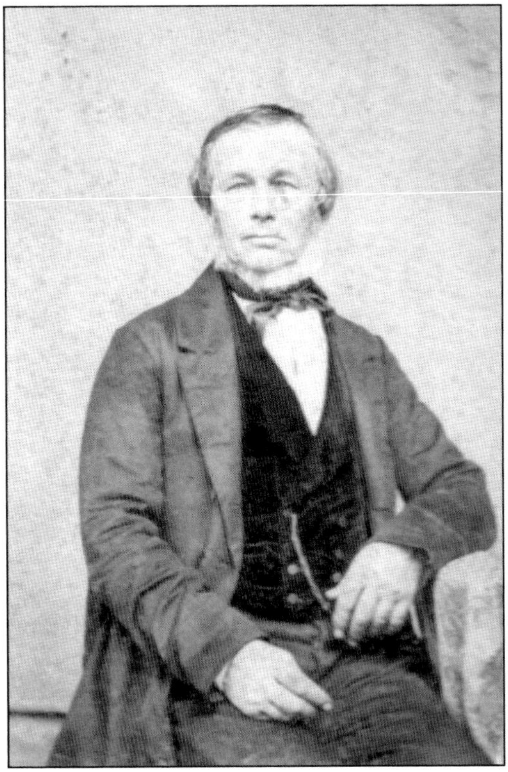

Rev. Josiah Adams was pastor of the Trinity Methodist Church in Elmore from 1860 to 1862. When Fort Sumter was fired upon, he walked down the aisles and shouted, "This is no time for inside meeting—let's get out under that blue sky on the commons and consecrate ourselves to our country and to our God." (HEPL.)

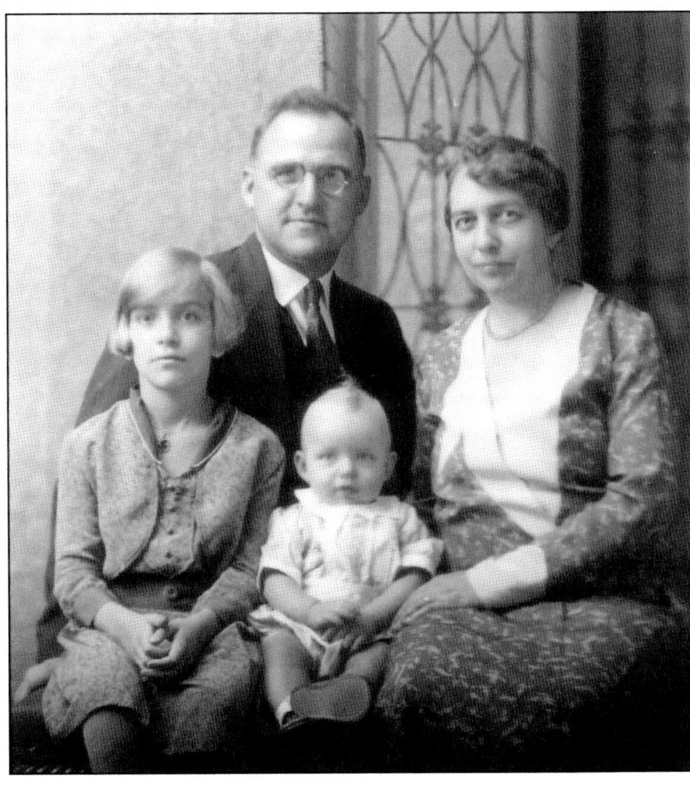

Rev. Karl W. Scheufler was the pastor of the Elmore Trinity Methodist Church from 1929 to 1934. He is pictured here with his wife, and children Jean (left) and Lowell. (Sara Grace Owen, HEPL.)

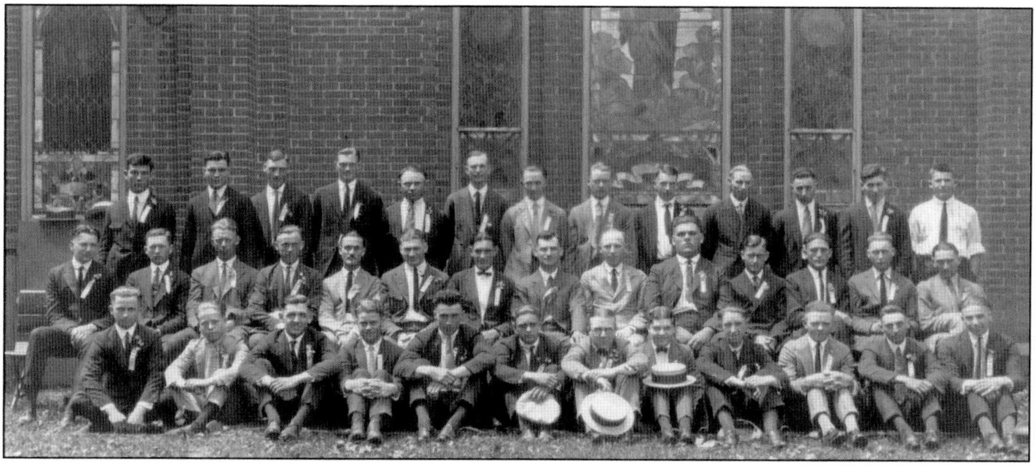

Pictured is the men's Sunday school class at Elmore's Trinity Methodist Episcopal Church during the 1920s. The class was taught by Henry House, and attendees included invited guests from other towns. In this image, from left to right, are (first row) Harmon Rozine, Stanley Damschroder, Ralph Rothert, Ted James, Clarence Villahuer, unidentified, Bill Damschroder, Karl Carsten, Kenneth Ames, Carlton Yeagle, Orville Lamale, and Matt Arnold; (second row) unidentified, unidentified, Richard Reynolds, ? Wagner, Arthur Flick, Clarence Fulkert, Norman Ling, Henry House, Howard Watson, Forest Sarnes, J. Kirk Luckey, Gleo Ling, Marion Reynolds, and Harold Croll; (back row) Caroll Sarnes, Clement Williams, Richard Rymers, Bruce Ling, Lester Damschroder, Clifford Weis, Carl Lehman, Ralph Willey, Roger Butt, unidentified, Arthur Lamale, Howard Neeb, and unidentified. (HEPL.)

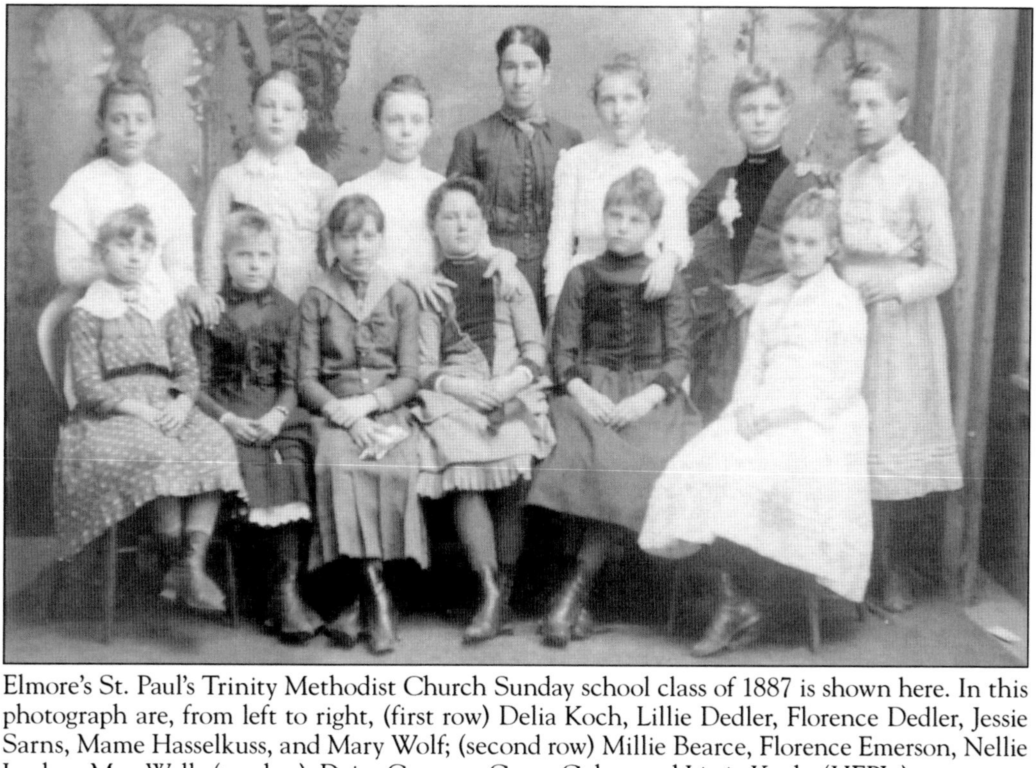

Elmore's St. Paul's Trinity Methodist Church Sunday school class of 1887 is shown here. In this photograph are, from left to right, (first row) Delia Koch, Lillie Dedler, Florence Dedler, Jessie Sarns, Mame Hasselkuss, and Mary Wolf; (second row) Millie Bearce, Florence Emerson, Nellie Luckey, Mrs. Wells (teacher), Daisy Cropper, Grace Gahn, and Lizzie Koch. (HEPL.)

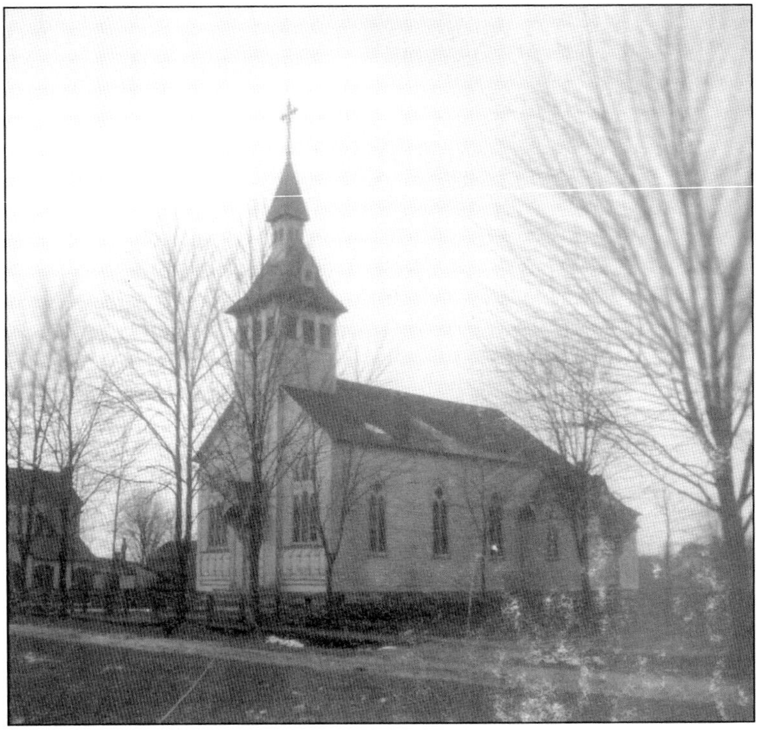

Early Catholics in Genoa had the services of a Toledo priest in 1856 and met in private homes until a room was secured above a blacksmith shop in 1872. In 1874, Our Lady of Lourdes Catholic Church (shown) was built on Superior Street; the congregation moved to South Main Street in 1924. The present church was built in 1950 on land donated by Henry Bergman. (Edna Turner Collection, GPL.)

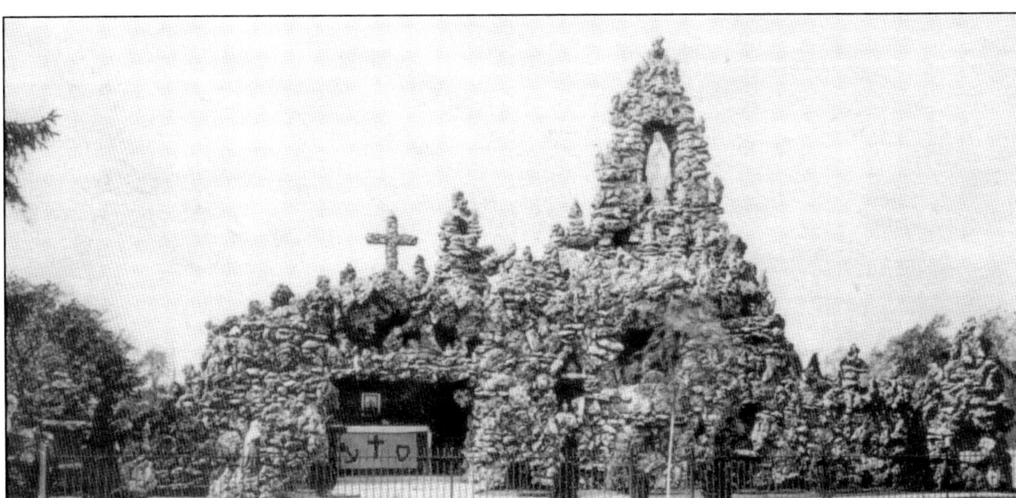

Toledo bishop Karl Alter visited the original Lourdes Grotto in Lourdes, France, and decided to build a replica of the shrine in his diocese. The grotto at Our Lady of Lourdes Catholic Church in Genoa was completed by parish volunteers under Father Jazwiecki's pastorship. It is made from one million pounds of tufa imported from the Blue Hole in Castalia, Ohio, and was dedicated on September 8, 1934. (Joe Badger.)

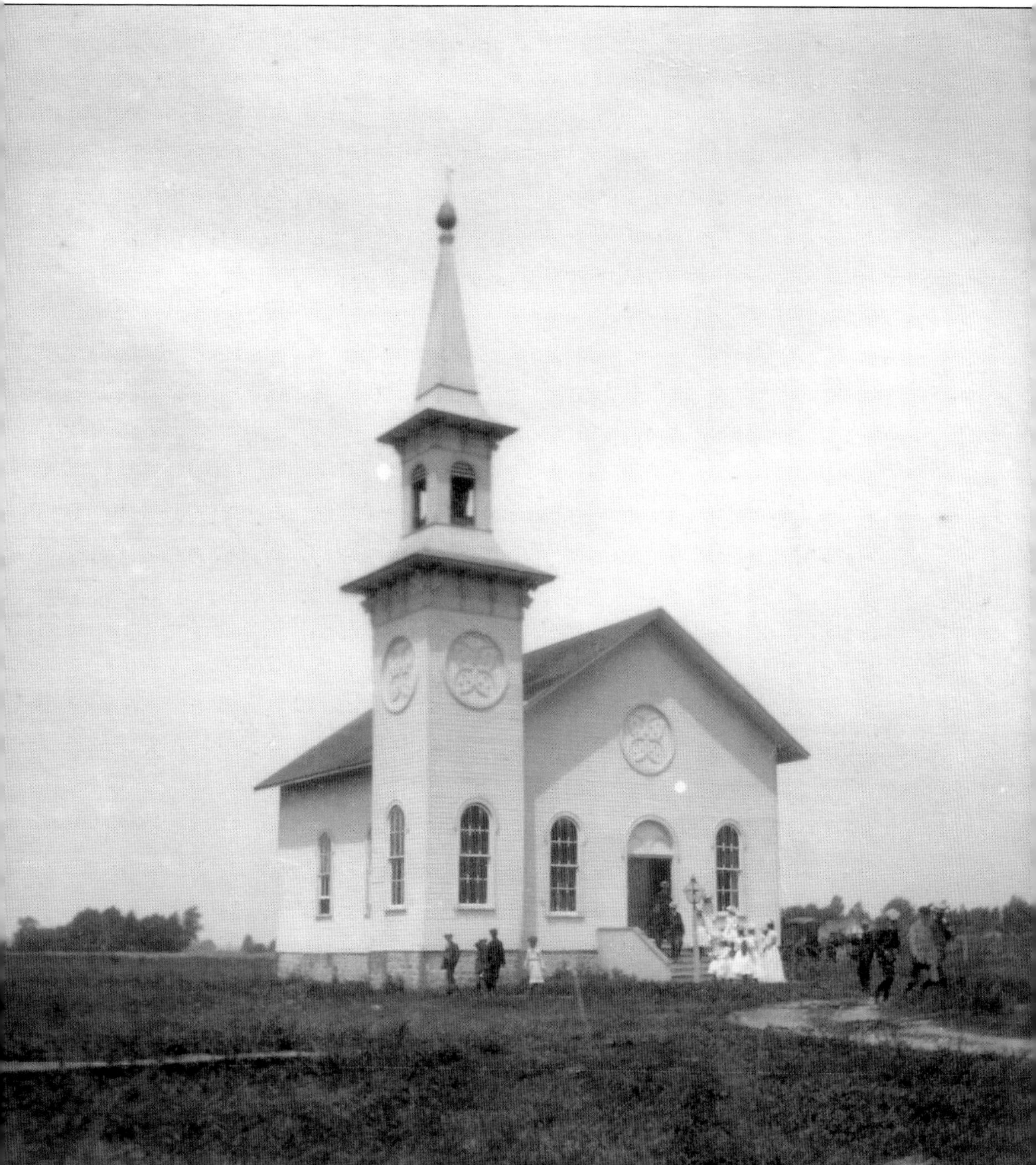

The Disciple Church in Genoa was also referred to as the Church on the Commons. It was built in 1874 on Third and West Streets but was moved in 1906 to Main and Fifth Streets, a more convenient location for members. This photograph was taken before 1906 when it was located at Third Street. (Edna Turner Collection, GPL.)

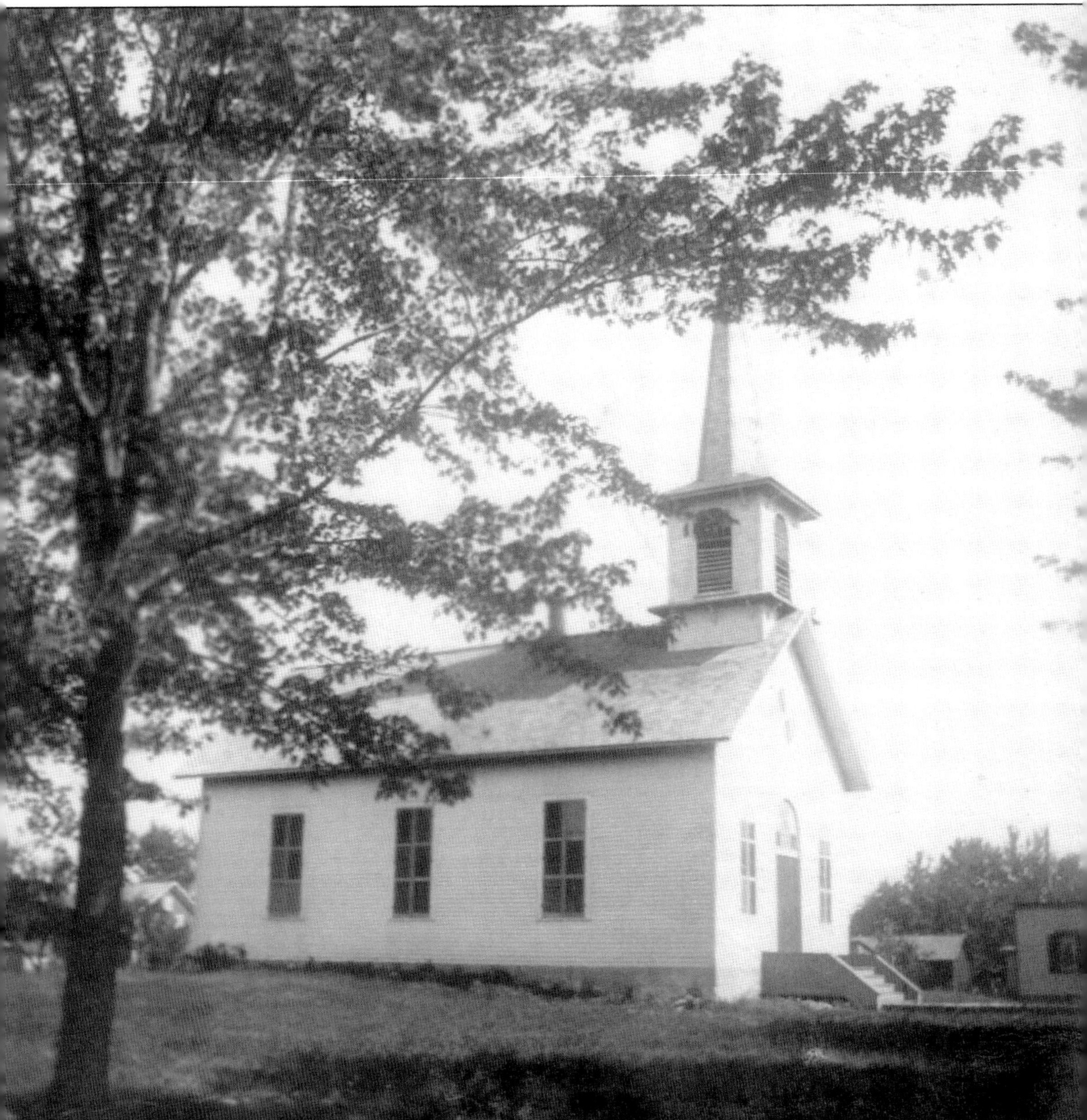

The Trinity Methodist Church in Genoa was built in 1869 on the corner of Fourth and Main Streets under the pastorate of Rev. Samuel M. Lynch. This frame building stood until 1926, when the current brick structure was built. This photograph was taken sometime before 1910, as the church parsonage was not yet constructed. (Edna Turner Collection, GPL.)

Rev. Frank Rowe was pastor of the Trinity Methodist Church in Genoa from 1950 to 1958. He is pictured here with his family around 1955. They are, from left to right, (first row) Steve and John Rowe; (second row) Beverly and Frank Rowe. (Eleanor Richards.)

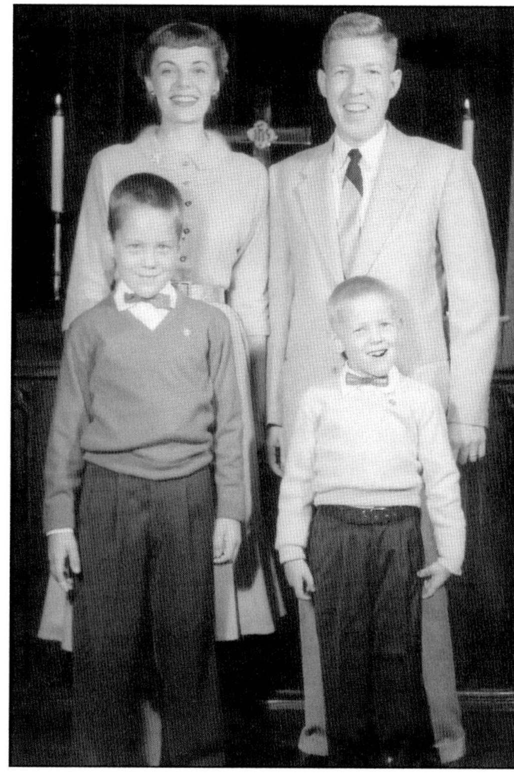

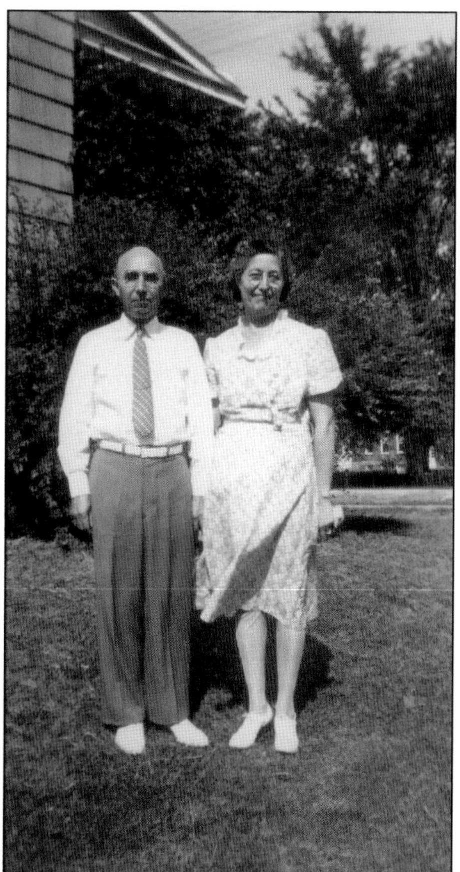

The Trinity Methodist Church in Genoa held the pastoral services of Rev. Samuel Brunner from 1939 to 1944. He is photographed here with his wife, Mildred, in 1940. (Eleanor Richards.)

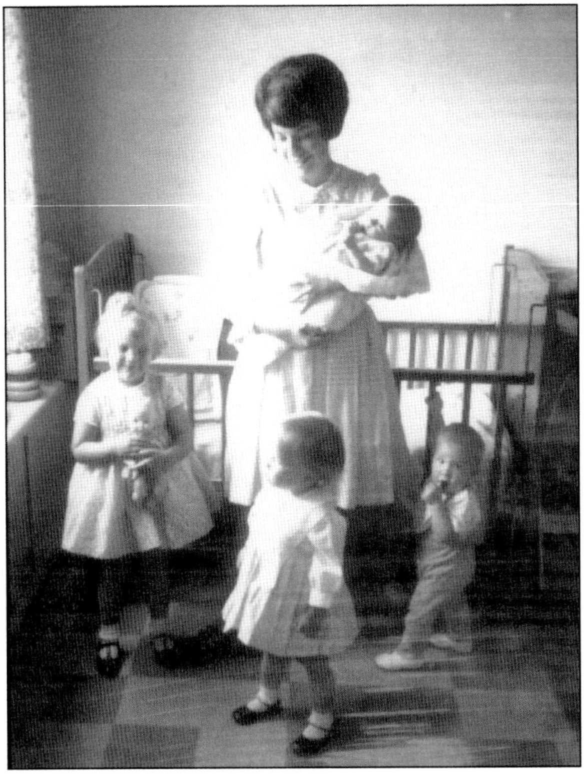

Phyllis Driver cares for the children of church members in the nursery of the Trinity United Methodist Church in Genoa. The children in the image include Heidi Driver (left) and Robbie Stone (right). (Eleanor Richards.)

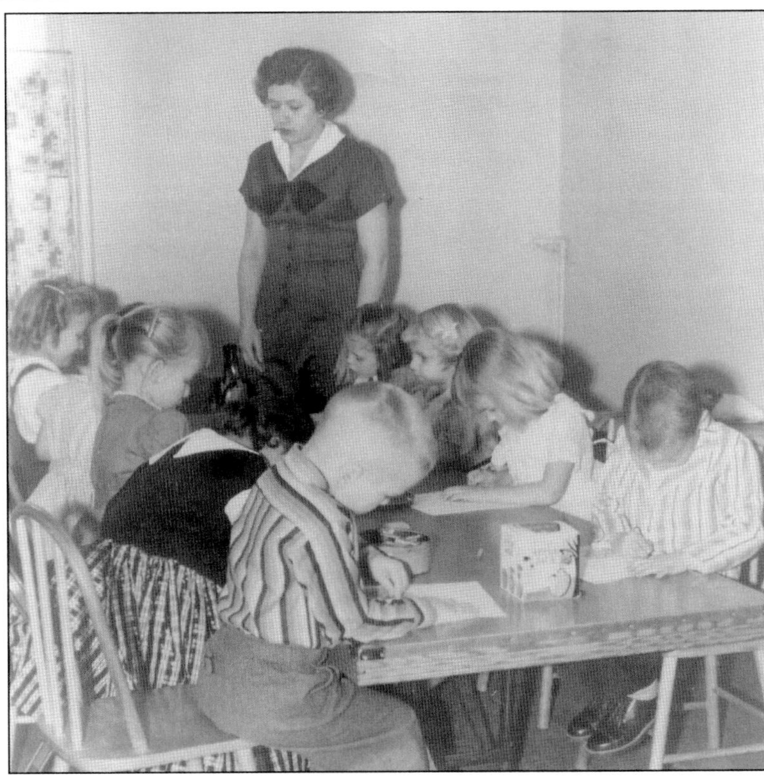

Florence Floro watches children of her 1958 Sunday school class at Trinity Methodist Church in Genoa as they color biblical pictures from the day's lesson. (Eleanor Richards.)

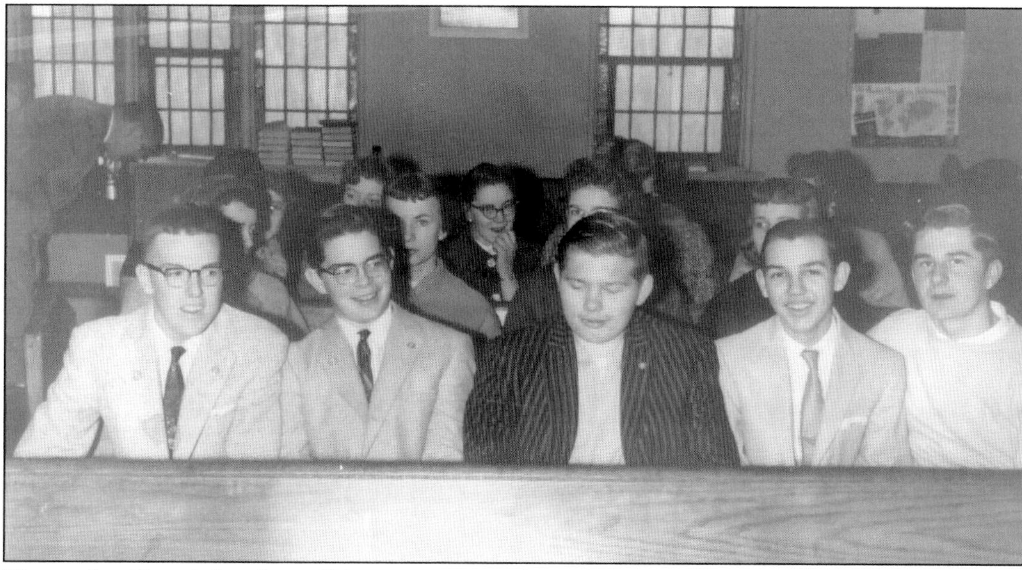

This is the Church Leaders of Tomorrow group from Genoa Trinity Methodist Church in 1958. (Eleanor Richards.)

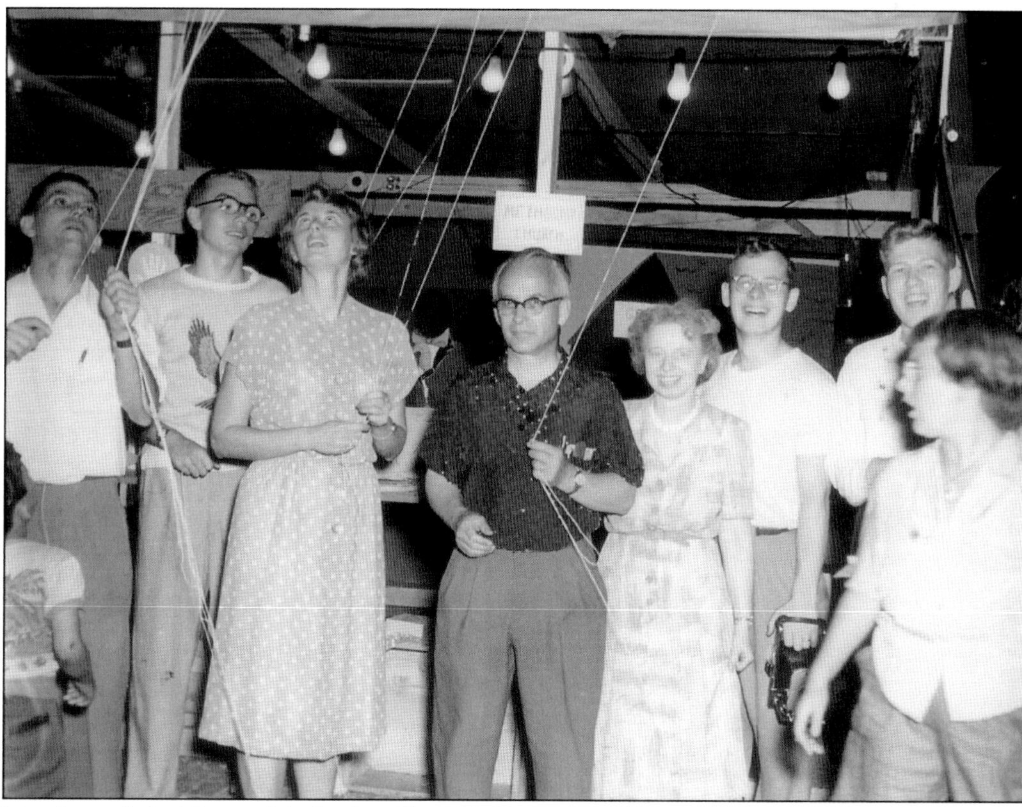

Members of the Trinity Methodist Church's Young People Social Club run the balloon stand at the 1951 Genoa Homecoming. In this photograph are, from left to right, Bill Wheelock, Jim Wetmore, Donna Mae Bergman Welch, Robert Skilliter, Marian Skilliter, Donald Skilliter, and Rev. Frank Rowe; the girl on the far right in front is unidentified. (Eleanor Richards.)

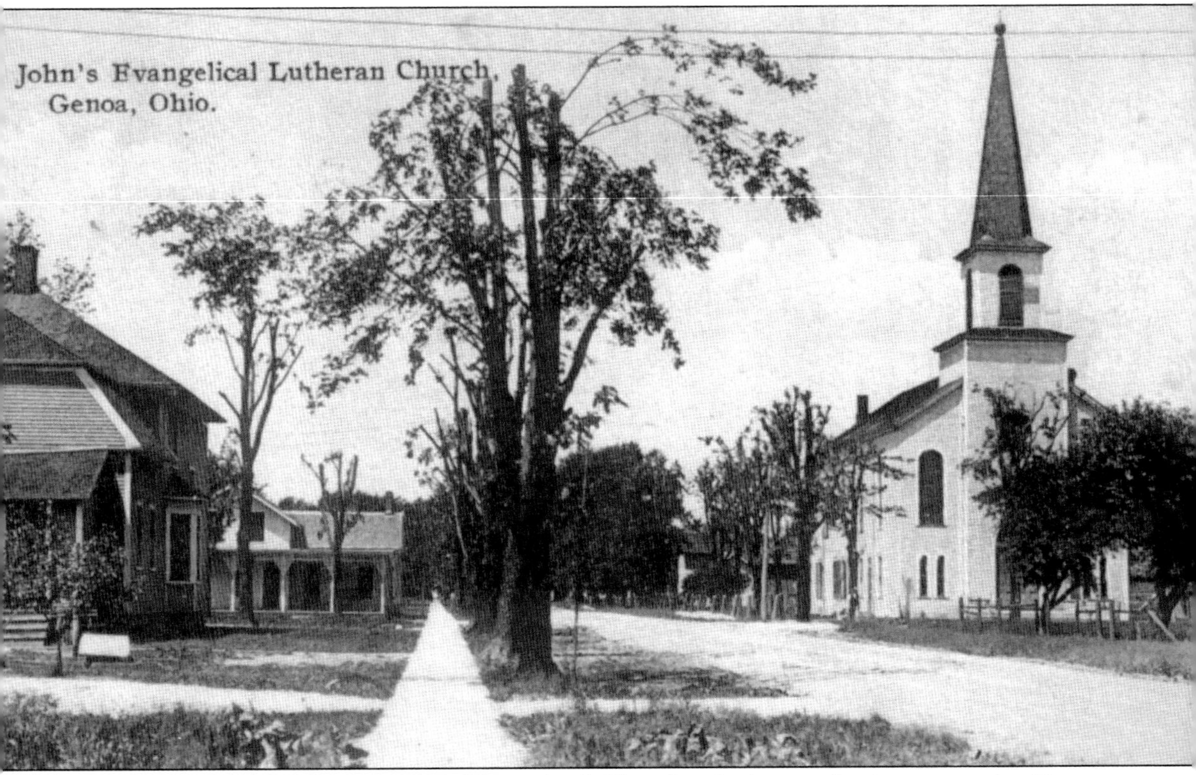

A 1906 postcard shows St. John's Evangelical Church, which was also known as the German Church. German families gathered in 1868 and founded the German United Evangelical Protestant St. John's Church of Genoa. The structure was built in 1871 on Superior Street and served the congregation until the 1950s. At that time, the name changed to St. John's United Church of Christ, and the church moved to Washington Street. (GPL.)

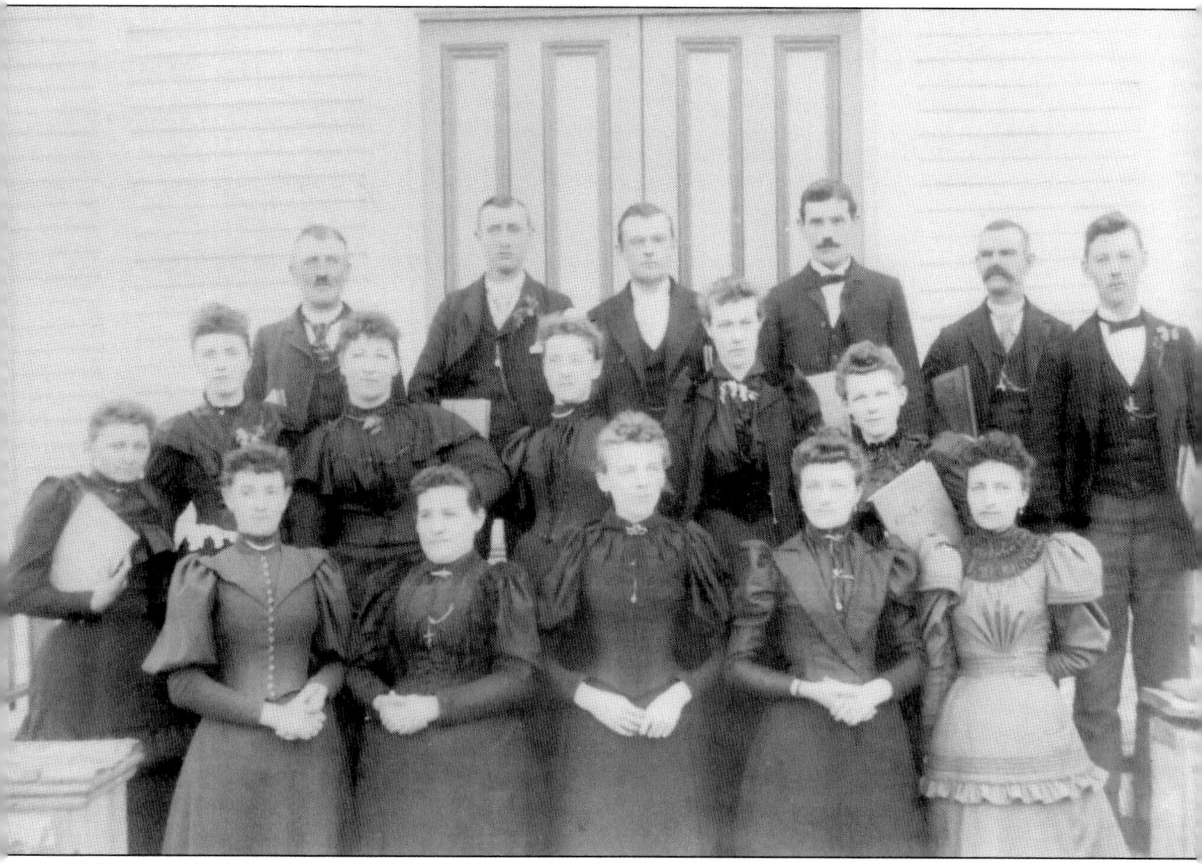

Choir members from St. John's Evangelical Church in Genoa are shown in 1894. They are, from left to right, (first row) Augusta Dreyer, Mrs. Otto Burkhart, Mina Uthoff, Ella Camper, and Minnie Camper Fork; (second row) Lydia Berndt, Reka Sartoris Niehaus, Mrs. Fred Werner, Louise Dreyer Sartoris, Edith Bachman, and Augusta Kasting; (third row) Henry Sartoris Sr., Louis Sartoris, Otto Burkhart (minister), William Berndt, Mr. Schaetske, and unidentified. (GPL.)

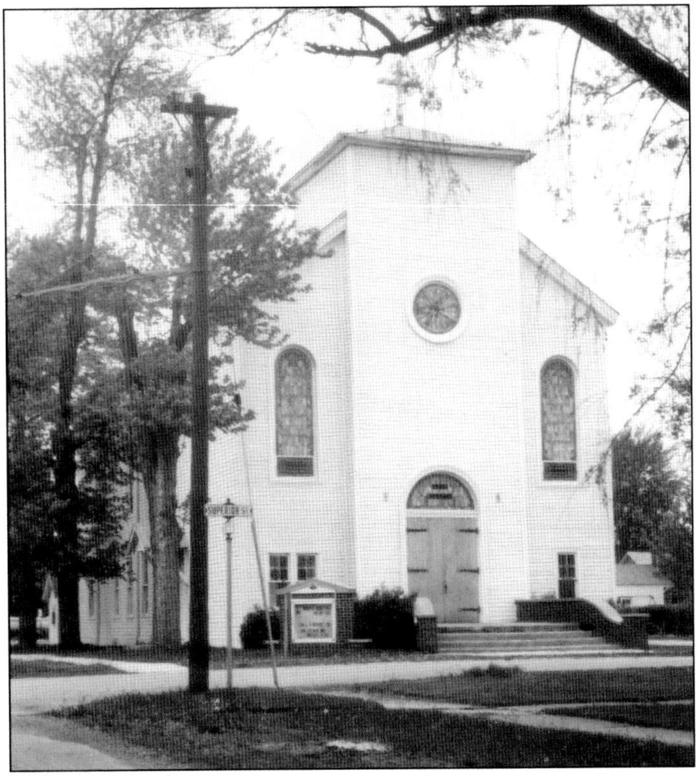

After taking possession of the old St. John's Church building in 1959, the Baptist Church of Genoa moved from its mission building on Seventh Street, its home for the previous two years. (Edna Turner Collection, GPL.)

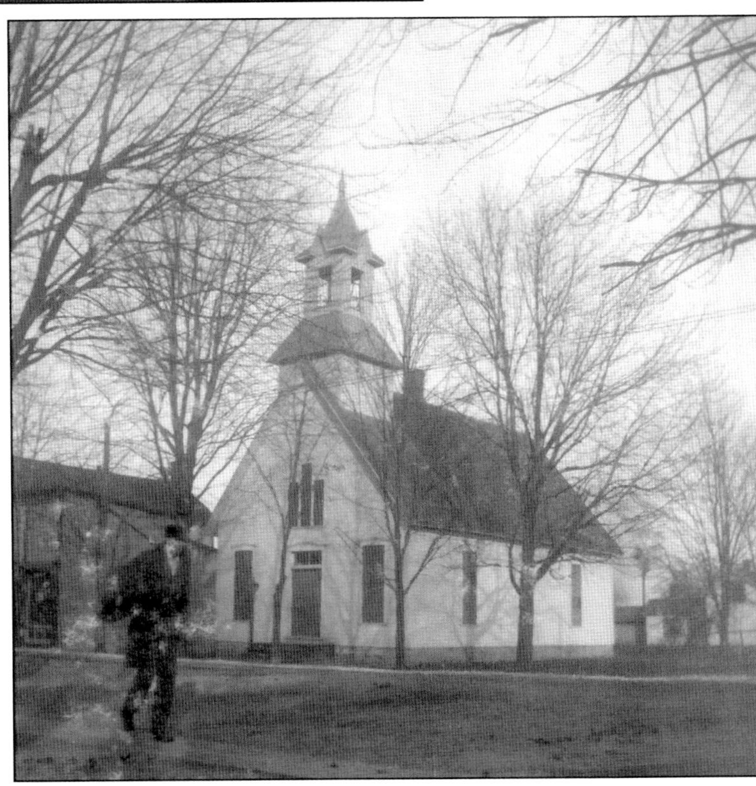

The Genoa Presbyterian Church was constructed in 1882 when Rev. C.K. Smoyer led the church. It was located next to the Christian Church on Main and Fifth Streets. The church disbanded after Rev. Homer Alexander left in the 1920s. The building was turned over to Genoa High School to be converted into a gymnasium, but it ended up serving several local business ventures. (Edna Turner Collection, GPL.)

Seven

Tragic Times and Those Who Helped Us

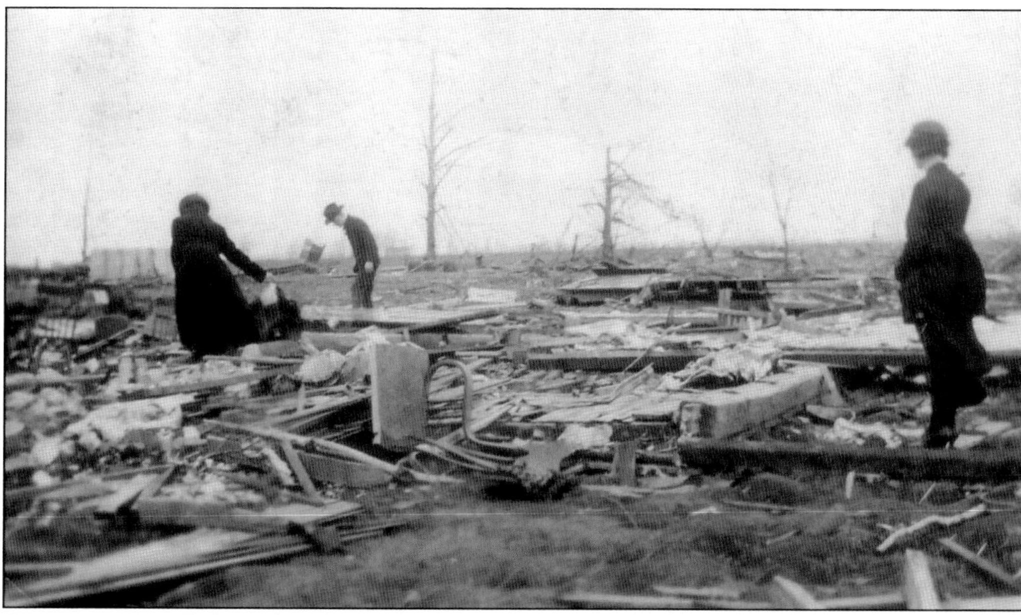

Genoa citizens sift through the debris of what was once a private residence after a tornado tore the house from its foundation. On Palm Sunday, March 28, 1920, the twister came through the western portion of town, beginning at the Englehart farm, and lifted after reaching the Holt homestead just north of Genoa (about two miles). It destroyed 12 homes and 20 barns and outbuildings. Due to the fact that it went through a sparsely inhabited section of town, there were only two deaths; however, several serious injuries were reported. None of the families affected had tornado insurance, and the homes were total losses. (GPL.)

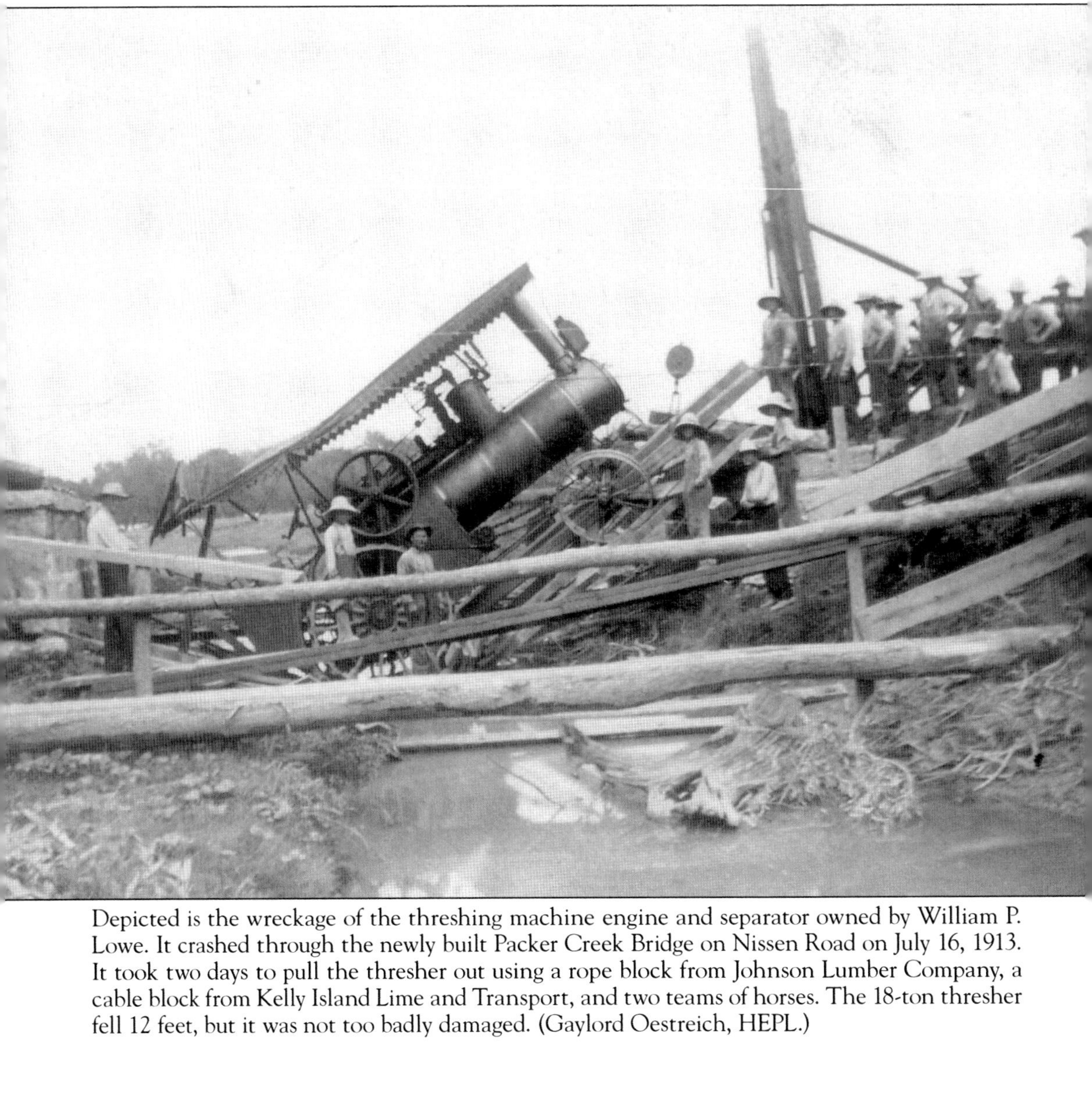

Depicted is the wreckage of the threshing machine engine and separator owned by William P. Lowe. It crashed through the newly built Packer Creek Bridge on Nissen Road on July 16, 1913. It took two days to pull the thresher out using a rope block from Johnson Lumber Company, a cable block from Kelly Island Lime and Transport, and two teams of horses. The 18-ton thresher fell 12 feet, but it was not too badly damaged. (Gaylord Oestreich, HEPL.)

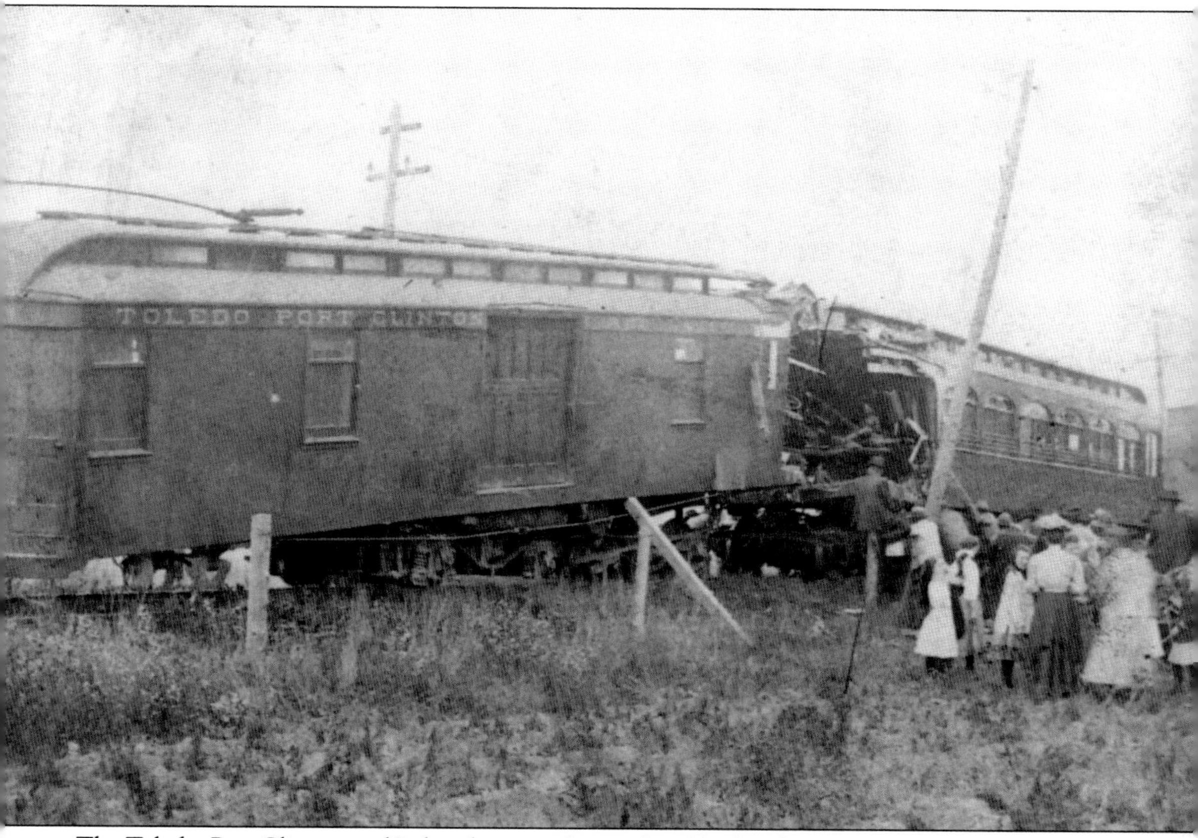

The Toledo, Port Clinton and Lakeside interurban railroad had its first major wreck on September 28, 1907, when it experienced a head-on collision at Linker's Curve near Elmore. Car no. 23 and boxcar no. 41 crashed due to impaired visibility at the curve and disobeyed orders. Several passengers were injured, but only motorman Harry Null died. Both cars were repaired and returned to service within months. (EHS.)

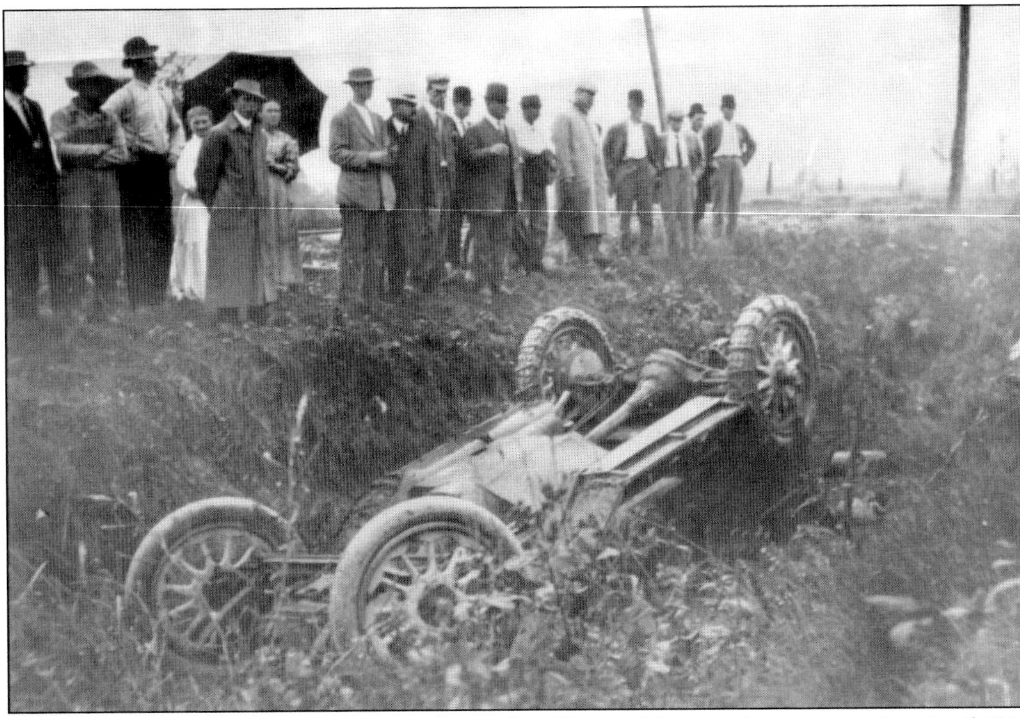

A crowd oversees an overturned car on the road to Elmore. The accident occurred in April 1912 and left the two passengers dead at the scene. (HEPL.)

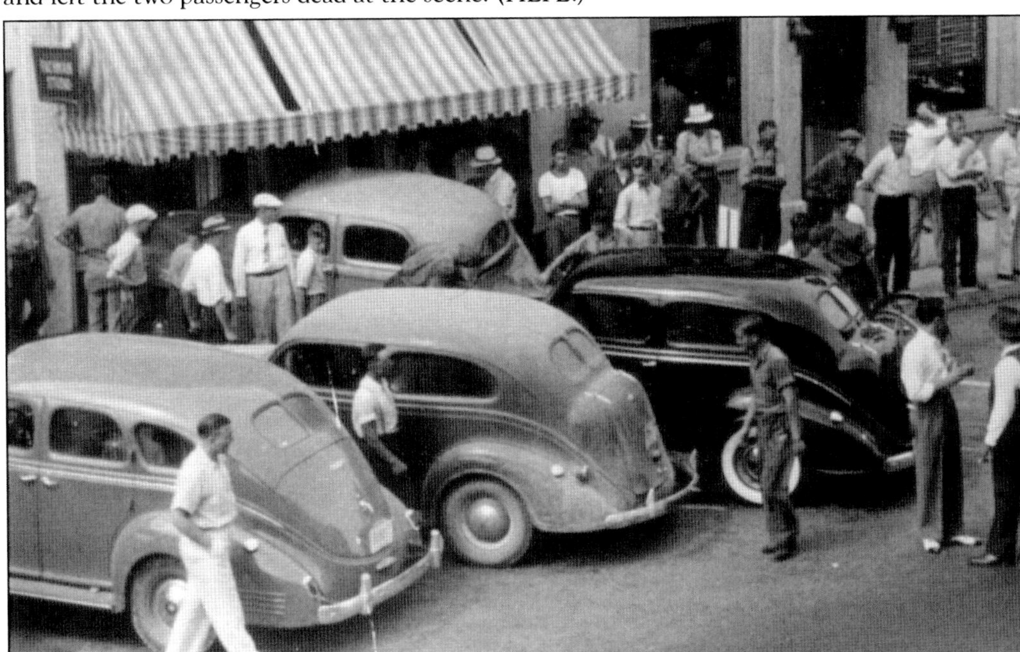

Three Toledo boys crashed their car through the entrance window of Barne's Restaurant in Elmore during a late-night drive in 1950. No one was injured in the accident, but the driver was slapped with a $10 fine and 10 days in the Port Clinton Jail. (Henry House Collection, HEPL.)

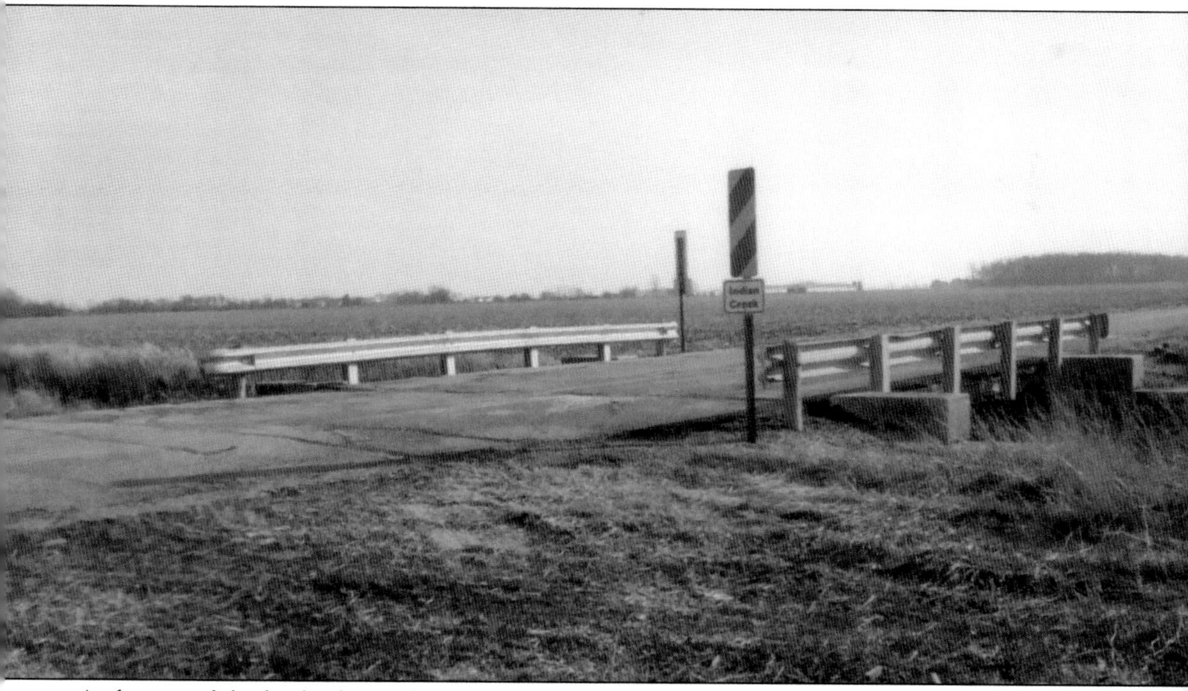

A glimpse of the bridge located on Portage Slemmer Road in Elmore shows where the Headless Motorcyclist is believed to appear every March 21 on the anniversary of his death. Legend has it that a man came home to the Elmore area from fighting in World War I to find his girl in the arms of another. He was so infuriated by the discovery that he rode out and crashed his motorcycle off of this bridge into the creek. His bike and body were mangled, and he was decapitated. Each year, many come out to the bridge to perform a ritual to bring back the motorcyclist. If one waits at the end of the bridge and flashes his headlights and honks his horn three times, a ghost light has been reported to be seen coming over the bridge and disappearing. Richard Gill of Bowling Green State University documented this phenomenon in 1968 and wrote about it in the *Journal of the Ohio Folklore Society*. (Don Wick.)

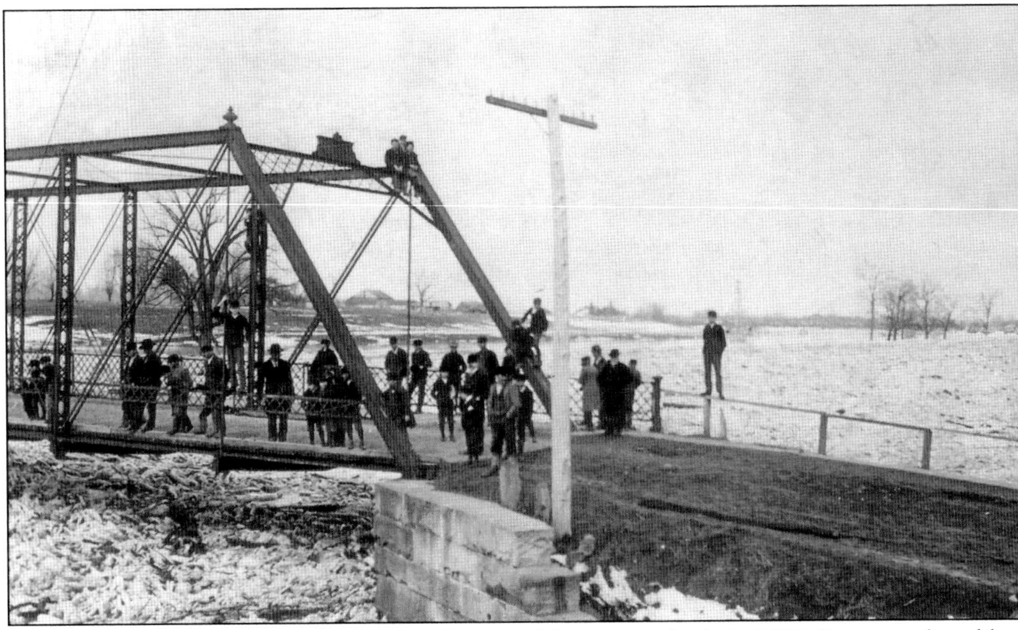

The iron wagon bridge over the Portage River in Elmore was built in 1883. It was replaced by a concrete bridge in 1927. The absence of substantial guardrails and light fixtures at the approach to the bridge made it common for carriages to miss the span at night and run into the river. (HEPL.)

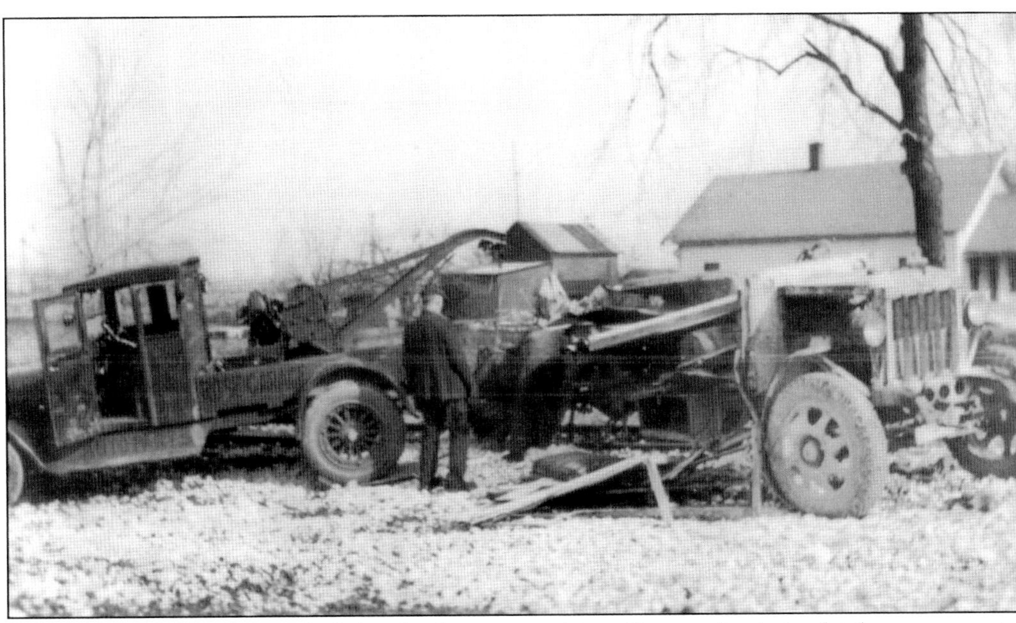

The wreckage of Emil Meyerholtz's vehicle was towed into Genoa after being hit by an oncoming train in town. The driver, Duke Reau, was not hurt. (Galion Jensen, via Gene Meyers.)

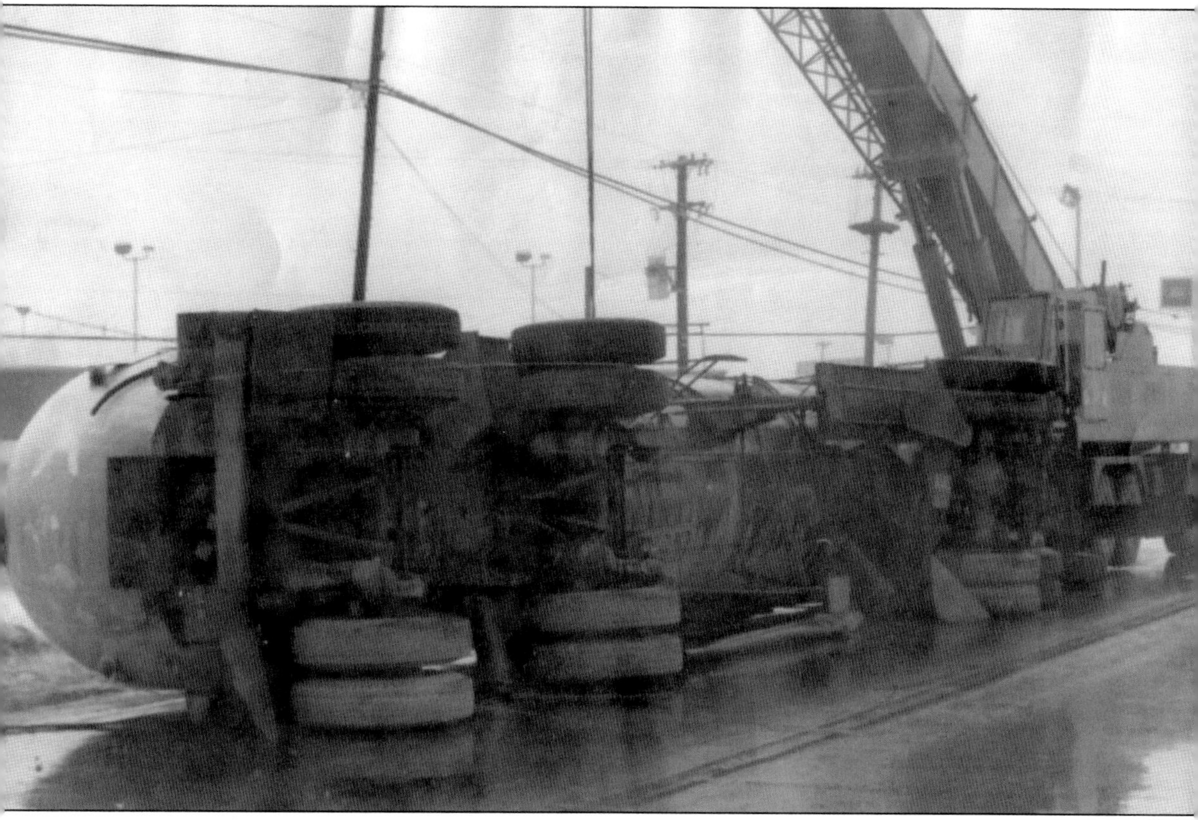

A propane tank truck was demolished in a three-car collision in December 1974 on Route 51 near Genoa–Clay Center Road. Four people were injured in the accident, but the propane miraculously did not catch fire. Genoa fire crews stood by for eight hours in case the truck did ignite. (Allen-Clay Joint Fire Department.)

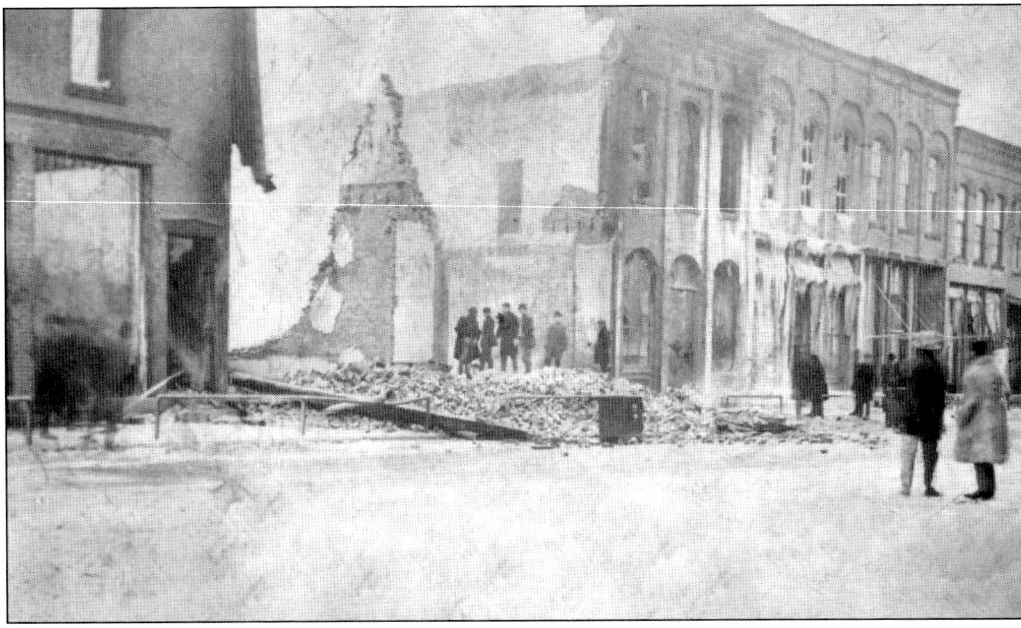

This image shows the aftermath of the January 1895 fire in the business district of Elmore. It began on a Sunday evening in Chadman's Meat Market, spread to Jaeger Hardware, the Peter Keil Saloon, the Sauerwein Building, and the Elmore Opera House—destroying them completely. The A.W. Luckey Fire Department, along with crews from Toledo, eventually put out the flames, but firemen were hindered by frozen hose lines and hand-pump fire engines. (HEPL.)

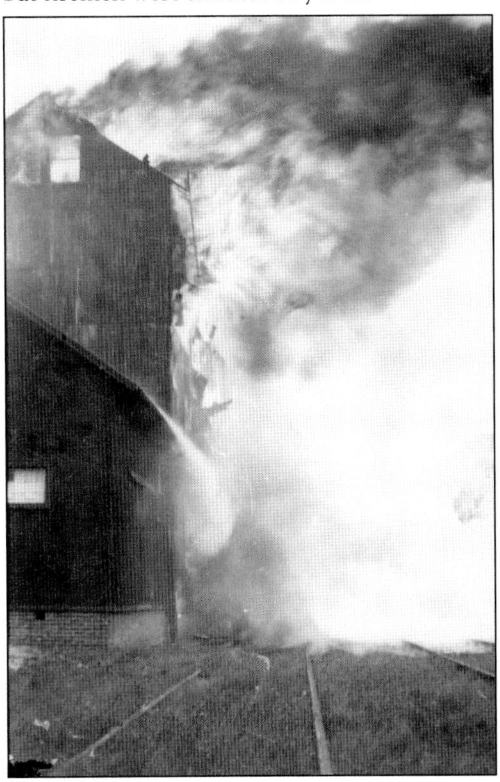

Having been acquired from Magee and Pafenbach, the Farmer's Elevator Company began in Elmore in 1911. As shown, the elevator caught fire in 1937, but it was soon replaced on-site the following year with permission from the town council. The elevator was then leased in 1974 to Lindsey Farmer's. (HEPL.)

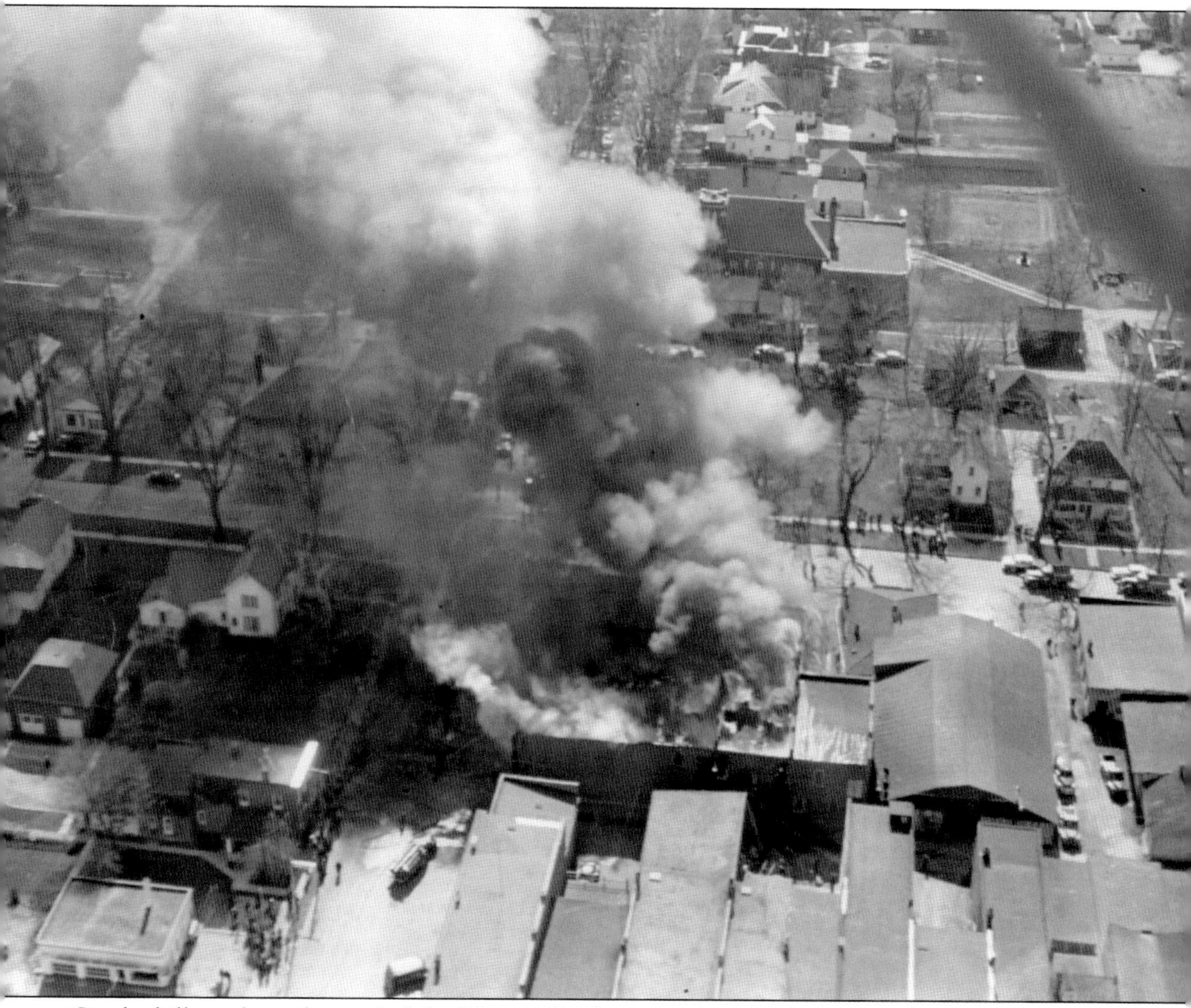

Smoke billows from the roof of the Elmore Hardware in this aerial photograph. The fire broke out in April 1955, and proprietor William Kontak lost the Toledo Street store he had run for 19 years. Kontak rebuilt the next year on Rice Street. The store was formerly owned by the Banting-Sanders Company and had suffered numerous fires over the years. (HEPL.)

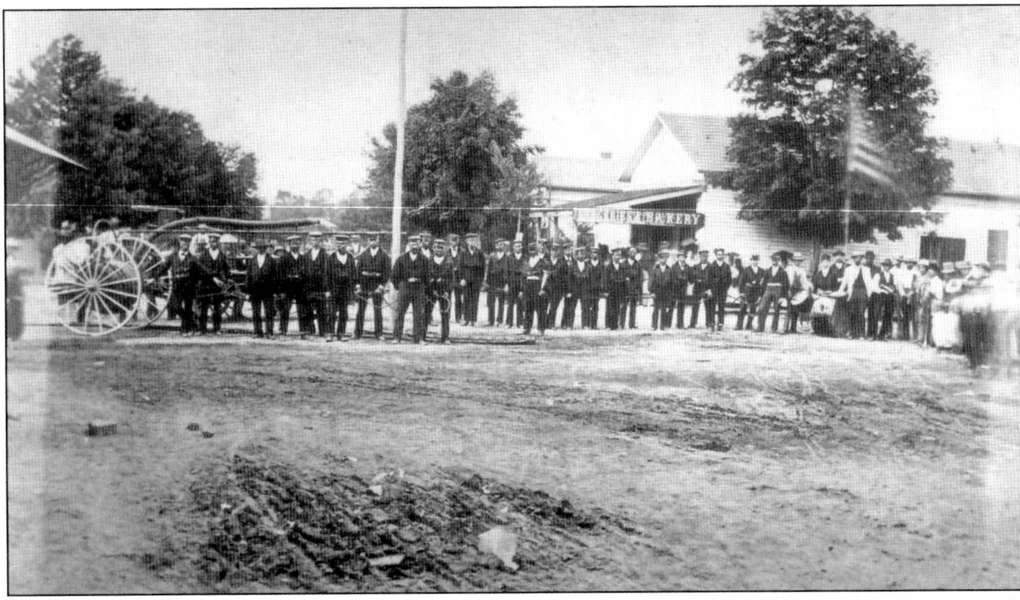

The A.W. Luckey Engine Company stands next to the old Elmore band in the early 1870s. As the first official fire department in Elmore, the Luckey Company was established in 1868 after a flourish of arson throughout the village that would unfortunately continue for the next few decades. (Linker Collection, HEPL.)

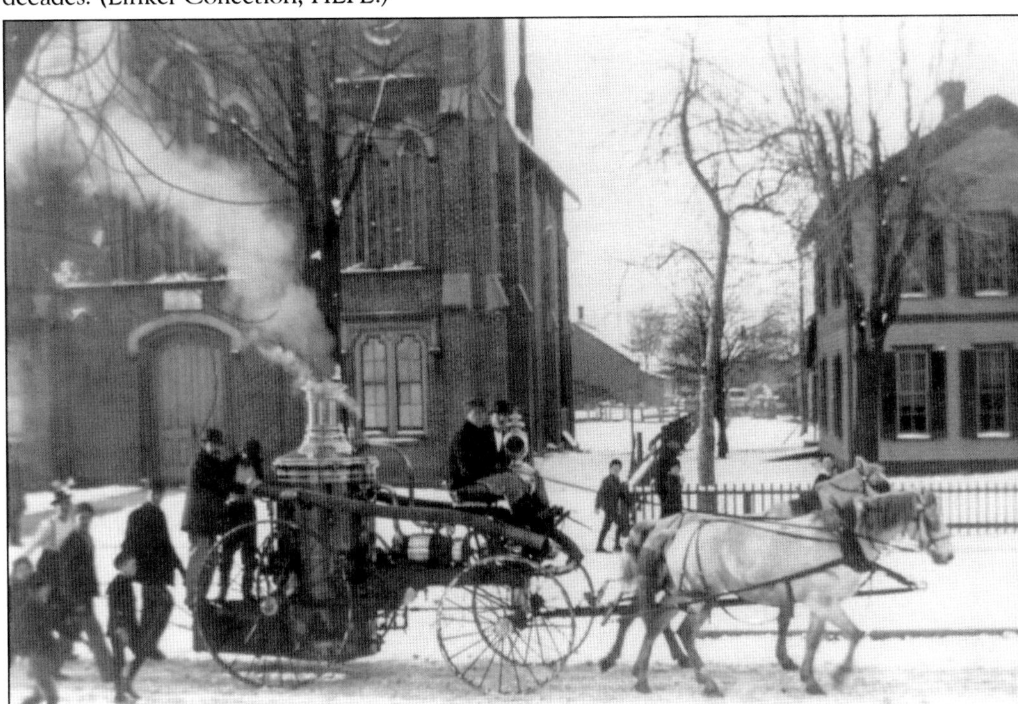

This photograph was taken in 1895 and shows the Silsby fire engine and pump brought to Elmore from Oberlin, Ohio. William Bothe drives the wagon, and on the end is R.J. Crozier, who is in charge of the new engine. The brand-new engine was named "Old Betsy" and was used successfully until 1911, when the waterworks was built and the truck's use discontinued. (HEPL.)

The Clay-Genoa Volunteer Fire Department in 1930 includes, from left to right, (first row) August Johnson, Ray Wyse, Sherell Holcomb, Rufus Waldron, and unidentified; (second row) Paul Haar, Donald Cashen, Vallie Miller, Harry Earl, and Vern Plantz. (Allen-Clay Joint Fire Department.)

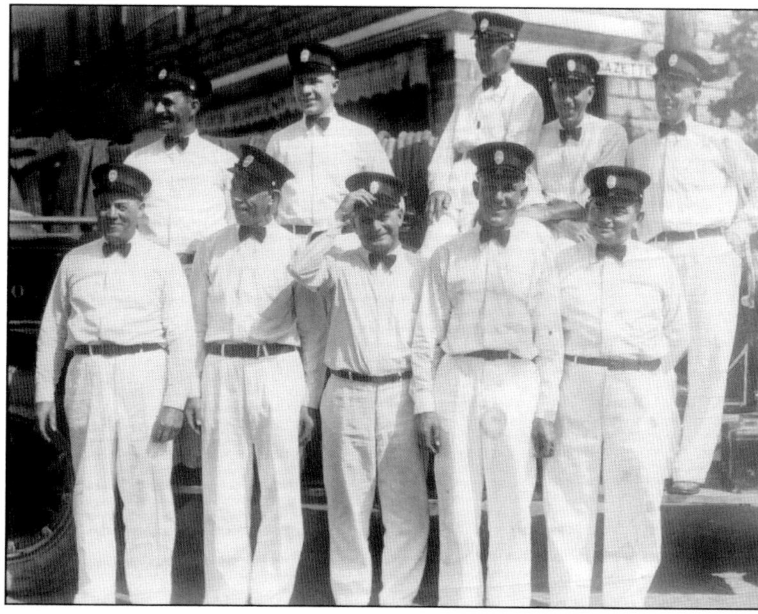

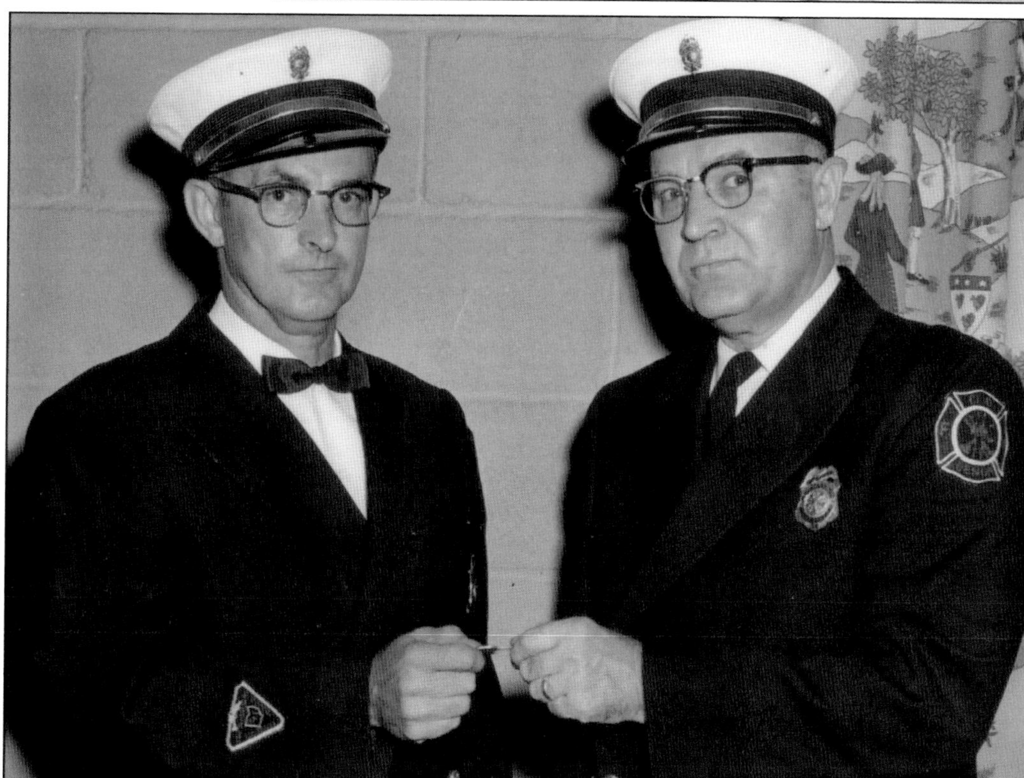

Former Clay-Genoa fire chief Donald "Baldy" Cashen (right) passes the torch to new chief Warren Hesslebart in 1962. Having served for 34 years, Cashen had been chief of the fire department since 1928. Firefighting became a family tradition for the Cashens and many others. Donald's son Ronald, brother Paul, and brother-in-law Robert Hille served in Genoa. His granddaughter Janet Crawford serves in the Elmore department. (Ron Cashen.)

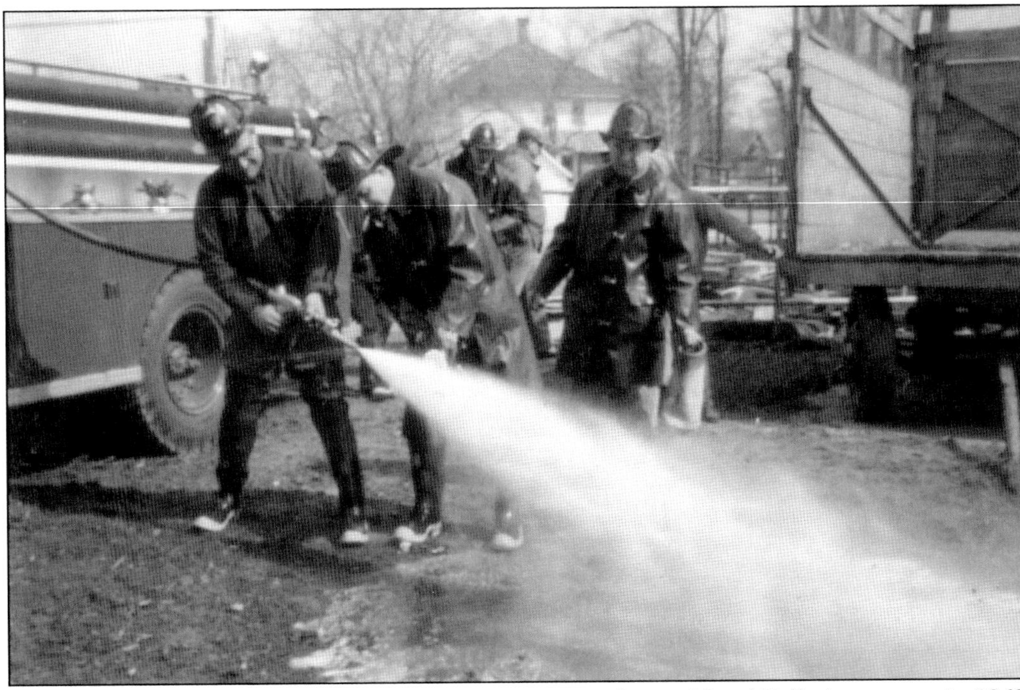

Genoa firemen test the hoses before putting out a grass fire on Virgil Zeller's property in 1962. The men in front are Jake Coleman (left), Ken Schmidlen (center), and Jack Musolf. (Allen-Clay Joint Fire Department.)

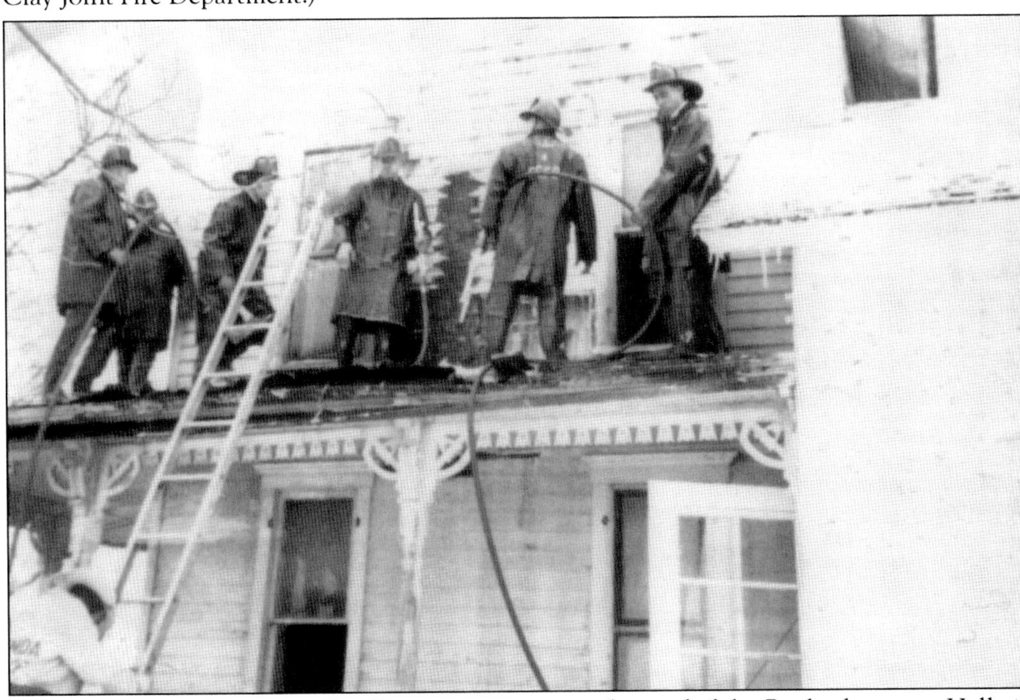

Members of the Clay-Genoa Fire Department inspect the roof of the Bagley home on Hellwig Road after extinguishing flames. The blaze took place in March 1966. (Allen-Clay Joint Fire Department.)

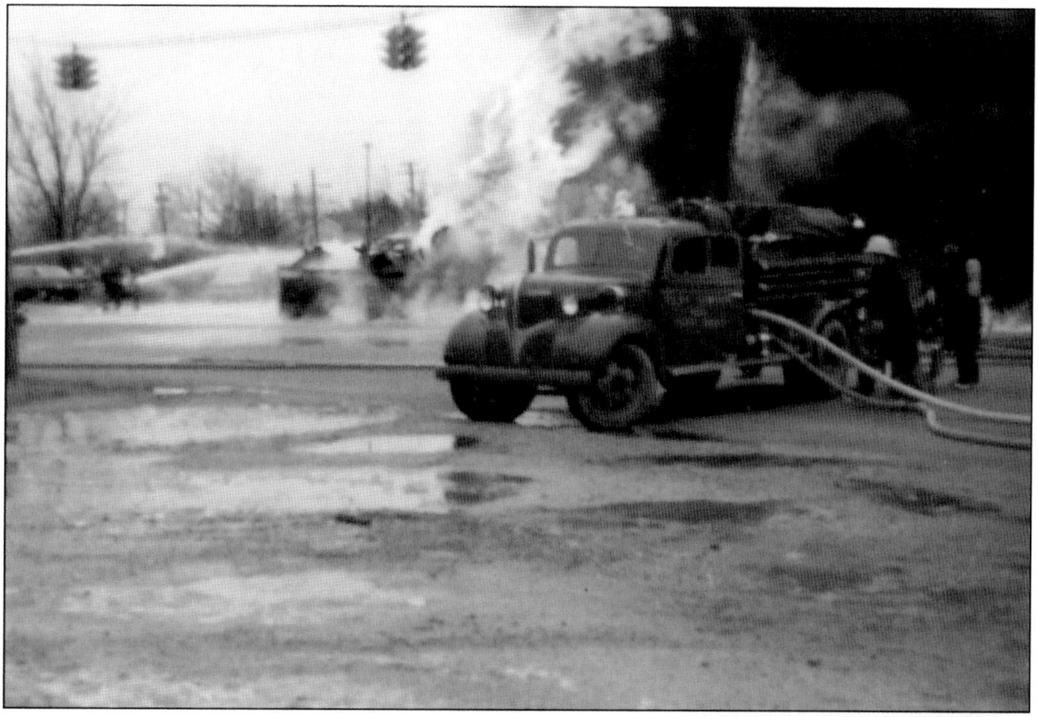

On January 21, 1972, a gasoline-tank trailer overturned on Route 51 in Genoa and caught fire. The blaze became nearly uncontrollable and destroyed the Nolte service station, two trucks, and six cars and knocked out phone service to most Genoa customers. No injuries were reported, but the Genoa, Elmore, Millbury, Woodville, and Clay Center Fire Departments battled the flames for hours. (Allen-Clay Joint Fire Department.)

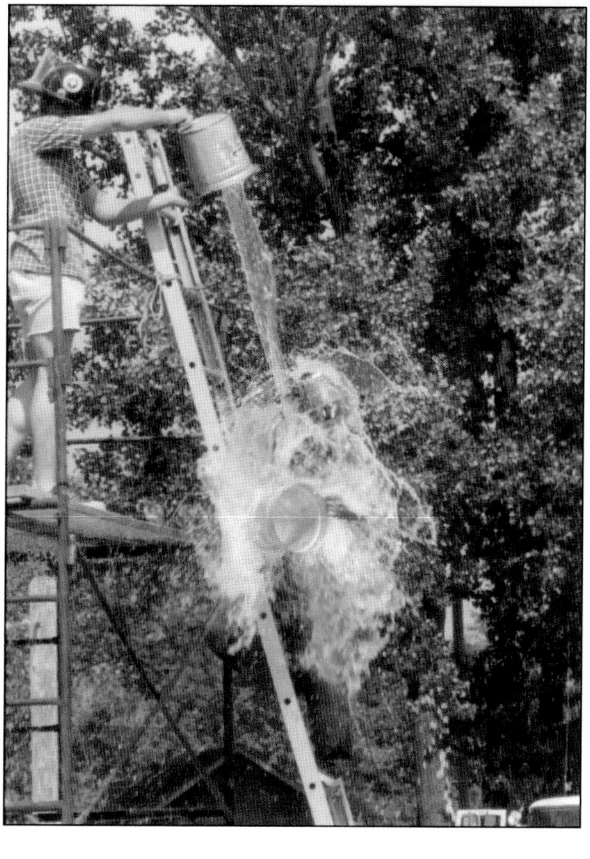

Genoa firemen have a little fun while performing training exercises in fire rescue. This photograph was taken during the summer of 1977. (Allen-Clay Joint Fire Department.)